Studies in German Literature, Linguistics, and Culture:
Literary Criticism in Perspective

Editorial Board

Literary Criticism in Perspective

James Hardin (*South Carolina*), General Editor

Eitel Timm (*British Columbia*), German Literature

Benjamin Franklin V (*South Carolina*), American and English Literature

Reingard M. Nischik (*Mainz*), Comparative Literature

* * *

About *Literary Criticism in Perspective*

Books in the series *Literary Criticism in Perspective*, a sub-series of *Studies in German Literature, Linguistics, and Culture,* trace literary scholarship and criticism on major and neglected writers alike, or on a single major work, a group of writers, a literary school or movement. In so doing the authors — authorities on the topic in question who are also well-versed in the principles and history of literary criticism — address a readership consisting of scholars, students of literature at the graduate and undergraduate level, and the general reader. One of the primary purposes of the series is to illuminate the nature of literary criticism itself, to gauge the influence of social and historic currents on aesthetic judgments once thought objective and normative.

German Socialist Literature 1860–1914

Illustration from a "Mai-Festzeitung," 1897

H.-J. Schulz

German Socialist Literature 1860–1914

Predicaments of Criticism

CAMDEN HOUSE

Copyright © 1993 by
CAMDEN HOUSE, INC.

Published by Camden House, Inc.
Drawer 2025
Columbia, SC 29202 USA

Printed on acid-free paper.
Binding materials are chosen for strength and durability.

All Rights Reserved
Printed in the United States of America
First Edition

ISBN:1-879751-34-8

Library of Congress Cataloging-in-Publication Data

Schulz, Hans-Joachim, 1938-
    German socialist literature, 1860-1914 : predicaments of criticism / H.-J. Schulz. -- 1st ed.
    p. cm. -- (Studies in German literature, linguistics, and culture)
    Includes bibliographical references and indexes.
    ISBN 1-879751-34-8 (alk. paper)
    1. German literature--19th century--History and criticism.
2. German literature--20th century--History and criticism.
3. Working class writings, German--History and criticism.
4. Socialism and literature--Germany. 5. Socialism in literature.
6. Socialism--Germany--History. I. Title. II. Series: Studies in German literature, linguistics, and culture (Unnumbered)
PT345.S38 1992
830.9'358--dc20

92-32532
CIP

Acknowledgments

The production, dissemination and reception of German socialist literature of the turn of the century did not attract scholarly attention until the 1960s. Despite efforts by scholars in the former German Democratic Republic to make a representative sample of this literature available to a modern public, the vast majority of primary texts, as well as of the socialist literary criticism of the time, is still difficult to identify and to access, especially in the United States. I owe special gratitude to those who helped me overcome these difficulties. The Vanderbilt University Research Council provided funds to extend a sabbatical leave and to visit archives in Germany. The staff of the Interlibrary-Loan Department of Vanderbilt University's Central Library responded with patience, intelligence and efficiency to a steady stream of requests; and I would like to take this opportunity to thank three of its members for many years of assistance and friendship:

>Lois V. Griest
>James E. Toplon
>Marilyn P. Jackson

Finally, thanks go to David Shepherd for reading the manuscript and to Barbara Schulz for supplementing my meager word-processing skills.

For Anke and Phillip Schulz

Contents

Preface		xi
1	Revolution and the Canon	1
	Canonicity and Reception Study	6
	Literature and Literary Life	11
	The Reception of Socialist Literature 1860-1914: A Problem of Method	20
2	The German Labor Movement 1860-1914: Class Struggle vs. Integration	23
	The Political Emergence of a Class	24
	The Trials of Legality	31
3	Cultural Theory and Cultural Practice	43
	The Conquest of Knowledge	43
	Associational Culture	50
	A Culture of Celebration	57
4	Literature: Theory, Criticism and Dissemination	61
	Franz Mehring	61
	Some Debates	70
	Literary Dissemination and Consumption	82
5	The Literary Genres	93
	Poetry	96
	Drama	102
	Fiction	108
	The Proletarian Autobiography	115
Works Consulted		122
Index		147

Preface

*T*raditional literary criticism is a form of reading that seeks to overcome the historicity of texts and to establish their timeless validity. To write the history of criticism of an author or of a group of works, then, implicitly means to read critics against the grain of this intention, to restore the historicity of their voices and to describe the historical limits of their judgments. In most cases, the historian will note significant changes in critical approach and evaluation which permit one to read critical texts back into the larger texts of the political, social, cultural, and esthetic discourses of the period. In this form of metacriticism, the historian usually moves from critically recognized literary works to their critical reception and from there to the historical environment of that criticism.

The reception of early socialist literature in Germany is one of those cases where the historian departs from this procedure. There is no consensus about the characteristics of "socialist" literature, and there is no canon of recognized texts. Both during the period 1860 to 1914 and in later decades, the literary texts written in and for the socialist movement were judged by the extent to which they assisted the cultural or political work of the movement or by the political "correctness" of their content. Changes in the body of texts discussed and shifts in the patterns of evaluation reflect — quite directly — changes in the ideological disposition of the Social-Democratic movement or in the political agendas of later critics. To gain access to the specific nature of a literary criticism so closely tied to the ideological discourse of German socialism and its critics, then, the procedure described above has to be reversed: from an understanding of the development of the socialist movement and its political philosophy we proceed to the cultural theory and practice of the movement and to the role literature played in both. Only in that manner can criticism of early socialist literature in Germany — both contemporary and later — be fully understood as political readings of literary texts which both conformed to and at times resisted these forms of reading.

Chapter 1 outlines some of the theoretical and practical difficulties encountered by critics who apply traditional principles of evaluation to early socialist literature, a literature whose values were political and social as much as esthetic. This insistence on classical and non-political norms of literary excellence is found not only among non-socialist critics but is also typical of socialist literary criticism and literary politics. The reasons for this socialist perpetuation of a non-political literary esthetics are discussed in chapters 2-4 that trace the gradual separation of art from politics in the political and cultural ideology of the German socialist movement, a separation that was finalized in its literary theory and critical practice. Chapter 5, finally, presents a sketch of the genres of early socialist literature in Germany, of their peculiar social and political functions, and of a criticism slow to recognize that these literary works devoted to social and political aims cannot be adequately assessed by the standards of traditional textual criticism. As the history of criticism of early socialist literature shows, the development of a methodology that combines analysis of the textual qualities of literary works with a description of their social functions is still in a preliminary stage.

1: Revolution and the Canon

THE HISTORY OF THE German socialist movement is a history not so much of organizational growth, social struggle and political events as it is a history of the constitution, reception and transformation of ideas. Few political movements, if any, are seen to have stood under the obligation of an unalterable canon of ideas as German socialism has. It is but a slight exaggeration to say that at times historians of the German socialist movement, especially Marxist historians, have not presented its organizational life and political activity in terms of changing socio-political conditions and Social Democracy's responses to them but rather have "read" its development as forms of an attempted exegesis of the works of Marx and Engels. The historians' verdict of the ability of German Social Democracy to understand Marxist theoretical texts and to apply that understanding to the political and social praxis is pervasively negative. Their judgments tend to echo those of Marx and Engels themselves (the "old men in London") who — from the vantage point of exiles unencumbered by the tangible complexities and dangers of political agitation — accompanied the constitution of an organized workers' movement in Germany with a running commentary which at times was acerbic and in all cases professorial.

The duplication of the critical posture and of the judgments of Marx and Engels by later historians of German socialism perpetuated an implicit model of the relationship of philosophy to politics more Lassallean than Marxist: that of philosophy as a legislative and politics as an executive agency. This view privileges theory, its articulators and articulations, and presents politics as speech and speeches; here the history of the movement is the history of its articulated (and misarticulated) ideas, of the orations and writings of its theorists (Marx and Engels, Lassalle, Bebel, W. Liebknecht, Kautsky, Bernstein, Mehring, Luxemburg, Zetkin), of party programs and resolutions, and of the discussion ritual at annual party conferences. The history of the reception of Marxist theory in the German labor movement is a legitimate concern of *Geistesgeschichte*. But where the description of the movement is keyed to the reception of Marx as a normative standard, the rich organizational life of a movement is slighted which adopted Marxism only late, hesitatingly and never fully, and which by necessity tended to isolate revolutionary theory from political pragmatics.

However, the notion of politics as "hermeneutics," as the attempted *understanding* of canonical texts and the *application* of their meaning to the social and political environment, is not an approach imposed upon the historical material by later historians. In a movement which began in the 1860s with the establishment of liberal education clubs for craftsmen and workers, the original and paradigmatic act of proletarian emancipation was not the strike or street protest but the reading of authorized texts, the acquisition of approved knowledge for the intellectual, moral and esthetic improvement of the individual. The equation "knowledge is power" attended the birth of the socialist movement and remained, despite all criticism, a central metaphor of its discourse. As the German labor movement split away from its bourgeois liberal tutors and became increasingly politicized and class-oriented, a double canon of political and scientific texts emerged: Lassalle and Marx and Engels on the one hand, Darwin and his epigones on the other; to which, in the political area, minor classics (Bebel, W. Liebknecht) were added in due course. The fact that the conceptual relationships between the Lassallean and Marxist political philosophies, and between these philosophies and popular versions of Darwinism, are highly conflictual was never explicitly thematized in the early decades of the movement (except, of course, by the London critics), and could therefore not serve to problematize the notion of political action as textual fidelity. The progressive worker who entered the movement was obliged to become, first of all, a reader of canonized texts. He was taught to approach each of these texts as containing coherent, self-evident and class-transcending *scientific* truth. His posture would remain that of a passive reader since his class, without the means to create material conditions for a culture of its own, did not, according to Rosa Luxemburg and others, have the capacity to expand the theoretical limits of the canon bequeathed to it by progressive bourgeois thinkers — its job was to protect this heritage from reactionary "vandalism" (Luxemburg 1903, 367).

What we have described here briefly was, of course, a complex and evolving relationship of political theory and political practice. And as both the party and its allied unions grew in strength (or at least in membership), the exclusive fight for their legality (which lasted until 1890) was later complemented and gradually replaced by the day-to-day activities of organization, parliamentary maneuvering and union work (all of it reformist rather than revolutionary). Revolutionary theory (its canonized texts and the hermeneutic reverence they commanded) slowly assumed a different function in the ideological life of the movement: its function changed from providing conceptual, terminological and metaphorical guidance to revolutionary political action in a political system presumed on the verge of collapse to providing a discourse of utopian prophecy, of future certainty within a bourgeois-capitalist system which had proven impervious to the notion of impending revolution. The status of revolutionary theory changed from an ideology of action to a rhetoric of invocation, expectation and hope; it did not, however, lose its formal primacy in the public life of the party.

Eduard Bernstein's much-maligned "revisionism," which relegated Marx' work to the status of a major *historical* classic and became an official issue in 1898-99, was iconoclastic not because he advocated a departure from dominant (i.e., reformist and integrationist) practice but because that practice was made the basis of a new theory of class relations: thus the traditional relationship of theory and practice was reversed, the status of the canonical texts vis-à-vis an evolving social reality was called into question and with it, implicitly, the legitimacy of canonicity, of historical texts providing historically transcendent norms. According to Rosa Luxemburg (1899a), this constituted an attack on theory itself (441). The fiction of a revolutionary canon of texts and their enduring legislative power had to be preserved; Bernstein's revisionism, as a formal theoretical proposition, was therefore rejected even by some of the most dyed-in-the-wool revisionists.

Both the ideological development of the movement and much of the historical writing concerned with it, then, can profitably be analyzed in terms of the changing functions of canonicity. The movement's need for canonical sources of identity and certainty has its historical reasons: after the failed bourgeois revolution of 1848, the fourth estate as a political body existed merely as an appendix to the bourgeois liberal movement — tolerated, patronized and kept in political naivete. The language of the *Communist Manifesto* and of Lassalle's speeches provided the means to articulate political goals not only in opposition to the forces of reaction but also in opposition to the bourgeoisie as a class presiding over the modern forms of capitalism. In the understanding of early labor leaders, Lassalle's ethical idealism and his effective evocation of the invincible power of truth was complemented by Marx' historical materialism which appeared to elevate Lassalle's ideal of emancipation to a historical necessity. As this "homogenization" of two thinkers as substantially different as Lassalle and Marx shows, the theory which provided the language of the early movement was understood only superficially.

Much has been made of the "wrong" hermeneutics of the movement, its adherence to false prophets, its misreading of the right ones. But the importance, nature and changing functions of canonicity itself tended to be overlooked by historians of the movement. It is, of course, true that the canonical status of certain texts lent authority and coherence to the language of the movement and provided that degree of communality of word, concept, perception and even experience which is a necessary condition of any lasting solidarity. However, the acceptance and, in a sense, duplication of canonical thinking on the part of historians becomes problematic in the sphere of the cultural, artistic and literary values promulgated in the movement. No matter how little the membership, or even the leadership, of the movement understood Marx or Lassalle (or had read them), the latter had provided a number of "scientific" concepts (class struggle, the inevitable evolution toward a classless society, the "iron law of wages") which — in conjunction with the classical revolutionary slogans of freedom, equality and fraternity — could be readily invoked in political agitation as scientific and ethical laws. But beyond Lassalle's call for a "coalition" of workers and science, the movement's canonical sources of truth offered no guiding concepts for an understanding of the role of culture (literature and art in particular) either in the period of revolutionary struggle or in the emancipated society of the future. Nor did these sources show how the socio-economic laws described in them could be used to define form, content and functions of a political or socialist art.

Thus the authority of the socialist canon did not extend into the area of literature and the arts. Except for the works of the "freedom poets" associated with the revolution of 1848 (Freiligrath, Herwegh, Weerth, Heine), no literary or artistic models existed that could have become sources of canonic authority. This circumstance, of course, could have facilitated a redefinition of inherited concepts of art and of standards of judgment, encouraged experimentation with new forms and social functions of art, and might have led to the beginnings of a proletarian class culture, a counterculture not only in opposition to prevailing bourgeois norms but also, in time, capable of producing its own authority. As the socialist movement, which laid emphatic claim to the title of a cultural movement (*Kulturbewegung*), grew stronger, it developed the organizational and physical means necessary to sustain experiments with art forms specific to the life-experience of the proletariat and its political aspirations as a class: cultural associations in many cities, libraries, theaters and theater associations, magazine and book publishing. But despite the occasional lip-service paid to the idea of a "new" or "proletarian" culture, the force of a traditional canonicity prevailed in the cultural area as it did in the political.

The need to herald, defend and "apply" a "scientific" canon (not one based on the self-interest of a class but on universal truths) was essential to the hermeneutic posture of this cultural and strongly ethical movement. But since the revolutionary gesture was not sustained across the full spectrum of ideological life and no "political" canon of texts, ideas and values was available to guide the reception and production of art, the resulting "canonical vacuum" was filled by the standards of a past which the party viewed as the pre-history of the movement and, negatively, by a formal and wholesale rejection of a contemporary bourgeois culture and art as commercial, immoral and decadent. The adoption of the esthetics of German idealism and the rejection of any coalition with progressive bourgeois art movements encouraged the separation of art from politics, discouraged experimentation and enshrined a classical canon which privileged "understanding" and devalued "application": by looking devotedly to the art of the German classical era as a first embodiment of values which would hold triumphant sway in the emancipated society of the future, the hermeneutic gaze became fixed on a point above history, above the specifics of contemporary political life, a point where past and future mirrored each other in a stasis which denied the present any power to act and create, and reduced that present, in the cultural sphere, to an era of passively understanding, conserving and defending a transcendental canon of texts, values and forms of consumption.

I have used canonicity here — in theory, historiography and the cultural sphere — as an initial access to an aspect of the ideological dynamics of the German socialist movement, to its tensions between revolutionary and conservative impulses. For a reception study of early socialist literature in Germany, however, the question of canonicity possesses a special methodological relevance. Two canonical authorities provide the standards of classification and judgment of the reception of texts within the movement: in the area of politics the perceived theory of Marx, in the literary area a select corpus of classical texts (primarily Schiller and Goethe). These two authorities ruled separate realms and did not, explicitly, interact. With the adoption of a "classical" literary and esthetic canon a wholesale importation of traditional bourgeois conceptions of the role and nature of artist, art and "reading" took place so that the printed reception of "socialist" literature within the movement can be seen and reconstructed as the defense of a historically given canon. Literary reviewing, specifically, followed closely the standards of literariness and canonical stature of the bourgeois cultural establishment and press, without, however, emulating the latter's readiness to submit canonical standards to the test of new movements and styles.

Since the two canonical authorities of the movement (the political and the esthetic) remained separate prior to World War I, a vocabulary to discuss a specifically socialist literature could not be developed. In the period following World War I and the split of the movement into Social-Democratic and Communist parties, however, the retrospective reception of the literature of the early movement begins to become politicized: here the canonical authority of Marxist theory replaces to some extent that of classical esthetics and a sorting of texts into properly revolutionary ones on the one hand, and revisionist, petty-bourgeois, etc., on the other, begins to take place. This revision of the canon becomes pronounced in the present, with West German Marxists and East German literary historians setting different accents in accordance with their separate agendas but agreeing in principle that a canon of properly socialist works needs to be extracted from the mass of ideologically faulty material —

with both groups ending up with a minimal canon of ideologically (and esthetically) acceptable texts, a canon surrounded, so to speak, by a vast "canon" of missed historical opportunities.

Canonicity and Reception Study

The reception of theory, the depoliticized role of literature in the movement, and the dominant form of the history both of the movement and of its literary activity — all these have in common a certain reliance on traditional hermeneutic principles. These same principles also underlie traditional reception studies which tend to be studies of the formal, informed and printed readings of historically sanctioned texts. It stands to reason, therefore, that a reception study of early German socialist literature not only take account of the movement's systemic tendency toward a canonical hermeneutics but also question the extent to which traditional reception study is capable of giving an account of the nature and role of literature within a movement most of whose readers did not possess the readerly competence which an H. R. Jauss, for instance, or Hans-Georg Gadamer envision (and represent). Reading, reciting and singing workers of that period made up an "interpretive community" (Stanley Fish) quite different from those communities to which literary theorists, critics and historians (including those of the socialist movement) belong. Traditional reception study tends to privilege a form of literary communication which is the exception, rather than the rule, of literary consumption. It is based on an exclusive model of reading, that of a highly literate reader interrogating a text whose autonomy as a universe of coherent and historically transcendent meanings is assumed and whose mimetic impulse, generic identity and relationship to formal and thematic traditions are taken to be relevant concerns of the reader. This socially authorized form of reading also accentuates its values as a contemplative, non-utilitarian ("esthetic") activity, an activity generically different from other kinds of perception, reaction and action. This view of an "adequate" reading of a literary text places the text outside the framework of interests and needs which inform our daily lives, and views it exclusively in terms of its inherent significations, i.e., meanings supposed to exist independent of the reception process. Where these essentialist meanings are not realized in the reading, or where a text becomes functionalized within a framework of extra-literary interests, a "trivial" reading is supposed to have occurred, a reading that may be of interest to psychologists or sociologists but not literary scholars proper. It is, then, not surprising that the form traditional reception study takes is that of a reiteration of formal, printed reactions to individual texts, authors or movements by critics of authorized competence; this is a form of reception study which constantly reauthorizes the exclusivity of classical hermeneutics and implicitly condemns other personal and social functions of literature and art to marginal relevance. This self-perpetuating circularity of method, of course, is that of traditional literary history and literary pedagogy, and it is inherited by the German socialist movement. The difficulty of a reception study of early German socialist literature lies in the fact that it must account for conditions of production, dissemination and reception ("reading") significantly different from those posited by classical hermeneutics and traditional reception study and that — within literary study — few methodological tools are available to do so.

Within reception study, two basic communicative situations have served as bases of investigation. The first is characterized by a cultural competence presumed to exist in the informed reading, for example, of a poem by Gottfried Benn or Ingeborg Bachmann. Here author and reader share, in Robert Escarpit's terms, a "cultural circuit," or, in the terminology of Gadamer (and later Jauss), a high-cultural "horizon of expectation" shaped by the "authorized consensus" of the Western cultural tradition. The hermeneutic process here envisioned transcends and transforms not only the historicity of two moments which "merge" in that process — that of the origin of the text and that of its later appropriation by the reader — it also transcends the specific "non-literary" interests and motivations that may have occasioned the one, the other or both. While the whole cultural posture of the movement and its educational efforts were devoted to the grand agenda of teaching workers the competence necessary to participate in this kind of high-cultural hermeneutics, all accounts of workers' reading habits circulating within the movement testified to their lack of cultural competence and evoked the ghost of a form of reading presumed to be the "negative" of competent reading: "trivial" reading. In this second basic communicative situation, one characterized by cultural incompetence, the reader (and sometimes the text) is not shaped by high-cultural traditions but rather by interests rooted outside the esthetic realm, resistant to esthetic transformation and impervious to temporal transcendence. *Trivialliteraturforschung* (especially in the form of *Ideologiekritik*) often attempts to determine the needs such "unesthetic" reading meets (escape, consolation, etc.) and the ways "trivial" texts meet these needs. The interest that underlies the historical concern with trivial literature and trivial reading (beginning with Goethe's and Schiller's complaints of dilettantism) is in "trivial" reading as a mockery of "proper" reading, as an inversion or perversion of classical hermeneutics. Where this view dominates, the received values of "proper reading" are not problematized but perpetuated, and the opportunity to investigate other functions of literature (both personal and social) is slighted.

The methods by which the two types of reading are investigated in reception studies are necessarily quite different. Reception as the "effective history" (*Wirkungsgeschichte*) of canonical works is read entirely in the form of printed criticism, i.e., accounts of the reception process purified of all "improper," incidental or functional forms of appropriation. Since such forms of criticism are usually not available for "trivial" literature or non-sanctioned uses of literature, the reception study of "trivial" literature is based, on the whole, on the "trivial" texts alone. These texts are analyzed mainly in terms of their inadequacy of content and ideology, both of which are assumed to be appropriated without any kind of mediation (personal, social, cultural or literary) intervening between text and reader. In this latter form of reception, an "adequacy" between "trivial" reader and "trivial" text is assumed to exist which is comparable to the adequacy presumed to exist between a "competent" text and its "competent" reader. Since there is a systemic unwillingness in reception study (and not only there) to widen the concept of hermeneutics to include uses of literature other than the presumed readerly realization of essential textual meanings in a moment transcending all historical specifics and situational demands, the reception study of both "high" and "low" literature posits the exclusive value of "classical" esthetics, even when studying forms of its absence.

The present study of the reception of early German socialist literature is not the place to challenge systematically the principles of classical hermeneutics and the forms of reception study derived from those principles. It is, however, important to identify two concepts of reception ("competent" and "trivial") and to understand the exclusive role these concepts have played in the movement itself and in most accounts of its literary life. While there was an insistence in the labor movement on the need to acquire traditional hermeneutic competence, more typical and consequential was the realization of the "deficiency" of proletarian reading and of most of the literature circulating within the organizational spheres of the movement. The deficiency was increasingly identified with the "trivial" values of entertainment and sociability. This division of literature into "proper" and "trivial" functions persists not only throughout the literary discussion in the movement but is recapitulated and varied in later evaluations of early socialist literature and becomes ideologically charged: the designation changes to "revolutionary" (proper) and "bourgeois" or "revisionist" (trivial). It is important, then, for a "metacritical" study of early socialist literary activity not to proceed in tautology with the process to be described, merely reiterating judgments most of which are bound to principles which did not, or did not exclusively, inform the cultural and literary life of the early socialist movement, but rather to facilitate an understanding of the organizational and cultural space created by the movement in which literature assumed a number of different functions.

The attempt not to treat an essentially extra-canonical literature and its functions in traditional canonical terms is always problematic; one may become implicated in canonical values by the use of concepts or procedures of apparent methodological neutrality. An example here is the *definition* of socialist literature, i.e., the determination of the object of reception to be described. What is (early) socialist literature? Most answers to this question seek a determination of the nature of socialist literature either in terms of ideological content or in terms of the author's class standing (socialist literature = proletarian literature).

The first approach, which seeks to identify a corpus of socialist literature by its revolutionary or socialist content, permits — if the concept "revolutionary" is a liberal one and the concept "socialist" synonymous with social protest — the inclusion of a number of "political" writers who either preceded the movement or remained at its margins, such as the liberal-bourgeois "freedom poets" of 1848 or the early G. Hauptmann and other Naturalists. The inclusion of the "freedom poets" as a kind of "pre-history" of socialist literature is very much in agreement with their reception in the movement by critics, by the organized literate proletariat and especially by the early poets of the movement who owe much of their tone, gesture and metaphorical resources to them. The inclusion of Naturalists, however, is not in agreement with the official literary ideology of the movement which rejected Naturalism categorically as "unesthetic" and pessimistic. The content-based creation of a corpus of early socialist literature, then, is not necessarily in agreement with the *Selbstverständnis* of the socialist movement or the functions literature had within it; it is, rather, a formal construction. In this approach the bourgeois literary canon is scanned for works of those authors who either befriended the movement or deplored the social conditions it addressed; and these works are segmented out to create the fiction of a socialist tradition as a subset of the inherited bourgeois literary canon. The works of writers active in the movement and identified with its political agenda are then measured against the esthetic standards set by these monuments of bourgeois literary history; the result is their dismissal from canonical respectability with varying degrees of finality and regret. Since the literary life of the movement is not reflected in the bourgeois literary canon, that canon cannot account for its peculiar forms of literary dissemination, reception and valuation.

This (at bottom formalistic) approach to the creation of a "canon" of early socialist literature corresponds to the canonical traditionalism of the movement discussed above. When this approach is adhered to strictly, even with the usual apologies for the lack of cultural competence of early writers in the movement or their intended audience (apologies which reinforce traditional standards by "exempting" some works or writers from them), the resulting corpus of socialist texts is either very small —

or non-existent. A reception study based on this approach would reiterate critical responses to the "socialist" content of some works by bourgeois writers, responses possibly incidental to the tenor of the reception of these works as canonical literature.

There is a version of this approach, however, which refuses to assimilate (and lose) socialist literature in the bourgeois canon. It is a contemporary attempt to recover the true revolutionary impulse in the literature of the movement (or, rather, traces of such an impulse). Here the literary life of the movement is narrowed down to the rare literary expressions of what a later generation considers a genuinely revolutionary attitude — in "operative" poems or some proletarian autobiographies — in order to construct from these fragmented expressions a countercultural canon. This is an "archeology" of unrealized historical potentialities, a kind of "utopia history." Whatever textual canon we construct on this basis would be one without historical authority since these revolutionary impulses left only faint traces in the movement's historical consciousness and recorded memory.

An alternative to the content-based methods described above is a sociological approach to the determination of early socialist literature in which the term "socialist literature" is usually replaced by "proletarian literature" (*Arbeiterliteratur*). The assumption made here is that true members of the proletariat would not or could not express anything but their own life-experiences and would do so in their own language. Their productions, then, are seen as authentic partly by virtue of their lack of literary or cultural "competence." This method of "defining" socialist or proletarian literature is often, of course, more than a scholarly approach to a vexing problem of definition; in many instances, there is an insistence on the "proper" social origin of socialist literature which reflects traditional tensions between educated party leaders and the masses. As far as the question of definition is concerned, however, this approach merely shifts the burden of definition from "proper" textual content to "proper" social origin: who or what is a worker (or proletarian)? The concept has always been an ambiguous one: the movement's first generation consisted mostly of craftsmen, petty bourgeois and bourgeois intellectuals; and even when urban industrial workers made up the majority of the membership of party and unions, the political enlightenment, education and elitism of the qualified worker implied a rejection of pure proletarian life-forms and possible art forms indigenous to those life-forms. In any case, those members of the working class who published poetry, fiction or plays in the socialist press had already moved away from ordinary proletarian existence not only by their degree of literacy but also by their position within the movement: most of them were, or soon became, editors in the socialist press or other kinds of functionaries.

There is a body of literature, of various kinds of writing, by workers untutored and relatively untouched by the conventions of literary expression, popular or classical. Most of these texts are lost in the numerous socialist provincial newspapers; some of them, however, constitute a small but remarkable body of indigenous proletarian literature accessible today. Among these texts the early proletarian autobiography is perhaps the closest thing we have to a genuine literary voice of the proletariat. But here again there is no forgotten canon to be brought back to memory: literature by true proletarians, or literature expressive of a truly proletarian social experience, was never cherished, encouraged or recognized in the socialist press, was never seen as anything more than a form of dilettantism to be discouraged in favor of established notions of formal excellence and universal themes. As much as the equation socialist literature = *Arbeiterliteratur* may satisfy an urge for formal tightness of definition, it is hardly suitable for a description of the forms of production, distribution and reception of literature within the organizational and ideological boundaries of the early socialist movement.

Literature and Literary Life

Content-based approaches to identifying a historical body of literature as "socialist" (or "proletarian") are grounded in notions of text which separate literary works from the uses made of them and which seek to describe the attributes "socialist" or "proletarian" exclusively as textual qualities rather than as social functions of the text. Even using very loose notions of "socialist content" as criteria, the corpus of works between 1860 and 1914 evidencing such content is extremely small and does not constitute a literary-historical body of works; many of the texts thus identified were not widely or lastingly received either in the bourgeois or socialist cultural circuits. On the other hand, during these same decades, the German labor movement grew from tentative liberal beginnings to a system of mass organizations boasting millions of members and the strongest political party in the second *Reich*. As a socialist political organization, it became not only the strongest in Europe, it was — for Lenin and other foreign socialist leaders — a model of organized political culture. This rich and complex organizational culture of the German socialist movement provided the milieu within which literature was produced, disseminated and appropriated; and this milieu comprised a loosely connected set of structures, from the party leadership and its conferences, journals and pamphlets down to singing, hiking and biking clubs and *their* social events and publications. It is this organizational culture, and the ideological forces which informed it, which shaped to a considerable extent the communal and individual uses of literature.

By the turn of the century, German Social Democracy had produced a wide range of alternatives to the social and cultural organizations of bourgeois society in an attempt to shield workers from the harmful influences of bourgeois ideology and to strengthen worker solidarity. Most of these organizational structures — educational or theater clubs, associations of teetotalers or freethinkers — were not based on political or ideological principles specific to their interests. They drew their political identity from their formal association with the party; they were separate but not fundamentally distinct from their bourgeois counterparts. In a sense, then, Social Democracy's elaborate and successful attempt to pit its own organizational totality against bourgeois society resulted in some new forms of organizational life but also in a partial duplication of that society's organizational and ideological structures, a fact particularly evident in the literary life of the movement, in the functions and uses of literature.

It would be wrong, then, to look for an explanation of these uses and functions exclusively in those areas seemingly appropriate for their theoretical discussion: the literary debates at party conferences, for instance, or the pages of the party's theoretical journal *Die Neue Zeit*, Franz Mehring's critical essays or the pronouncements of cultural commissions. The socialist establishment took official and positive note only of those uses of literature which conformed to the canonical reverence so typical of its liberal *Bildungspolitik*; other uses — when noted at all — were tolerated at times but always suspected of trivializing this very reverence. It is indeed important, for an understanding of the literary life of the movement as well as for a reception study of its literary production, to give an account of the official politics of culture and literature and to extract from that politics a theory of literature and its social and — possibly — political functions. But this theorizing about literature and art which took place within the movement (and which is largely systematized in Mehring's writings) neither reflects nor adequately conceptualizes the cultural praxis of organized workers.

It has been established so far that a study of the reception of early German socialist literature which adheres strictly to the primacy of textual qualities in literary communication would end up with a very small corpus of primary works and an equally small group of critical texts interrogating these works. While the scholarly and journalistic reception of certain pre-selected texts constitutes an important aspect of the reception of socialist literature, the full meaning of this form of reception is revealed only when seen as a part of, and partly in contrast to, other forms of literary uses within the movement. Moving away from the narrow "essentialist" position, which must begin with the question: *what* is socialist literature, we are guided toward the other end of the scale: *when* is (was) literature "socialist," i.e., what were the "socialist" uses of literature, or: what functions did literature assume within the context of early organized socialism? This last form of the question, of course, includes the uses of *all* forms of literature, past and present, high or low, political or non-political; it provides a necessary contextual aspect to more specific forms of reception study. The questions appropriate to the reception of early socialist literature within the movement are: what literary functions did the organized culture of the movement privilege for the purpose of imbuing, sustaining, strengthening and shaping a sense of the social, political and cultural identity, purpose and end of its organization (such as representation of social reality, enlightenment, agitation and propaganda, celebration of future victory, pride in the proletarian conquest of culture); which were the texts perceived to provide these uses; and, finally, what other values — peculiar to the movement, but not specific to its perceived social, educational and historical mission — shaped the practice of literary production, distribution and reception?

There is no alternative to the shift proposed here from an essentialist to a functional definition of socialist literature if our interest is in the substantial literary activity of the pre-World War I socialist movement rather than in a small body of texts on the margins of traditional literary history. The common-sense choice of simply accepting as our corpus of literature those texts which the movement labelled socialist or at least perceived to be so, does not offer an alternative either: the socialist establishment until 1914 did not favor the politicization of art to a point where a socialist art or literature could be defined as fundamentally different from traditional art, let alone be instrumentalized as a weapon in the class struggle. The term "socialist literature" is avoided or, as in the case of Mehring, dismissed as a kind of contradiction in terms. The mastery of the monuments of German literary classicism was considered the highest level of literary activity for a culturally and socially emerging working class; its historical mission was the appropriation of the cultural heritage of the past. All other literary concerns were seen as subordinate to this essentially passive and contemplative activity. The literary life of the movement, then, stood under the obligation of two sets of values difficult to reconcile, one — to use well-worn terms here — integrationist (aiming, ultimately, for an assimilation of the proletariat, or its organized part, into the bourgeoisie), the other revolutionary (aiming to overthrow and replace the bourgeoisie and its values as a first step on the way to a classless society). The integrationist orientation in the cultural politics of the movement goes back to the workers' clubs of the 1860s which were run by liberal bourgeois benefactors and dedicated to improving their members' social status primarily through their professional and cultural qualification. The one area of perceived power not contested by the classes was that of *Bildung*, of the scientific and cultural knowledge thought necessary to function in the bourgeois sphere. This is why the organized acquisition of scientific, historical, philosophical and literary knowledge, of "cultural power," took precedence over political action and became emblematic of the fight of the working class for dignity and power and, *at the same time*, of its apolitical and integrationist ideology, of a denial of the class character of its socio-political and cultural situation. In the area of art, literature in particular, equality with the privileged classes seemed possible without political and economic struggle.

However, the fiction of the early educational associations of a community of political and social interests of liberals and workers could not be maintained for long. The history of the German labor movement can be read as the history of its (more or less complete) separation from its liberal parent. Since approximately 1860, a growing movement embarked on a course designed to separate workers from the bourgeoisie and its ideology, enclose them in an organizational culture resistant to outside influences and to permeate their lives with the consciousness of a class destined either to inherit the state from a decadent and dying bourgeoisie or to acquire power by revolutionary action. The separation of the Social-Democratic movement from bourgeois liberalism, its increasing politicization, organizational independence and sophistication, did not, however, lead to a formal reconsideration of the assumed political extraterritoriality of the scientific and esthetic realms so fundamental to the educational aspirations of the early labor associations. But these developments did generate and sustain a strain of the movement's cultural discourse marked by revolutionary, countercultural, even iconoclastic impulses. Where this strain becomes evident, we witness a sort of seepage from the political revolutionary rhetoric of the party and its actual political struggles into the realm of esthetic culture or, in times of reformist acquiescence to the political status quo, a transfer of the revolutionary impulse from the political to the cultural discourse and sphere of action. While any such extension of a revolutionary ideology into the realm of the arts ran counter to the cultural politics of the movement, and the idea of a revolutionary art was never able to unseat or even challenge that politics in any lasting fashion, at the same time the revolutionary temperament could never be expurgated entirely from the cultural discourse of a movement dedicated to radical social change. The official ideology of cultural acquisition rather than production, of preserving inherited values rather than creating new ones, is never without a suppressed or muted counterpoint of revolutionary impulse and gesture; and it is this counterpoint which accounts for certain omissions of theory and the remarkable metaphoric shifts of rhetoric which we can observe in Mehring and other literary critics and theorists.

The relationship between the two strains of the cultural discourse of the movement marks the ideological space of the movement's literary life.

The "integrationist" ideology separates significant esthetic production not only from politics but also, quite emphatically, from the present: the classical perfection of the revolutionary bourgeoisie of the 18th century, represented by Lessing, Schiller and Goethe (and, to some extent, the "freedom poets" of the 19th century), has been perverted within the present late-bourgeois culture; the proletariat must therefore preserve and cherish this perfection and wait for a liberated future in which it will, once again, flourish. This view, expressed systematically by Mehring, not only pits political literature against the universal and historically transcendent significance of great art, thereby reducing it, ipso facto, to the status of the trivial; it also precludes the creation of valid art in the present, not only by the decadent bourgeoisie but also by a proletariat still subject to bourgeois tastes and busy with the political and economic struggle. In the integrationist mode literature appears either as the finished and lasting product of a great past, unmatchable in the present, or as a decadent or otherwise trivial product of the late-bourgeois present. The literary activity proper to the organized proletariat, therefore, is not in the area of production — condemned to be trivial — but in the acquisition of the cultural competence necessary to read, cherish and preserve the classics. This is the historical mission of the class — a noble one but also one essentially alien to what constitutes it as a class: its political and social class consciousness, its cultural experience and its political aspirations.

The two strains are mutually constitutive within the ideological dynamics of the movement's literary life: thus, from the dominant integrationist perspective, all explicitly political literature and all political uses of literature are "revolutionary" to the extent to which they subvert, implicitly or explicitly, the reigning paradigm of the transcendent universality of "true" art and the disinterested contemplation it elicits. "Revolutionary" here does not mean a concept of literature or of literary function derived from a political theory — Lassallean, Marxist or anarchist — or a praxis based on such a theory. There was no theory of revolutionary art in the early movement. The revolutionary element is dialectically constituted within the literary life of the movement by the dominant ideology itself: by its ambiguities, the implicit tensions between political activity and cultural passivity, by the factual and psychological impossibility of containing the revolutionary impulse within the areas and languages of politics and economic struggle. The dominant discourse itself is ideologically fractured and so are the various forms of literary life. It is therefore of limited heuristic value to divide, as many critics have done, the literary products and activities of the movement into integrationist and revolutionary categories: each of these products and activities, as indeed the literary life in its entirety, are characterized by the tension to both conserve and transgress received values, to both challenge tradition and seek legitimation from it. Each activity and product is the result of a transaction between the integrationist and revolutionary strains of the cultural discourse of the movement.

Even the historical mission of appropriating the classics and defending the classical canon against bourgeois decadence, this supposedly proletarian cultural activity *par excellence*, shows the interaction and tension of its integrationist and revolutionary strains. From the days of the early workers' associations on, the image of the worker who — after a day's debilitating work — sits in his ill-heated attic bent over Schiller's heroic *Wilhelm Tell* is an icon, frequently invoked, of the ideology of a possible cultural equality with the bourgeoisie and of a realm above the economic and political struggles between the classes in which human nature, untainted by the narrow interests of the moment, can be contemplated in its timeless esthetic forms. From this perspective, art appears as a sanctuary from politics and as a consolation for its pains. But the image of the worker reading the "poet of freedom" Schiller is also a militant image, one expressive of a fight against educational and cultural deprivation and its causes, and of an appropriation of culture which implies the cultural dispropriation of the bourgeoisie. The proletariat, which — in the words of a later phase of German socialism — "storms the heights of culture," means to hold the conquered territory and to expand it. In that sense, the conquest of the classics is a process symbolic of a wider conquest; and Schiller's dramas in particular, read steadfastly by the proletariat as prefiguring its own fight for freedom, are subject at times to a form of appropriation which instrumentalizes them into weapons in the *political* struggle. When such a (rare) reversal of the ideologeme of classical hermeneutic reverence into political instrumentalization occurs, institutional strictures are not far behind, as the so-called Schiller debate of 1905 demonstrates. There Rosa Luxemburg, Franz Mehring and other socialist intellectuals had to defend, in a manner of speaking, Schiller's historical irrelevance against an effective political and revolutionary use made of some of his dramas.

Other forms of the literary life of the movement exhibit a similar ambiguity of conservative, transgressive and revolutionary tendencies. While on the highest level of cultural sophistication the proletariat was to learn to read the classics, on the lowest level it was to unlearn the reading of penny dreadfuls and other forms of supposedly harmful literature supplied in large quantities to the lower classes, especially to women. The fight against "bad" literature began in the early stages of the movement and remained a major element of socialist cultural policy during the period under consideration here. At no time, however, did the movement create a sustained critique of "trivial" literature: charges of obscenity occurred regularly, as did those of an unacceptable primacy of entertainment over instruction, of misrepresentation of social reality (proletarian reality in particular), of an intellectual paralyzing of the worker with an "opium for the mind and poison for morality" (Liebknecht 1872, 73). Frequently socialist critics of popular fiction implied that the production and sale of such literature constituted a bourgeois conspiracy to keep the proletariat in a state of intellectual and emotional immaturity and to distract it from its political mission. But the campaign against popular fiction lacked specificity of definition: neither the harmful ideological and political effects of this product of bourgeois commercialism were identified and analyzed, nor did its critics advance an idea of fiction, popular or otherwise, which could counteract these effects with specifically socialist ones. The alternative to the growing popularity of "pulp" fiction, then, were the literary classics of the past or a contemporary fiction defined primarily by the *absence* of certain kinds of offensive content.

The campaign against a literature thought capable of contaminating the political disposition of workers is one of the few instances of an acknowledgement of the involvement of literature in the political and ideological milieu in which it is read, of some political and social functions of literature. The exemption of the arts from the movement's philosophy of radical change and the enshrining of canonical reverence as the supreme literary activity of the proletariat could not be expected to create a large worker's elite with the cultural competence of the educated bourgeois, a sort of sub-class of cultural bourgeois in overalls. Workers, as the use of socialist and public libraries showed, indulged in non-approved literature more than in the reading of the classics of socialist theory or bourgeois literature. This kind of literature came to its readers in the form of slick fiction and general-interest magazines. The national consumption of this literature of artificial refinement, melodrama and pseudo-aristocratic outlook far outstripped the consumption of "highbrow" literature or truly subcultural literature such as pornography; its commercial success attracted many high-brow artists and sustained an army of competent hacks. Here is the front at which the party decided to wage its war against harmful literature; the particular target was the most successful of the German fiction magazines, *Die Gartenlaube*. In 1873 already, the Lassalleans had added a literary supplement (*Social-politische Blätter*) to their party newspaper to fight dime novels and fiction magazines like *Gartenlaube* which, according to the former's initial editorial, had "poisoned the mental health of the people and damaged Social Democracy even more than the bourgeois political press" (Loreck 1977, 18). The magazine was eventually merged with the *Volksstaat-Erzähler* of the "Eisenach" branch of the socialist labor movement to produce a singularly successful "socialist" version of the *Gartenlaube, Die Neue Welt* (1876) which eventually appeared in editions far larger than those of its competitor (a run of 650,000 in 1914). It remains to this day the most successful literary undertaking of German socialism.

The co-opting of a successful bourgeois formula proved once again that Social Democracy was able to duplicate bourgeois enterprises. It did not, however, represent a successful attempt to change workers' reading habits or to politicize literature. The *Gartenlaube* affected a literature and style ostensibly free of politics and propaganda but it did glorify country, war, the monarchy, the aristocracy and the officer's corps and permitted itself occasionally to ridicule domestics and other proletarians for their ignorance, defective speech and manners. The editors of *Neue Welt* succeeded largely in eliminating these features offensive to progressive workers from the popular fiction published in their magazine and even published a small number of texts by writers of the movement; but since there was very little popular fiction that could be called proletarian or socialist, the magazine had to draw on many of the same authors published by *Gartenlaube* and similar bourgeois magazines. This most notable fight against "bad" literature is again paradigmatic of the mutual constitution of progressive and conservative tendencies within the organizational culture of German socialism and its literary life. The Social-Democratic party fought a literature which presented capitalist society as a "natural" form of social organization and offered its disadvantaged members nothing but diversions, escapist consolations and a vicarious participation in pleasures and privileges alien to their class. The fight ended with a remarkable "victory" of socialist publishing; and this success is not measured by the size of editions alone: thousands of members of organized labor began their reading careers with *Neue Welt* in which they sometimes — albeit seldom — found themselves and their political orientations to be the heroes of fiction. The magazine fulfilled one function of literature within the movement which was not likely to be mentioned in discussions of literary esthetics: it served to rouse the interest of women in the socialist cause — not by its socialist content but by the implicit authorization of popular fiction — and thus helped recruit new party members. But this "anti-bourgeois" undertaking turned out to be, to a substantial extent, a duplication of its adversary; and its task — to stem certain forms of literature and literary consumption — was subverted, at least in part, to perpetuate and affirm them. This fact was an open secret frequently addressed at party conferences in the form of complaints about the "low quality" of the magazine's content. However, in the absence of any concrete notion of a socialist literature, "highbrow" or light, matters of esthetic and ideological concern receded behind a publishing success of bourgeois proportions and were finally silenced by that success.

As the example of the magazine *Neue Welt* demonstrates, the phenomenon of socialist literary life is not accessible through texts and their manifest meanings alone, nor can the study of its reception be confined to the criticism of "representative" texts. "Texts" here are components of organized activities; and these activities serve cultural-political purposes whose ideological content is definable but seldom obvious. The primacy, in the literary politics of the movement, of classical texts and their appropriation by the proletariat, itself a particular "integrationist" ideologeme, negates the possibility of creating literary "monuments" that narrate, in new forms, style and content, the story and world-view of contemporary socialism, as some of the works of Lessing, Goethe and Schiller were seen to have done for the revolutionary ideology of the 18th-century bourgeoisie. It is therefore inappropriate to analyze texts authenticated and circulated in the movement only in terms of their "bourgeois," "petty-bourgeois" or "revisionist" content or ideological narratives rather than to take account of their functions within the communicative totality of literary life as well.

This is particularly true for the poetry of the movement. Its cherished lyrical texts can be read as depositories of various classical, romantic and bourgeois-revolutionary traditions and their vocabularies; in that sense, their individual content, abstracted from their specific communicative contexts, frequently appears as an unconsummated marriage of various ideological strains. However, the value of these texts was not to be realized primarily in an individual interrogation of their meaning, in the coherence of their conceptual content; their value depended on their effectiveness in particular communicative situations, situations which also provided their generic identity. Some that succeeded brilliantly in that sense (the various proletarian anthems come to mind), may fail all tests of traditional literary judgment. Much of this poetry was meant to be recited before a group or to be sung by it in order to "tune" or motivate that group; and here a variety of specific functions can be made out. Some texts were meant to activate and motivate workers in situations of social or political struggle (strikes, demonstrations, elections), to strengthen their solidarity and courage, to glorify the struggles or to provide solace for their failures. Others (by invoking the vision of a conflictless future or the "natural" inevitability of victory) perform a ritual inducement of optimism; others legitimate a reformist movement by the use of military rhythms and rhetoric and a militant revolutionary metaphoricism. Many of them also contribute to a poetic discourse which to a large extent hymnicized and ritualized the movement by a poetic practice of invocation, incantation and religious metaphorization.

One poetic function, however, seems to overarch all others: celebration. Celebratory poetry is not, of course, a poetry of protest and struggle, of uncertainty and the creation of new visions and values; it designates or calls up certainties, imbues them with paradigmatic universality and thus turns them into ritual, shared sources of reassurance. In early socialist poetry both the past (e.g., the anniversaries of the great poets) *and* the future (the certainty of a revolutionary spring and a summer of fulfillment) are celebrated with equal assurance; thus by the alchemy of poetic celebration and the grand metaphor of the cyclicality of natural time, the struggles and losses of an uncertain extended present are "skipped"; the certainties of past and future, freed of the mediation of a troubled present, are blended into a timeless moment of quasi-religious faith. This kind of poetry, and this aspect of much of the poetry of the movement, does not constitute a rhetoric of persuasion but rather a ritual repetition of a dogma, of an article of faith, from which the solidarity of the community is constantly renewed and strengthened.

Few texts can be reduced to a single one of these functions and the ideological tasks they represent; most of them are multifunctional and as such they reflect, individually as well as collectively, the conflicted totality of socialist cultural practice and literary life.

The Reception of Socialist Literature 1860-1914: A Problem of Method

The functions of the movement's poetry indicated above are not immanent properties of individual texts abstracted from their historical functional contexts. Similar to the other two examples of socialist literary life cited here — the appropriation of the classics and the creation of a socialist fiction magazine — the meaning and function of literary texts is tied to specific communicative situations, organized activities and ideological values: the "tuning" of an activist group, for instance, or the cultural "short-cut" to equality with the bourgeoisie, or the use of popular fiction to attract and hold party members. These ideological functions of literary texts, of course, were not formally articulated in the movement and legitimated as valid bases of esthetic judgment. The formal criticism of the literature of Social Democracy, whether published in the socialist or bourgeois press, tends to reflect criteria of selection and valuation quite different from the functional values these texts had within the literary life of the movement. In essence, they were selected and judged by the standards of the bourgeois literary canon. A reception study, then, which is based exclusively on this body of formal literary criticism, implicitly constitutes the texts selected by this criticism as the corpus of "socialist literature," and thereby commits itself to an essentialist and traditional hermeneutic position and permits a kind of historical disembodiment of the literary life of the movement.

In a reception study of early socialist literature, then, the corpus of primary material and the reception it generated are not defined by a consensus of what the received object is. The determination of Benn's or Bachmann's poetry allows little room for dispute; even in the case of a reception study of "romantic" literature, involving fundamental historical changes in the concept "romantic," the *term* romantic may serve as the formal common denominator. The term "socialist literature," as we have seen, cannot serve that regulating function: criticism written under that label is extremely rare, especially in the time under consideration, and cannot do justice to the full range of literary phenomena unique to German socialism. That full range of what socialist literature is, or rather was, or was perceived to be, cannot be deduced from a small body of criticism formally devoted to socialist literature alone.

A study of the reception of the literature of early German socialism, in contrast to most traditional reception studies, cannot take its object for granted but must define that object even as it describes its reception. The critic cannot act as a mere compiler, cannot pose as an objective mediator of historical opinions; she is heavily implicated, as all reception scholars are to some degree, in defining the object of reception and indeed sometimes defining it to some extent *against* the prevailing trends of the history of its reception — in our case the canonizing tendency and the adherence to a traditional hermeneuticism which permeated the discursive practices of the movement and largely account for the institutional "forgetting," the extended non-reception of much of the literary life of the early movement. It is clear from what has been said so far that this deviation from prevailing trends involves, among other shifts, a shift of emphasis from individual literary critiques (few anyway) to systemic tendencies of reception within the contexts of the literary life of the movement and the larger ideological dynamics of Social Democracy as well as later assessments of these contexts.

In order to carry out such a study of the literary life of early German socialism and its reception, historical aspects have to be brought into view which would remain outside the parameters of a traditional reception study of early German socialist literature, namely the development of the German workers' movement from the liberal education clubs of the 1860s to the largest political organization of the second *Reich* and the evolution of its organizational culture which provided the space of socialist literary activity. Similarly, the organizational and ideological structures of this literary activity need to be made visible: the literary distribution system, especially the socialist press; the institutionalized ideology of culture and literature as it is formulated in Mehring and others and is ineffectively challenged in the rare official literary debates of the movement. Finally, the communicative situation of the individual genres of socialist literature need to be established, along with their formal and thematic properties.

The literature and literary life of the movement between 1860 and 1914 attracted little attention outside its organizational sphere; and even within that sphere, the dialectical relationship of cultural life and cultural theory, of literary theory and practice — having no model in Marxist or Lassallean theory — remained inert. Most of the literature of this period therefore disappeared quickly from the collective and recorded memory of Social Democracy. During the Weimar Republic there is virtually no reception of the literature of early socialism. After 1945, specifically after 1960, a renewed interest in this "forgotten" phase of socialist cultural life generated a considerable amount of research on the cultural and literary politics of early socialism but comparatively little criticism of actual texts. Especially in East Germany, however, a number of dissertations and reprints reopened access to a representative body of texts. This post-war development also must be seen in relation to ideological agendas then alive in the two parts of Germany: the writing of a pre-history of East Germany's cultural and literary politics in general and the ideology of Socialist Realism in particular and, in West Germany, the debunking of a social democratic establishment seen as hopelessly compromised, along with the concomitant search for a pre-history of genuine revolutionism suppressed in the accounts of bourgeois and party historians.

2: The German Labor Movement 1860 — 1914: Class Struggle vs. Integration

CRITICAL ACCOUNTS OF EARLY socialist literature in Germany generally appear as sub-texts of the political and ideological history of the Social-Democratic movement; and in many cases there is a massive and unmediated transfer of concepts and interpretive strategies from politics and political theory to the literary life of organized labor. The account given in this chapter of the development of Social Democracy as a political organization and as an organizational culture is necessary for a reception study of early socialist literature not only because the Social-Democratic "subculture" constituted a cultural circuit different, in some significant respects, from the bourgeois sphere of high-cultural consumption, but also because the dominant critical approach to early socialist literature treats the literary life of the movement as a kind of mirror to be held to its political life. And this is a mirror which magnifies especially the *embourgeoisement* (*Verbürgerlichung*) of the movement, its deviations from "correct" revolutionary standards; here — in the terminology of the preceding chapter — the hermeneutical failures and "textual infidelities" of a supposedly Marxist movement are elaborated in terms of the formal and thematic intertextualities and proximities of bourgeois and socialist literature. Only rarely, then, is the cultural life of organized labor seen as an autonomous sphere, with its own version of the ideological complexities of the movement; instead it appears as a privileged point of access to the petit-bourgeois values embedded in its organizational structures and literary texts. Consequently, in the descriptions of this culture the critics' own political-ideological agendas are frequently advanced with scant patience for the existential conditions and cultural needs of a disenfranchised but self-emancipating class.

The following account of the political development of the early socialist labor movement in Germany emphasizes the ideological performance of certain notions which are central to its *Weltanschauung*, are indeed nodes of its discourse. These notions mark the "switching points" of the transfer mentioned above from the political sphere to the cultural and literary areas which can be witnessed in the reception of early socialist literature. They are socially and historically disembodied notions of the state and legality, of freedom, justice, knowledge and art, of historical determinism and revolutionary freedom, of class and its limits.

The Political Emergence of a Class

The early German labor movement had no successful German revolution to draw on as a legitimating historical paradigm. In contrast to France, the implementation of enlightened ideas in the 18th century (such as the emancipation of the peasants) had not come from below, through revolution, but from above, in the form of state-ordered reforms. The then-dominant political ideal of an enlightened monarchy was based on an idea of the state as a legal structure above politics and class interests. This conception encouraged reverence for authority and the law and facilitated the ideological transformation of class problems into legal and administrative ones (Böhme 1969, 38). It is this "idealistic," class-transcendent conception of the state which the labor movement inherited from a liberal bourgeoisie which fought for it in 1848 in a revolution which — despite its military aspect — was the outcome and expression of a reform movement faithful to the law and the monarchy (Mann 1958, 194). The liberal conception of the state was subsequently reinforced not only by the first legislator of modern German socialism, Ferdinand Lassalle, but also and especially by the form of political struggle imposed on the movement by historical circumstances: that of a prolonged struggle for its legality. This is an idea of the state, as Marx put it in his critique of the "Gotha Program" of the unified socialist parties of 1875, which is "abstracted from its social conditions," "an independent entity [...] with its own *intellectual, ethical, libertarian foundations*" (Marx 1946, 29).

It is in the bourgeois revolution of 1848 that this liberal idea of the state became the basis of revolutionary activity and a revolutionary discourse. During the early phases of industrialization in Germany, the bourgeois and proletarian classes developed side by side, one necessary for the existence of the other (Rühle 1930, 20-21); and their common opposition to the reactionary and feudalistic powers of the German states minimized differences of interest between them. The extent to which early attempts at organizing the proletariat appear as an afterthought, indeed as a kind of mimicry, of the movement of bourgeois emancipation can be seen in the organization begun by Stephan Born and his "Central Committee for Workers" in Berlin in 1848. The "General German Labor Fraternity" (*Allgemeine Deutsche Arbeiterverbrüderung*) spread rapidly, published a journal and held national conferences in the two years of its existence. The aim of these organizational efforts, however, was not to constitute and empower a class separate from that of the bourgeoisie but rather to upgrade the social status of workers and to integrate them into state and society on the basis of equal legal rights (Balser 1962, vol. 1, 50). The bourgeois and proletarian classes suffered the persecutions and repression of the post-revolutionary reaction together; and this commonality of political experience sustained, for another decade or so, the idea of a grand, popular liberal movement in which the working class was a "natural" but inactive participant. However, the industrialization of the 1850s, with its "phenomenal increase in production" (Kuczynski 1946, 87), brought new economic power to the bourgeoisie and the first indications of a tendency to subsume the political ideals of 1848 under those of economic progress, to trade, so to speak, political power for the unhindered development of a modern system of capitalist free enterprise. Here the interests of the bourgeoisie and the propertyless masses began to diverge; and the labor movement began to see itself as the proper heir to the political ideals of 1848.

Since the "three-class" electoral system which prevailed in Germany granted the propertyless class only token power, the form its political organization took was that of the voluntary association (*Arbeiterverein* or *Arbeiterbildungsverein*), initiated, sponsored and guided by liberal organizations. These associations were devoted to educational goals and maintained, at least formally, the abstention from overt politics imposed upon them by law. But it was in the very nature of these clubs, as *proletarian* organizations, that a class-oriented concern with economic and social oppression would undermine political neutrality and the fiction that abandoning the liberal party line would separate workers from the "grand cause of civil liberties" (Schulze-Delitzsch 1862, 218).

By the early 1860s, the idea of class difference as a difference entirely of legal rights, education, social attitude and refinement, as propagated by such liberal labor leaders as Roßmäßler and Schulze-Delitzsch, had lost some of its power. This particular liberal ideology, however, survived the split of the liberal and proletarian political movements and accompanied, as an effective ideological sub-text, the entire development of German Social Democracy, surfacing at times in the form of various "deviant" ideological strains, such as "ethical socialism," revisionism etc. A comprehensive statement of the liberal position concerning the working class is Schulze-Delitzsch' "catechism for workers" (*Arbeiterkatechismus*, 1863), one of the most widely circulated political pamphlets of the 19th-century German labor movement. Here the power of capital is seen as a natural phenomenon, as a class-transcending source of progress benefitting everyone (43); workers' organizations should not engage in futile attempts to change the socio-economic structure but rather strive to *know* its "eternal laws" (112).

The decisive impetus for the development of a class-based labor movement came from Ferdinand Lassalle who had recently developed an interest in the "workers' question" (*Arbeiterprogramm, 1862*). He was approached by a group of labor leaders to serve as their spiritual mentor in the style of Schulze-Delitzsch, to be for the modern labor movement the "powerful mind in which everything is concentrated and from which everything emanates" (Dammer, Fritzsche, Vahlteich 1862, 352). Lassalle responded in a "grand" manner totally new to the halting discourse of proletarian emancipation, giving, in Mehring's words, the *"ordre de bataille* in the first battle of the great war of emancipation of the German proletariat" (1897-98, vol. 2, 43). In the language of the "Open Letter" (*Offenes Antwortschreiben*, 1863) with which he responded to the request, "large problems must be solved in a grand manner, never piecemeal" (84). Lassalle is the first highly visible spokesman for the working class to reject explicitly the laborious road to the social elevation of workers by way of savings and education as well as the liberal approach to minimizing class difference; on the contrary, he makes this difference the pivot of his political philosophy and strategy. In his "Open Letter" and subsequent statements, the separation of the proletarian cause from that of the liberal bourgeoisie becomes a compelling philosophical idea, a historical as well as ethical imperative; this "most important historical consequence drawn from the revolution of 1848," so a later Marxist, is an act whose importance "grows with the historical perspective" (Luxemburg 1904, 417, 418). Just as important as the content of his political agenda are Lassalle's language and rhetorical stance, his public manner and image. Lassalle claims the grand revolutionary style of the freedom poets of 1848 for the struggle of the working class, thus legitimizing and heroicizing, by implicit historical parallel, a political struggle not yet properly begun.

In contrast to Marx' historical materialism, Lassalle stresses the ethical and legal aspects of the workers' circumstances and consequently the fight for the general, equal and direct vote as the principal and sole aim of the party founded by him in 1863, the General German Workers' Association (*Allgemeiner Deutscher Arbeiterverein*, ADAV). Lassalle's idea of "revolution" means the establishment of new legal norms on the basis of existing ones (Na'man 1970, 333-34), a concept which links Lassalle and the modern labor movement with the revolution of 1848 and one which remains at the heart of its revolutionary discourse. The state — which would be conquered by legal means, and with the "drawn sword of science" (1863a, 89) — is a legal entity, removed from the historical forces that shape it, an "unhistorical fiction" which, according to Rosa Luxemburg (1904, 419), was actually an idealization of the Prussian state.

The history of the German socialist labor movement can be read, as much orthodox historiography does, as the successful overcoming of Lassalle's theoretical heritage by Marxism. What this narrow view obscures (or merely relegates to the category of "error") is the fact that Lassalle's writings initiated the theoretical understanding of most early labor leaders (such as Bebel) and remained at the very core of the socialist canon of texts at least until 1918; and many of his slogans became part of the essential ideological vocabulary of socialist discourse and literature, a vocabulary quite impervious to the theoretical changes in the party program. One of Lassalle's important functions in the development of German Social-Democratic ideology was that of conduit to the revolutionary tradition of 1848 which both branches of the movement claimed as their heritage. The resilient heroic icon of Lassalle is at the center of a mythical narrative of potential poetic and dramatic power: the agon of a heroic defense of freedom and justice before a court of law and the ultimate triumph of the word, of knowledge and truth over selfishness and ignorance. Here the historical reality of power is transformed into a narrative of contesting ideas.

Most *Arbeitervereine*, however, continued to submit to the tutelage of bourgeois liberal leaders and supported the national congresses of labor associations, the first few of which were totally dominated by bourgeois elements (Bebel 1910-14, vol. 1, 106) and confirmed the liberal agenda. The congress movement, however, came under the influence of Liebknecht and Bebel — recent founders of the petit-bourgeois, liberal Saxonian People's Party (1866) — and joined the First International (founded in 1864) at the Nuremberg congress of 1868. The key statements of the program approved at that congress — that class rule must be abolished and the emancipation of the working class must be accomplished by the working class itself — separated this branch of the German labor movement from the liberal establishment. One year later, in 1869, the congressional movement voted to join the Social-Democratic Workers' Party, founded by Bebel and Liebknecht and some renegade Lassalleans in Eisenach that same year. The Lassalleans and the Eisenach party did not collaborate to advance the cause of labor but rather devoted much of their energy to fighting each other. Their controversies seldom dealt with conceptual or theoretical issues.

The events of 1870-71 became the first defining experience of the young labor movement. The Franco-Prussian war and its conclusion confronted party leaders with choices fraught with risk. After the capture of the French Emperor, Napoleon III, the party considered the objective of the war to be accomplished and voted against additional war credits in the Imperial Diet (*Reichstag*). Following Marx' lead, the party also condemned the intended annexation of Alsace-Lorraine, and campaigned vigorously, in the language of a slogan run repeatedly in the *Volksstaat* in 1871, for "A just peace with the French Republic! No annexations!" This was an attitude of considerable courage but also, in a climate of triumphant nationalism and chauvinism, one which earned the "socialists" a reputation for unpatriotic internationalism, for being — in the terms of imperial invective — "fellows without a fatherland."

An even more defining experience during this period was the uprising of the Paris proletariat in March 1871 and its brutal suppression by French government troops at the end of May, an act tolerated and aided by the German occupiers. Encouraged by Marx, Social-Democratic leaders had greeted the Paris Commune enthusiastically as an example and harbinger of proletarian revolution: the *Volksstaat* reported the events and their aftermath as a political myth in the making and Bebel defended the Commune in the *Reichstag*. As Bruno Kaiser's and Ursula Schulz' documentations (1958, 1968) show, the Paris Commune was celebrated, mourned and invoked in the German labor movement as the paradigmatic revolutionary experience of the epoch. The endorsement of a violent uprising was to haunt Social Democracy for years to come. Leaders were arrested and interned. The high point of these persecutions was a charge of high treason against Liebknecht, Bebel and Adolf Hepner. The trial, known as the *Leipziger Hochverratsprozess*, took place in March 1872 and resulted in two-year jail sentences for Bebel and Liebknecht. Its transcript became one of the canonical documents of the movement.

This document is remarkable in two ways. By reading forbidden socialist texts into the court record, the defendants provided the only legal access then available to some of the important "subversive" texts of the movement, thus turning a governmental act of suppression into a propaganda victory. In addition to this representation of the socialist textual canon, the eloquence, erudition and ethical posture of the defendants created the impression, not unintended, of a re-enactment of Lassalle's famous judicial defenses of truth and legality against ignorance and the perversion of the law. The link is made explicitly: Bebel appropriated Lassalle's claim for the *Eisenacher* that all uses of the term *revolution* had been peaceful ones; and Liebknecht, in an autobiographical statement submitted to the court, proves that the *Communist Manifesto* only describes natural processes and opposes any "mechanical" making of a revolution (26). This comprehensive, well-argued defense of socialism, "framed" by a canon of authorizing texts, reinforces the Lassallean narrative of class struggle as a rhetorical exercise, as a dispute essentially of verbal exchanges, as a heroic defense of pre-existing concepts of legality and justice. Here social struggle appears as ethical action and socialist theory as a reading of the "natural laws" of an inevitable social evolution.

The liberal establishment accepted Bismarck's authoritarianism as a price to be paid for unification, for an increased rate of industrialization and Germany's rise as an economic power. The short-lived boom after unification (*Gründerjahre*) seemed to confirm the wisdom of this political pragmatism. The perception of an alliance of state, aristocracy and segments of the liberal bourgeoisie against the labor movement led to a rapprochement of the two socialist parties; the two branches of German Social Democracy finally merged in 1875. The so-called "Gotha Program," which was to serve as the theoretical basis of the party until 1891, is seen in traditional histories of the party as a compromise forced upon the Marxists by the Lassalleans. In the verdict of Marx and Engels, it represented a temporary defeat of Marxism. Both views presuppose the importance, to the framers of the program, of theoretical questions over those of agitatory efficacy, an assumption not confirmed, for instance, by Bebel's memoirs. Moreover, most of the Lassalleanisms found in the Gotha Program were neither imposed on the discourse of the party nor did they disappear from it after the official "defeat" of Lassalle.

Official persecution of the party increased in proportion to its organizational consolidation and the growth of its electoral appeal. The time spent in safeguarding the legality of organizations and organizational activities, spent in jail and in preparation of legal defenses absorbed a large portion of the socialist leaders' attention. There was a Lassallean kind of heroism in evading and defeating prosecutors — as well as in losing to them, of course. Even before 1878, if we can trust Bebel's detailed account in his memoirs, the political life of the party centered on legal questions and practices. Next to the legal safeguarding of the organizations of the movement, legislative work in the *Reichstag* constituted the mainstay of the party's political work, and this work consisted largely of speeches, the submission of bills which had no chance of approval and the rejection of the government's budget. With the ratification and enactment of the anti-socialist law in October 1878, which forbade all party activity except legislative work, the narrow emphasis on the legal and largely symbolic parliamentary aspects of politics, inherent in the movement from its beginning, had become "law."

The law suppressing all non-parliamentary political activity of the Social-Democratic party was renewed until 1890. The devastation which its rigorous enactment wreaked can hardly be imagined. With very few exceptions, all local associations were closed down and 40 newspapers and other periodicals, as well as 1,200 other publications, were banned. Labor leaders were expelled from their cities and home districts, violently disrupting their personal, professional as well as political lives. As the results of national elections show, illegality did not weaken the movement but strengthened it against all expectation: Social Democrats emerged from the election of 1890 as the strongest party, with almost 20% of the popular vote. This result, along with substantial gains by other oppositional parties, hastened the end of Bismarck's regime, an end celebrated in party histories as the defeat of the "Iron Chancellor" at the hands of Social Democracy. In these histories, the period of partial exile from political life (1878-90) appears as the "heroic age" of Social Democracy, as a time when — struggling against overwhelming odds — its historical mission became clear and its true character as a class organization and revolutionary party was formed.

There can be no doubt that during this period the Social-Democratic movement came of age, so to speak, in terms of forming a lasting ideological and organizational identity. The theoretical separation of labor from the liberal-bourgeois cause, which Lassalle had initiated, and the subsequent development of independent political organizations had established the notion of a separate class with separate goals. However, the siege mentality which the movement developed under the influence of its prolonged status as a political and cultural pariah shifted its emphasis from changing society to creating a counter-society. Especially in the area of organizational culture, the formal separateness of socialist organizations from their bourgeois counterparts outweighed the importance of their content. After the banning of newspapers and organizations, many of them were revived and forbidden again until ways had been found to safeguard their legality by making them politically "neutral." Considerable ingenuity went into reviving and preserving the old political organizations as politically neutral ones. Here a veritable culture of legalization developed which inverted the official condemnation of Social Democracy: not the party was illegal, rather its illegalization was. The legality of the party's aims and means was the guarantee of its eventual victory. In the words of a proclamation of Hamburg party leaders going into exile: "Our enemies will perish of our legality" (Miller, 1964, 179).

This aspect of the development of Social Democracy during the period of the anti-socialist law contrasts sharply with its description as the heroic age of the movement, as a phase in which its radicalism and irreconcilable antagonism to bourgeois society, in short, its Marxist character, became firmly established. The latter view is not confined to orthodox Marxist historians. Schorske (1955, 3), for instance, subscribes to it as much as does the official history of the movement of the GDR (*Geschichte der deutschen Arbeiterbewegung*, vol. 1, 352-94). Both cite as prime evidence the official deletion from the party program, at the first exile congress in Wyden, Switzerland, in 1880, of the phrase that the party strives to accomplish its goals "by all legal means." This rhetorical response to an imposed condition of illegality did not, however, amount to a declaration of revolutionary violence against Bismarck's state. The party made every possible effort not to be provoked into violence. Here, as during the Leipzig treason trial, the idea of socialist revolution is dissociated from an abstract, dehistoricized concept of violence: "violence can be a reactionary as well as a revolutionary factor, it is the former more often than the latter" (*Die Kongresse*, vol. 2, 155). Marx did not provide the movement with a guiding concept of revolution which could have served to problematize the ideological practice here described. In his Inaugural Address to the International (1864), for instance, the key terms are "conquest of power" and "emancipation of the working class" (12-13), an "empty concept" of revolution which leaves the tension between historical determinism and revolutionary activism unresolved (Miller,

1964, 120, 121); and nowhere, according to Scharrer (1976, 23), does Marx describe "the proletariat as acting revolutionary subject."

The need to argue for a categorical difference between socialist revolutionism and the "pitchfork-wielding" variety of an actual uprising became an important motivating element of socialist discourse. Freeing the notion of revolution from its traditional component of substantial willed action left a gap between the radicalism of the movement's revolutionary language and the reality of its ideological performance which consisted of *administering an expectation of social change*: "it is not our task," so Symmachos (i.e., Karl Kautsky) in the *Sozialdemokrat* in 1881, "to *make* revolution but rather to *use* it" (Steinberg 1967, 61). This phraseology persists with Kautsky, the chief theoretician of the party, until World War I. In 1893, in an article on a "Social-Democratic catechism," he coins the phrase: "Social Democracy is a revolutionary party, but not one which makes revolution," which is repeated with equal assurance in his *Der Weg zur Macht* (The Road to Power, 1909, 53). The party's legalism and parliamentarianism was authenticated with some finality in Engels' preface to the 1895 edition of Marx' *Klassenkämpfe in Frankreich 1848 bis 1850* [*The Class Struggles in France (1848-1850)*], in which the impossibility of a successful violent revolution is as much taken for granted as is the continued growth of Social-Democratic electoral power which will encompass new segments of the middle class and which will unfold "as unstoppably and as quietly as a natural process" (Engels 1895, 524). Despite some later modifications to its "peaceful" language (Kautsky 1909, 49-52), this text was both symptomatic and normative.

With the emphasis on legality in the official discourse of the party, and in its rebuilding of a devastated organizational structure, then, the movement did more than merely "hide" its true revolutionary intentions from the watchful eyes of the police, as nostalgic views of the "heroic age" would have it. Under the pressure of the anti-socialist law, the movement systematized, in its discourse and institutions, the principle of revolution which it had inherited from Lassalle and the bourgeois revolutionaries of 1848. And since the threat of a recriminalization of socialist activities persisted well into the 20th century, the rejection of a *making* of revolution, of *initiating* social and political change by any means other than parliamentary legislation, became the hallmark of Social-Democratic revolutionism. The primacy of the survival of the organization over matters of "theoretical content" had become a constituent element of German Social Democracy.

The Trials of Legality

The period of emergence from legal exile offers an opportunity to test the theory of a new socialist revolutionism nurtured in and by that exile.

This is a period marked exclusively, in many histories of the movement, by the formal adoption of Marxism in the party program of 1891. In the narrative of orthodox Marxist historiography, Marxism had finally prevailed over Lassalleanism and "vulgar-socialist traditions," and the movement had been firmly placed, as far as its theory was concerned, "on a foundation of contemporary science" (Engels 1891, 227); and, of equal importance, theory and its informing texts had assumed the primacy appropriate to them in a scientific *Weltanschauung*. But for Schorske (1955, 4-6), as for other non-party historians, the Erfurt Program encodes the movement's double agenda, its compromise between revolutionary and long-term objectives and the immediate needs in an unrevolutionary period, a compromise between revolutionism and reformism which held as long as the socio-economic realities permitted the illusion of their compatibility. The program consists of two parts, one devoted to theoretical, the other to practical matters. The lack of mediation between them, as Miller (1964, 217) has pointed out, is prefigured in the Le Havre Program Marx had written for the French socialists (Marx 1880b). The "dialectical unity" of revolutionism and reformism and, in a sense, theory and practice, which orthodox histories assume to exist in the conceptual structure of the program (e.g., Füllberth 1974, 8; Abendroth 1978, 32), was never spelled out or demonstrated by Marx (Miller, 1964, 216) — the "dialectic" remains unfulfilled not only in the political practice of the movement but in the theoretical part of the program, as annotated by Kautsky, as well.

In these annotations (1892), Kautsky, architect of the theoretical section of the program, attempts to maintain a balance between political action and a passively experienced teleology; however, political activism of any substantial kind is theoretically devalued: societies are not constructed like buildings, they are the result of historical processes (132); they are not merely something to be wanted, they are inevitabilities (136). The historical evolution may be aided somewhat by willed action and thought, but principally ideas play a part only as an accompanying process of *understanding* (138). This theoretical basis of the party leaves no room for revolutionary activities that may initiate historical processes; and, apart from the certainty of a future public ownership of the means of production, it withholds all concrete views of that future from the workers' imagination: "speculation" on the nature of the "future state" (*Zukunftsstaat*) is pronounced futile. This refusal to "show" the socialist future not only provided political opponents with a ready-made target, it also seemed to violate the "scientific" posture of modern socialism, its presumed power to extrapolate and project. This vague utopianism of expectation constituted an imaginative void readily filled with "pre-scientific" utopian content, popular and literary.

Kautsky's version of Marxism, as codified in his annotations of the party program, was widely distributed in the movement. It represents a reading of Marx mediated by another "text," that of Darwin and his epigones, a mediation in turn facilitated by Engels. In the afterword to the second edition of *Das Kapital* (1872), Marx speaks of the understanding which this work had quickly found among large portions of the German working class, "which I consider the best reward for my work" (19). The historical facts are quite different. Not even the leaders of the movement had read much Marx, and what little of his thoughts figured in their theoretical considerations was appropriated through a scientism, typical of the late 19th-century liberal intellectual, of which various popular forms of Darwinism — this "most eminently democratic science" (Bebel 1891, 195) — are probably the most important concretizations. Bebel's and Liebknecht's early writings, for instance, show the extent to which *The History of Civilisation in England* by the English social Darwinist Buckle provided a Darwinist model of history for the leadership of the movement.

As Steinberg (1967) demonstrates in his chapter on the reception of Marx in Social Democracy (43-86), party intellectuals received Marx primarily through Engels' so-called *Anti-Dühring* (book version in 1878). Whatever concept of socialism workers had came principally from Bebel's *Die Frau und der Sozialismus*, first published in 1879 (1891). Both emphasize the evolutionary aspect of Marxism. Especially the former flattened the dialectic of socio-economic evolution and human activity down to a "synthesis of nature and history," to social history as natural history. In his memoirs written in the early 1930s (1960), the 82-year-old Kautsky still describes Darwinism as the decisive formative influence on his *Weltanschauung*; the move from this position to Marxism entailed only a "modification" of the latter (216). What Kautsky's version of Engels' Marxism signifies is the canonization of a "revolutionary attentism" (Groh 1973), a form of "passive fatalism" (Scharrer 1976, 22). According to Edmund Fischer, both Darwinism and Marxism teach that evolutionary processes are very slow. That fact destroys the illusion that the world may be changed through revolution. The patient nurturing of reforms is therefore the proper form of Marxism (Fischer 1909, 576, 583).

The Engels/Kautsky transmittal of Marx is one example of the need to revise the notion of a "pure" hermeneutical relationship between the movement and the Marxian texts then available in favor of a serious study of typical forms of mediation. The Darwinistic version of Marxism in turn is mediated by other, less theoretical, "scientific" and abstract forms of popular socialism. Here Bebel's *Die Frau und der Sozialismus* plays an eminently important role. The book was *the* underground classic of the exile years. It is the only canonical text of the movement which does not refuse to "show" the future: Bebel sketches out a *Zukunftsstaat* (261-336) with a concreteness and enthusiasm which anticipates Edward Bellamy's utopian novel *Looking Backward* (1888). Clara Zetkin's translation (1889) became a classic text for the literate segment of organized labor and influenced the temperament of popular socialism more than any of the movement's theoretical texts could have done. Not only the myth of a triumph of Marxist theory in 1891 needs to be revised but also the underlying myth of a hermeneutic posture toward classic texts. This latter myth became norm in the official history of the labor movement in the GDR, in which the reception of every Marxian text is studied as if the movement had been, by some higher fiat, transfixed in a permanent posture of Marxian hermeneutics. Schieder (1964, 336-37) finds that such an exclusive emphasis on the Marx-reception in the movement detracts — in Conze's terms — from the larger "field of tension between state and society"; and Steinberg (1967, 124), in a provocative inversion of the orthodox hermeneutic axiom, proposes that the "history of Social Democracy between 1890 and 1914 is a history of emancipation from theory itself."

This latter view presupposes that the relationship to theory had ever been a constituent of the movement in any substantial sense. Social Democracy derived its "scientific" legitimacy from Marx (and Lassalle); but this ritually invoked *Wissenschaftlichkeit* was that of a popular, deterministic natural history of society deprived of all traces of Marxian dialecticism. Beyond this central metaphor and its attendant slogans, theory — although enshrined — was largely ignored and often resented. Bebel tells us that the hectic schedule of party leaders left them no time for "private theoretical considerations" (1910-14, vol. 1, 117, 118). The resistance to theory can be traced in the congresses of the Social-Democratic party. It frequently took the form of a resentment against university-trained intellectuals (*Akademiker*) whose education placed them under the suspicion of retaining bourgeois values and of a half-hearted commitment to the proletarian struggle: they are seen as people who often bring to the movement nothing but "a ruined bourgeois existence and a Ph.D." (*PPT* 1896, 88). Their insistence on theoretical discipline contradicted the practical requirements of the "daily political battle": "not the writing of big books represents genuine party discipline but the involvement in the daily struggle" (*PPT* 1893, 120). In the prolonged *Akademiker-Debatte* at the congress of 1903, the issues of bourgeois academic training, cooperation with bourgeois journals, revisionism and freedom of thought all became issues in a vicious fight in which representatives of all fractions of the party (Mehring, Bernstein, Bebel, Kautsky, Göhre, Vollmar among others) were similarly accused of theoretical rigidity.

The first formal problematization of the presumed primacy of theory in the movement came from the leader of southern reformists, Georg v.

Vollmar, in 1891 and prefigured in some ways Bernstein's later challenge. In the first of his so-called Eldorado speeches, Vollmar affirms the purpose of theory "to represent an idea in its purity [...], to state the ultimate goal"; but he finds that in the era of legality the obvious discrepancy between electoral strength and practical political weakness calls for a transition from the primarily theoretical approach to a practical one, from the general to the particular (6). Responding to criticism of his address in his second speech, Vollmar especially opposes one aspect of received Marxist theory codified in the Erfurt Program: the primacy of an eschatological future over the present which he compares to the ultimate consolation of Christian teaching (20). The belief in an imminent collapse of bourgeois society and the expectation of "jumping directly into the future state" does not strengthen political activity but leads, on the contrary, to a "tactic of political abstinence" (21).

The year 1891 — the year of the Erfurt congress — is indeed a historical moment in the evolution of organized labor in Germany. The party had emerged from exile with a heroic posture, was rapidly increasing its electoral appeal, and had given its liberal-revolutionary practice a "scientific" basis. But there is more to this moment than the "adoption of the principles of scientific socialism by organized labor" (e.g., Füllberth 1874, 7); this is a historic moment particularly because it is rich in ambiguity which can be seen in the famous Erfurt congress itself. The discussion of the new party program did not take place; the program was adopted, at the end of the congress, without debate. Delegates had more important things to talk about. What did cause controversy and debate were Vollmar's speeches mentioned above and the attacks by a group of Berlin radicals, the so-called *Jungen* (Young Turks) on the leadership for its lack of revolutionary fervor. The campaign of the Young Turks was short-lived and quickly dismissed from history as a revolt of misguided *litterateurs* (Engels). However, the *Jungen* make up a significant ingredient in this moment's ambiguity. Both Vollmar's pragmatism and reformism and the Young Turks' charge of a death of revolutionism at the hands of party bureaucrats addressed the problem of the party's exclusive emphasis on a formally radical, legalistic ideology and the socially self-contained political life of the movement. But while Vollmar's reformism became the dominant mode of Social-Democratic politics, the revolutionary voice that had spoken inarticulately through the *Jungen* accompanied the further development of the movement as a muted but dialectically active strain of its ideology.

The increasing conservatism and political pragmatism of the party — whether in the form of "reformism" (Vollmar), "revisionism" (Bernstein), "practicism" (Ignaz Auer) or, at a later date, Kautsky's "centrism" — is to a considerable extent a result of its organizational development. In contrast to the bourgeois political parties of Wilhelminian Germany which consisted mainly of local dignitaries, the Social Democrats were a mass party devoted to political enlightenment (Ritter 1959, 45). Together with its associated unions and specialized workers' associations, it constituted a growing network of organizations and publishing outlets. This institutional growth required an increased bureaucracy and resulted in an increased bureaucratization of its life, a process first analyzed by Robert Michels in 1910. Unlike early popular leaders (Bebel, Liebknecht), full-time officials and parliamentarians were understandably committed more to the growth and survival of organizations than to their original "revolutionary" mission: organization became "the only vital function" (Michels 1910, 470 & 473).

An important factor in the development toward bureaucratism and reformism in the movement was the growth and centralization of affiliated labor unions after 1890. The practical work of unions had always been viewed by party politicians as reformist in nature and therefore inherently integrationist. The early Lassalleans saw unions as a detraction from high politics; and even the Marxists considered them useful only as "schools of socialism" (Marx) from which workers would "naturally" emerge as socialists (Bebel 1910-14, vol. 1, 193), as subsidiaries subject to party control. With the establishment of the General Union Commission under the leadership of Karl Legien in 1890, the Social-Democratic unions gained in organizational strength and independence, a development which already at the party congress of 1893 led to attacks on their independence and reformist tendencies. The complicated relationship between the two organizations had been "contained" in the metaphor of the two "pillars" of the movement (one representing the political fight of the party, the other the economic struggle of the unions); but since both were Social-Democratic organizations, the party's intellectual (theoretical) leadership was tacitly assumed. This fiction of a subservient partnership held as long as the party showed no signs of developing tactics commensurate with its revolutionary rhetoric. When this seemed to change, as in the mass-strike debate of 1905, the unions turned out to be an effective and powerful opponent.

In such situations of internecine conflict, the reformist agenda of the unions became articulated without apology. In 1899, for instance, Legien declared, in pointed opposition to the party's revolutionary language, that the unions had no interest in the "imminent" collapse of bourgeois society; they do not want to "build new social structures on the rubble of the old ones" (Varein, 1956, 20). The unions, so Legien at a later date, want a "higher culture and want to achieve it by way of a quiet development" (Legien 1911, 18). The party continued to uphold, by the efforts of its orators and editorialists, the idea of a "revolutionary expectation." But the greater the gap between its electoral triumphs and its political impotence, the more the appeal of unions grew since their work was visible, understandable and relevant to everyday concerns.

With the rapid rise of the unions and southern reformists under Vollmar's leadership, the ideological impasse of an institutionalized revolutionary passivity became increasingly problematic and engendered various attempts to restore conceptual coherence to Social Democracy's agenda. Of these attempts, Bernstein's "revisionism" and Luxemburg's revolutionism (especially as it is formulated in the course of the so-called mass-strike debate) are the most significant since both, from opposite perspectives, point to the seminal forms of ideological ambiguity which informed the socialist discourse. Bernstein saw the concept of socialism as science, the presence of a canonical theory with its power to hereticize, as an obstacle to the progress of the proletarian class. "Theory owes more to practice than practice owes to theory" (*PPT* 1903, 391). He pits an unencumbered reading of the changing socio-political reality against the hermeneutic exercises of reading theory. Bernstein problematized canonical theory by questioning its functions and by attacking some of its cornerstones. Among these cornerstones is the theory of an inevitable collapse of bourgeois society and the theory of the progressive "immiseration" (pauperization) of the working class — both principles sine qua non of the revolutionary theory of the time.

Despite the reputation of Bernstein's revisionism as a particularly heinous betrayal of Marxian principles, Bernstein's attempt was to free revolutionism from the fetters of a passive determinism and to restore its vital function as an ethical activity. While he grants the close relationship of science and socialism, he insists that the latter, "as a theoretical concept of the future, contains in large measure an element of the will" (*PPT* 1901, 176). In his insistence on placing ethics in the center of socialist discourse, Bernstein is not alone. Despite being derided by the orthodox as "emotional socialism," ethicism had always been an important component of that discourse; to the aged Kautsky it was the very "origin of all socialist aspiration and thought" (1960, 187). The ethical tradition, exemplified by such associates of the movement as F.A. Lange, Johann Jacoby and the party's long-time benefactor Karl Höchberg, becomes prominent again at this time under the influence of Neo-Kantianism, especially its chief proponent Hermann Cohen. The young Eisner stood under its influence and Friedrich Stampfer, in his memoirs, speaks of the "strong doubt" among opponents of party radicals "of the correctness of a purely deterministic view of history which sees only the 'inescapable must of history' and leaves no room for the creative urge of the human will" (Steinberg 1967, 100). Against the view of a self-initiating and self-regulating historical process, and the Marxian contention that the working class had no ideals of its own to realize, Bernstein holds a concept of socialism as an ideology of ethical action.

The party's version of Marxism was defended by Kautsky and others; but it was young Rosa Luxemburg who most clearly articulated the depth of Bernstein's challenge. In Marx, according to her, social reform is a means to the end of revolution. Since in Bernstein this relationship has been reversed, revolution has been reduced to a "condensed version of reform" (1899a, 369-70). Bernstein's much-quoted phrase, "the final outcome, whatever it may be, means nothing; the process is everything" (Bernstein 1897-98, 556), is the basis on which he advocates a petit-bourgeois version of the proletarian movement (Luxemburg 1899a, 370). If the theory of the inevitable self-destruction of the capitalistic system is given up, socialism ceases to be objectively necessary (376) and the scientific basis of the movement has disappeared. The fact that Bernstein was rejected at the party congresses of 1899, 1901, and, resoundingly, of 1905, did not mean, however, that through Bernstein, in Luxemburg's strangely idealistic terms, the proletariat had "expressed its temporary hesitation *in order* to look at [that hesitation] in its proper light and cast it away, with mocking laughter and a toss of its curls" (1899a, 445). While the theoretical voice of reformism had been muted, the practice continued.

Bernstein's revisionism was an attempt to have the reformist practice of the movement adequately represented in its theory. The attempts, spearheaded by Luxemburg, to transform the party's verbal radicalism into a truly revolutionary practice were occasioned by changed socio-political circumstances at the beginning of the 20th century. Labor conflict had intensified and become more brutal: in 1905, one-third of union membership was involved in work stoppages — more than in the entire 1890s. The time for mass strikes seemed to have come. They had been used in Belgium, Holland and Sweden; during a spontaneous and massive strike of western coal miners (which spread rapidly and forced itself on a reluctant union leadership), news came of the Russian revolution of 1905. Rosa Luxemburg, who had visited the site of the uprising, became the party's expert on this first revolution of the century and attempted to transplant its tactics to Germany.

For many German Social Democrats, the mass strike was an idea tainted by its anarchist origins. The party had rejected it at several meetings of the International. Since conditions in 1905, however, seemed to favor it and radicals had succeeded in placing it on the agenda of the party congress, the unions at their own congress unilaterally declared a need for peace in labor relations, rejecting even the propagation of the mass strike (*Dokumente und Materialien*, vol. 4, 146-47). The party congress approved the mass strike — but only as a defense against attacks on the suffrage system or the right of association (*PPT* 1905, 142-43).

Even in this most radical phase of pre-war Social-Democratic history, revolution was conceived only as defensive, never as initiating activity. A year later, a legitimate occasion for its use presented itself: new suffrage restrictions in various states, especially Saxony, causing spontaneous strikes across Germany. At a joint meeting of the leadership of party and unions, held secretly, both pledged to prevent a mass strike "as much as possible."

The debate on the mass strike and its de-facto rejection by party and unions represents more than the result of intra-movement power-plays and diplomacy. It is in this debate that an attempt is made to return the party to its presumed revolutionary origins, to test the revolutionary potential of its Marxist theory. And it is not only in the inconclusive outcome of the debate that the ambiguities and conflicted nature of Social-Democratic ideology became visible, but in the radical propagation of the mass strike itself, as it was presented by Luxemburg. Her view of the Russian revolution was that of an essentially spontaneous, quasi-natural event; this view removed the mass strike from the arena of organizational deliberation and control: it is a "historical product of class struggle" which the party may guide but not initiate (1905, 581). In her theory of the mass strike, the hierarchically constructed organization of skilled labor is implicitly pitted against a concept of the proletariat as a natural phenomenon: its revolutionary activity does not need pre-existing organizational structures, it produces them through revolutionary activity (1906, 117). Social Democracy, in its emphasis on organization, underestimates the political instincts of the proletariat. Ironically, the class instinct in the unorganized masses of the Russian revolution proved stronger than that of the organized, skilled and enlightened workers of Germany (144). Luxemburg does more here than challenge the leadership's interpretation of the current political situation. A few years earlier she had opposed Lenin's cadristic party structure (1903-04); now she questions the whole organizational system which is both a concretization of class awareness and an obstacle to its revolutionary expression. On one level Luxemburg's agitation for the mass strike pits revolutionary activism against the bureaucratic inertia of party and unions; on a deeper level, however, it removes modern revolutionary activity from the realm of conscious and organized action by presenting it as a historical inevitability, a spontaneous, self-generating process. Revolution, then, once again is a process to be expected, to be administered but not *made*; and once again the systemic separation of political theory and the daily struggle of party and unions remains unmediated (Scharrer, 1974, 78).

During the last decade before World War I, a further weakening of traditional revolutionary concepts of German Social Democracy can be observed. Thus the anti-militarism and anti-imperialism of the party was dealt a severe blow in the national elections of 1907 which the conservatives had choreographed as a referendum on national pride and power: the party lost almost half of its seats in parliament. The elections of 1912, however, which the party contested jointly with the liberals, brought a gain of 67 seats and made the party the largest in the *Reichstag*. In a party which increasingly identified itself with its parliamentary strength, these developments lent credence to the reformist majority and further isolated a left wing whose radical agenda, built around mass action, anti-militarism and anti-imperialism, took shape during these years.

When, on August 4, 1914, the Social-Democratic *Reichstag* delegation voted for the government's war credits and thereby became a de-facto supporter of the war effort, the degree of the movement's ideological integration into Wilhelminian Germany had become dramatically visible and the eventual collapse of an organizational synthesis of theoretical radicalism and practical reformism had been initiated.

The account given above of the ideological development of the Social-Democratic movement as it appears in its theoretical reflections and political tactics excludes from consideration its character as a "subculture" or "counterculture," as a complex organizational totality which offered, "beneath" the level of enlightenment and agitation, a number of political "life forms" not readily measured by the standards of hermeneutic fidelity. The incorporation of this aspect into the history of the labor movement is a recent development which has yet to affect the study of its literary life to any profound degree. The dominant forms of its history, whether by apologetes or detractors of the movement, measure its successes by the extent to which theoretical precepts were translated into political action; and, depending on the historian's perspective, theoretical discourse itself may appear as political action, or all political action may be read as reflecting theoretical awareness.

This privileging of theory as the structuring moment of historical narrative is not contemporary to the early movement itself. In Mehring's comprehensive history of German Social Democracy (1897-98), for instance, the theoretical discourse accompanies its organizational development as a secondary phenomenon. Even more representative of the historical narrative of the early movement are the autobiographical accounts of Bebel (1910-14), Blos (1910-14), Bernstein (1907-10) and Kautsky (1960). In these books, the theoretical basis of the movement is taken for granted as "natural" and self-evident; the decline of bourgeois society and the concurrent ascent of the organized proletariat as its historical heir is seen as a natural process whose conceptual content need not be given any particular attention. There is, in Bernstein's terms, no "celebrated combat heroism" here. The greatness of this mass movement is in its "consistency," a consistency which may create "an impression of monotony" (1907-10, vol. 2, iv). The history of the movement, then, is not so much a history of ideas, or even of general political events, as it is —

first and foremost — an *organizational* history, one of administering and registering its growth and electoral triumphs. Here the closed historical discourse of early Social Democracy becomes evident: history of the movement = organizational history; organizational history = natural history.

The failure of history to deliver the collapse of bourgeois capitalistic society, and the movement's failure to prevent World War I or to shape decisively post-war German society, changed — in fact inverted — the central narrative paradigm of the history of the movement. Instead of tracing the natural history of an ascendent class, modern histories of the labor movement tend to either trace its necessary integration into bourgeois society or to tell an ethical story of theoretical and revolutionary failure, and even of betrayal. This approach may serve to legitimate different political positions after Word War II. In the GDR, the history of the early movement is rewritten to create a pre-history of the Socialist Unity Party and to legitimate *its* revolutionary language, to teleologize the GDR present and to recover the Marxist assurance of a future classless society. Among West German socialists, the critique of a Social-Democratic Party seen as a pillar of modern capitalist society is deepened by tracing its history as a history of *embourgeoisement*. As far as the "bourgeois" interest in the German labor movement is concerned, beginning very late with Werner Conze in the early 1960s, the dichotomy of theory and practice became its informing concern (Ullrich 1972, 119). What many versions of this approach have in common, explicitly or implicitly, is an essentially un-Marxist concept of history as ethical performance against an immutable revolutionary standard (rather than as the development of complex ideological systems), enabling historians to narrate, in accordance with their present political agenda, a tale of heroes or knaves or both — but especially of knaves: of the corruption of an essentially pure movement by petit-bourgeois elements (Kuczynski 1946, 232-36) or its "infiltration" by revisionists (Füllberth 1974, 21).

Many of these approaches to the history of the labor movement involve a principle of segregation: in GDR accounts, the opportunistic chaff is separated from the true and heroic Marxist wheat: "[This] history of the German labor movement is a book of heroes" (*Geschichte der deutschen Arbeiterbewegung*, vol. 1, 39*); in West German accounts, the whole movement is separated from its missed revolutionary opportunities (e.g., Miller 1964, Steinberg 1967, Scharrer 1976, Hagen 1977, Emig 1980). This segregation of "proper" and "improper" ideological strains on the basis of a fixed theoretical standard, and their reification under such labels as revolutionary, class-conscious or bourgeois, opportunistic, revisionist, etc., tends to limit an understanding of the historical totality of the movement as a system of interdependent organizational spheres, of cultural forms of political life and of the symbiotic relationship of diverse ideological strains and their vocabularies. It also prevents the view of the socialist subculture as an independent phenomenon and as the environment of literary consumption. It is the recent interest in the lifestyle of the 19th-century proletariat and the "culture" of the movement in its widest sense which has made possible a consideration of its literary activity beyond the strictures provided by a historicism of hermeneutic orthodoxy.

3: Cultural Theory and Cultural Practice

ALTHOUGH THE SOCIAL-DEMOCRATIC movement in Germany began with the workingmens' educational associations of the 1860s and continued to stress the importance of knowledge and *Bildung* in the fight for proletarian emancipation, culture and *Bildung* remained theoretically unattended concepts until the end of World War I. To the extent that one may speak of a Social-Democratic theory of culture, this theory was articulated primarily in three texts which — at least in orthodox Marxist historiography — are taken to mark three phases in the movement's conception of culture: Lassalle's *Die Wissenschaft und die Arbeiter* (Science and the Working Class, 1863b), Wilhelm Liebknecht's *Wissen ist Macht — Macht ist Wissen* (Knowledge is Power — Power is Knowledge, 1872) and the guidelines on "Volkserziehung und Sozialdemokratie" (Popular Education and Social Democracy), submitted by Heinrich Schulz and Clara Zetkin to the party congress of 1906, which led to the establishment of a Central Education Commission and eventually of local commissions (*PPT* 1906, 134-37). Much of the reception of Social-Democratic cultural policy is based on these texts, as well as on the work of the commissions after 1906, and duplicates the attempt to separate bourgeois and revolutionary tendencies discussed above. While West German scholarship favors the description of socialist cultural policy as a sphere in which a liberal ideology proved particularly resistent to revolutionary ideas, GDR scholars take great pains to establish the historical unfolding of a correct revolutionary concept of culture from Lassalle to Liebknecht to Zetkin.

The Conquest of Knowledge

Lassalle's speech on "Science and the Working Class" is part of his legal defense against the charge of having incited class hatred in his *Arbeiterprogramm* of 1862; as such, it serves to establish the legality of his concept of revolution. Just as the possession of the vote will lead to the political power to transform society, Lassalle maintains, so will the possession of knowledge, hitherto denied the proletariat. In modern capitalist society, only two forces have remained unsullied by selfishness: science and the proletariat; Lassalle declares it to be the aim of his life to accomplish an alliance of the two (248). The transformation of a potentially violent class struggle into a fight for knowledge and truth will benefit both classes (250-51). In contrast to Engels, who emphasized the importance of social experience and the political activity that leads to such experience (Stirner 1979, 172), Lassalle narrows the contested realm to that of class-neutral knowledge, "truth." Lassalle is not referring here to the kind of knowledge which the educational associations attempted to transmit to enhance workers' professional qualifications and general cultural competence; and as his two highly philosophical and quotation-studded lectures on proletarian education, *Arbeiter-Lesebuch* (1863c), amply show, Lassalle also had no intention of training progressive workers in the various forms of social and political class struggle, but rather proposed to educate them in science and philosophy — Lassalle's philosophy in particular. Since the under-educated proletarian of this era had no realistic chance of implementing this educational agenda, the invocation of knowledge and truth as chief weapons in the class struggle became a rhetorical gesture, a poetic metaphor of the discourse of proletarian emancipation. The reduction of class struggle to a fight for knowledge and against ignorance reenforced the "knowledge-is-power" ideologeme so prevalent in the early movement. The "ignorance of the masses" as the chief enemy of the proletariat is a stereotype which lent coherence and legitimacy to a practice of appropriating bourgeois culture.

The political discourse as well as the poetry of the early socialist movement fed off Lassalle's highly metaphorical style which conveys the notion of revolution as a spiritual event, as the actualization of a historical idea. To participate in such an event intellectually is a form of esthetic production. His grand Schillerean elocution lifts the notion of revolutionary activity above the specifics experienced by the workers and onto an abstract and universal plane where it may be consumed esthetically. While, as Stirner points out, Marx' language in the *Communist Manifesto* is as rich in metaphor and other rhetorical devices as Lassalle's, it is not the language of the "pre-socialist" ethical hero and his pathos, of the mediator between "idea" and historical reality; rather, the proletariat is addressed here as historical subject, as the bearer of social progress (Stirner, 59-60). However, Lassalle's "estheticization of political propaganda" (Stirner, 1979, 248) shaped the public discourse of the movement more decisively than did the "imaginative power" of Marx' "revolutionary dialecticism" (Mehring 1908c, 202). When emulated on a level of lesser rhetorical and philosophical competence, it reveals clearly the ideologemes, frequently fixed in metaphorical gesture, which Lassalle's eloquence bequeathed to the movement. The controlling ideologeme is that of revolutionary activity as acquisition of historical and scientific knowledge.

Lassalle's formula of revolution as a vanquishing of ignorance and his alliance of science and workers as the essential structure of the socialist movement is one of the sources which feed the complex ideology of socialism as epistemological and scientific enterprise. This *Wissenschaft-*

lichkeit is an ideologeme polyvalent enough to allow a variety of uses. Rosa Luxemburg (1899a, 371) invokes the authority of Lassalle's *Die Wissenschaft und die Arbeiter* in her fight against Bernstein — who, incidentally, is the first editor of Lassalle's works. Bernstein's ally Paul Kampffmeyer (1903) invokes the same text to "revise" the Marxian theory of class struggle and to restore to the movement an agenda of "cultural progress." The liberal conception of social progress as educational and cultural progress — propagated in the early educational associations and authenticated by Lassalle's alliance of workers and science — remained unchallenged until Liebknecht's programmatic *Wissen ist Macht — Macht ist Wissen* whose title already indicates an intention to reverse the liberal slogans of "freedom through knowledge" and "power through knowledge." This text by the acknowledged and unchallenged expert in education and cultural policy and chief theoretician of the early movement was disseminated by the party, in full or in excerpts, until 1925. It became the seminal, canonical text which seemed to make additional concerns with the theoretical problems of socialist cultural policy superfluous. In orthodox historiography, it marks the "final rejection" of a liberal ideology of culture within the socialist movement (W. Friedrich 1964, 16). However, this assessment needs to be revised both in terms of the content of Liebknecht's speech as well as in terms of its reception in the movement.

The point of departure of much of Liebknecht's cultural policy is the enormous educational gap that existed between the German intelligentsia and the lower classes and the realization that efforts at educational self-improvement alone, without profound changes in the social and educational systems, may, in Roßbach's contemporary formulation, at best create an "inner freedom" quite useless in the social and economic worlds (Roßbach 1874a, 1). The reversal of the liberal slogan indicated in the title is stated explicitly twice in the text: "the main effort of workers should be directed at a transformation of the social and governmental structure, and the exclusive concern with education is nothing but wasteful play" (58); only "if the people seize power will the portals of knowledge open for them" (94). However, except for this formal move of reversing political priorities, Liebknecht leaves essentially untouched the liberal concepts of knowledge and culture as something politically neutral and class-transcendent. As with Lassalle before him and Mehring after him, certain metaphors dominate the discourse which reauthorize the liberal ideology of culture: there is a "temple of knowledge" which the proletariat must conquer and guard (94). "*There* is *Bildung*, knowledge for all. But state and society stand between us and our goal" (94). Liebknecht, then, does not problematize the liberal concept of knowledge and *Bildung* as politically neutral, as independent sources of political and social power. He merely changes a political tactic. By deciding the chicken-and-egg question (first political power, then *Bildung*), the dialectical complexities that exist between the socio-political and cultural spheres remain opaque in an unmediated either-or. The object of *Bildung*, in Walter Benjamin's phrase, was an audience, rather than a class (Benjamin 1937, 472); and no basis emerges here on which a discussion of *socialist culture* could be conducted. In this sense, Liebknecht's address to the educational association of Dresden is paradigmatic for the entire movement until 1918.

The "Guidelines on Popular Education and Social Democracy" which Zetkin and Schulz submitted to the party congress of 1906 (*PPT* 1906, 119-23), however, seem to articulate a theoretical break with the prevailing liberal notion of a class-transcending culture. "In view of its historic mission, the proletariat cannot merely appropriate bourgeois culture but must revaluate it in terms of its *Weltanschauung*" (*PPT* 1906, 122). The key term in this passage is "revaluate" (*umwerten*), a Nietzschean term Zetkin had already used in 1904. In a letter to Mehring she speaks of a proletarian "revaluation of all values," of a need to "liberate new cultural powers and to give them independent life" (1904a, 596). Does this party resolution, then, advocate a substantial transformation of culture and its social values based on the revolutionary needs of the organized proletariat? The rest of the guidelines quickly deflate any expectations of this kind: there is no demand here for the development of a proletarian culture; rather, the bourgeois state is urged to improve the educational and cultural conditions of workers, and the party is urged to intensify the dissemination of the principles of scientific socialism. As far as esthetic culture is concerned, the party is encouraged to "awaken and cultivate esthetic sensibilities" by making party publications more attractive, making reproductions of master paintings available, by publishing "esthetically valuable" entertainment literature, by the organization of concerts, lectures, museum visits and, last but not least, by the proper and attractive planning of social events (*PPT* 1906, 122).

The Central Education Commission proposed by Zetkin and Schulz began its work shortly after the party congress. Its membership consisted of prominent leaders of both the orthodox and reformist branches of the movement, with the former faction clearly in the majority. Judging by Lidtke's report on the unpublished minutes of the initial meetings of the commission, whatever their ideological differences may have been, there was general agreement on the unpolitical nature of literature and the arts and their irrelevance to the *Bildung* of workers (Lidtke 1985, 166-68). What is taken for granted by the members of the commission is an understanding of esthetic culture as generically different from political and scientific culture, as transcending class and historical conditions, as compensatory and escapist rather than cognitive. Culture is separated into a *Bildung* that facilitates the political struggle and — as a secondary phenomenon — one which provides esthetic enjoyment (Schulz, *PPT* 1913, 44). What is new here is the fact that some party leaders not only held art to be politically irrelevant but actually warned, as Korn did here emphatically (Lidtke 1985, 167), against its possible harmful effects on the political alertness of workers. The concept of *Bildung* which emerges from these commission meetings and is implemented in the next eight years consists essentially of political instruction to be administered to the leadership segment of the movement in extension courses and in the newly-established Party School (Maurenbrecher 1909a). The commission's program eventually included art, even a series of printed introductions to classical and modern dramas, but — as Lidtke's summary of sponsored festive events (poetry readings and concerts) for the years 1910-13 exemplifies (1985, 178) — these events were designed to provide access to the classics of bourgeois poetry and music, not to stimulate an interest in an esthetic counterculture.

The discrepancy between Zetkin's theoretical formulations concerning the historical relativity of all culture and the need for an emancipatory, proletarian art, on the one hand, and a cultural politics which excluded art from all emancipatory activity enacts, of course, the tension between verbal radicalism and reformist/integrationist practice which was central to the ideology of the movement. Schulz, for instance, concedes that at times art (in the form of revolutionary poetry) may seize the flag and issue a call for battle; but its primary function is to silence the noise of battle, to provide a refuge (1931, 88). Here, as in Mehring, art appears as a timeless sanctuary from the battles of history; where art does participate in these battles, it temporarily abandons its true identity. The only conception of a "socialist art" we find in these considerations of party intellectuals is one which is empty of content and bare of functions: it is the art of the future classless society, a society, as Rühle puts it in his explanation of the party resolution of 1906, which will produce a new consciousness and its own unique set of ideas (Rühle 1907, 12). "Socialist art" is postponed indefinitely.

Few voices were raised against this empty concept of socialist culture. Bernstein, in his introduction to Koigen's *Die Kulturanschauung des Sozialismus* (The Cultural Philosophy of Socialism, 1903), blames the "victory of Marxist doctrine" for a narrowing of the ideological horizon to topical economic and political issues (V). He pinpoints the "catastrophic" theory that no connections can be made between present society and the socialist future as the main reason for the postponement of all thought on the nature and content of socialist culture (VI). Koigen's own version of this dilemma is the "twin theory" of socialism and Darwinism which denies the freedom of creative activity (58).

The tension between revolutionary radicalism and a bourgeois cultivation of esthetic sensibilities is almost silenced in the cultural politics of the socialist trade unions. By 1923, a union official finds that most of the educational needs of the workers can be met by bourgeois institutions (Gumpert 1923, 113). Art, of course, is non-political, but it is useful. Music, for instance, benefits the worker by offering an alternative to the cinema, the pub and the boxing match. It brings "the emotional side of the workers [...] to pure life and elicits true humanity in all its depth. Similarly, poetry recitations improve the culture of the union members" (96). High art, then, can be used to detract from low art; both detract from or compensate for social and political reality. Gumpert's position is close to that of bourgeois advocates of popular education as exemplified in Siemering's study of socialist cultural activities in Vienna and Berlin (1911): "Social-Democratic cultural efforts are doomed as long as they are rooted in the notion of class struggle. [...] They should be directed at the entire population, not at individual classes" (177). In Zepler's reformist program of politically "purposeless" *Bildung*, the worker's striving, in the appreciation of great art, beyond political intentionality is itself a revolutionary activity (1910, 1558). Eduard David's primer for the self-education of future party functionaries, finally, recommends the master works of world literature as a "treasure trove of timeless wisdom in the finest formulations" (David 1907, 32). Here the problematic of art and socialism has dwindled to the comfortable dimensions of a concept of literature as the educated socialist's source of ready quotations.

As we have seen in the second chapter, the historiography of the movement tends to conform to a 19th-century model of *Geistesgeschichte* (history of ideas), rather than to an inclusive social-historical model. Its history is isolated from the rest of history; and the product is "an esoteric version of history" (Hobsbawm 1974, 373). This *Geistesgeschichte* of the socialist movement privileges the articulate personality, events of high political and theoretical visibility and legal and theoretical development, and draws from this "articulated" aspect of history its justification for viewing both the development of the movement and its historiography as hermeneutic exercises of selected articulations. This is also true for most of the descriptions of Social Democracy as a cultural movement (*Kulturbewegung*), which in West Germany tend to emphasize the assimilation of proletarian culture into that of the bourgeoisie and in the GDR stress the importance of socialist cultural organizations in the development of a proletarian class consciousness (Tenfelde 1982, 114).

As Schäfers' treatment of turn-of-the-century socialist cultural organizations in Leipzig (1961) demonstrates in exemplary fashion, the reception in the GDR of pre-war Social Democracy as a cultural movement was shaped, at least until the 1970s, by the need to legitimate present cultural policies. Cultural positions and activities are divided in terms of present categories of orthodoxy and heterodoxy. The latter are condemned as ethical failures, the former prove the continuity of a revolutionary tradition (Emig 1980, 13). Here, as in Moltrecht's account of the same organizations (1973) and Kühn's analysis of the revolutionary language of the proletariat (1974), the emergence of the present from the past is viewed, in Trommler's phrase, as an act of the present, not of history (Trommler 1976b, 15).

In West Germany, interest in the political, ideological and cultural history of the movement was similarly shaped by present ideological concerns. It was read, both by critical and neutral historians, as the prehistory of the failures (past and present) of Social Democracy as a revolutionary movement; and this failure was measured against a fixed theoretical standard. This approach is prefigured in Reisig's dissertation of 1933 which traces the dehistoricization of the idea of culture in the movement. In this historiographic tradition, exemplified more recently by Ritter (1959), Roth (1963), Feidel-Mertz (1964), Hagen (1974), Brückner and Ricke (1974) and Emig (1980), the complex and ambiguous relationship of revolutionary and integrationist strains in the cultural theory and practices of the movement have been reconstructed in some detail. Feidel-Mertz traces the persistence of a liberal concept of *Bildung* in the movement; Hagen isolates a particular strand of the Social-Democratic "ideological discourse," the appropriation and "dramaturgy" of Schiller as patron of German socialism; and Emig describes the relationship of socialism to the bourgeoisie as one in which the former attempts to wrest culture from the latter and in the process reproduces it (1980, 297). What these and other studies have in common is a replication of the movement's own primacy of theory and the consequent emphasis on the theoretical content of culture, as well as the assumption that alternatives to the historical reality (e.g., in the form of a substantially revolutionary culture) existed — without, however, being able to specify any of these alternatives.

These studies written after World War II do not take up Gertrud Hermes' attempt of 1926 to change the hermeneutic approach to the intellectual content of socialism to an investigation of socialism as popular ideology, an approach which attempts to account for the intellectual-emotional *Gestalt* of the politicized worker. In this book socialism appears not as scientifically coherent theory, but rather as a powerful and motivating system of simple ideas and images, held together by "pre-logical" analogies and metaphorizations, in which officially obsolete slogans ("knowledge is power," "the progressive pauperization of the proletariat," "the withering away of the state") prove impervious to doctrinal changes. Hermes is the first to attempt the description of socialism as a group-psychological phenomenon, and she explicitly rejects the traditional sorting in terms of correct and incorrect intellectual content. However, the force of the hermeneutic tradition is stronger than Hermes' challenge to it: the book is replete with criticism of the shallow intellectual content of the popular ideology of the workers. This criticism is delivered from a standpoint of theoretical omniscience which reinstates the primacy of correct theory over forms of political and cultural empowerment of a class to whom the movement was not a philosophical project, but rather a means to facilitate the formation of its social and historical identity. To the extent that it challenges interpretative traditions privileged in the party, Hermes' book anticipates a methodological change in our own time, initiated especially by the study of the everyday life of the proletariat and of the associational culture of the movement.

Associational Culture

The recent interest in the *Lebensweise* of the proletariat, however, does not necessarily lead to a problematization of what we have referred to as the hermeneuticism of historiography. Even in those GDR studies concerned with a reconstruction of the details of everyday life and the everyday cultural practice of the working class, for instance, turn-of-the-century Social Democracy is ultimately viewed as a stage in the teleology of "proper" class consciousness (Groschopp 1985); and the existence of a proletarian culture is largely attributed to the efforts of socialist agitation. In the fourth volume of his *History of Everyday Life in Germany* (1981), Kuczynski cites approvingly Göhre's contention that Social-Democratic agitation led to the complete collapse of the traditional culture of workers and asks: "Is there in our literature a better description of the power of Social-Democratic agitation and propaganda, of their effect and efficacy? This is what Marx and Engels had hoped for — and they lived to see it!" (240).

For Kuczynski proletarian culture is a self-realization of proper theory and its organizational forms are mere extensions of a party viewed as an institutional structure of hermeneutic activity. The result of this approach is either a simplistic translation of theoretical precepts into proletarian practice or a measuring of the theoretical deficits of that practice. In this conception of Social-Democratic culture, the cultural organizations of the movement are referred to as *Vorfeld-* or *Nebenorganisationen* (e.g., Wunderer 1980), a terminology which assumes a hierarchy of "primary" and "ancillary" organizations and functions. While this approach corresponds closely to the view the party held of its relationship with affiliated organizations (including the unions), it obscures the facts that their relationship was mutually constitutive and that for the majority of organized workers, the mere membership in an affiliated organization (cyclists, teetotalers, singers), and the sociability practiced there under the auspices of socialist *symbols* made up the extent and depth of their political-theoretical lives. For the party, these organizations were welcome to the extent that they disseminated political theory (a good knowledge of which was identified with class consciousness), provided a bulwark against bourgeois ideology and a means of class-conscious socialization. Any cultural activity which did not meet this prescription was held in suspicion. Since the party made no effort to define socialist cultural principles, the activity within these organizations was prone to emulate existent bourgeois models.

The various forms of a *Geistesgeschichte* of the movement which place Social-Democratic organized culture under a standard of theoretical propriety are an extension of the party's own sense of "scientific" mission, of a view of its history marked, as Kampffmeyer's pamphlet on the history and literature of the movement (1901) demonstrates, by the collective readerly experience of its major canonical texts. In this "scientific" perception, private and social spheres are either subordinate to the theoretical-political or they are considered politically irrelevant. More recent, inclusive social-historical forms of investigation which stress the *Lebensweise*, the everyday social and cultural realities of various classes, have made it possible to approach the cultural life within Social-Democratic organizations from a reconstruction of social experience rather than from a theoretical standard believed to be embodied in the party and its political actions. As Jacobeit and Mohrmann (1973b, 8) have pointed out, the "Questionnaire for Workers" which Marx constructed for a French journal in 1880 is an early indication of the need for an empirical approach to the actual conditions of proletarian life (Marx 1880a). It represented an approach that was not to be taken up seriously in the movement until the work of Levenstein (1909a & b, 1912) which in turn remained largely ignored in scholarship until recently. A reconstruction of social experience, of course, would not by itself explain the specific nature of socialist organizational culture; neither are proletarian culture and the culture of organized labor identical (Ritter 1979b, 19, 29). However, to view social culture from the perspective of everyday social experience can provide — in details and in principle — access to forms of political life not recognized by the party and many of its historians. An example here is the shortage of low-cost housing during the later 19th century and its effects on the social and cultural life of the proletariat. Engels had already pointed, in a series of articles in *Volksstaat* (1872-73), to the catastrophic social consequences of a development in which increases in housing costs far outstripped increases in workers' real income (Kuczynski 1946, 217-23). In the new industrial proletariat, mobility was extreme; and a large percentage of workers' households were shared with sub-tenants and "sleepers." The domestic sphere for these workers was therefore not a "refuge from the outside world" comparable to the residences of the bourgeoisie, but rather a temporary and fragile resting place (Brüggemeier/Niethammer 1978, 151). This explains to some extent the importance of the pub — the "extension college" of Social Democracy (Schult 1914, 42) — and the Social-Democratic *Verein* as spaces of socialization, educational, cultural and recreational activity.

The access proposed here to the organizational culture of the movement *as a form of political life* problematizes a concept of political activity largely normative for the party and its historians. This is a concept strictly confined to theoretically conscious and consistent (articulated) action in the public and legal arenas. From this level of high-political discourse, the private, professional and associational spheres of proletarian existence appear as "de-politicized" spaces of social life. One of the historians to challenge the exclusivity of articulated politics is Lüdtke (1982), who recognizes different "political arenas" (339) (including the work place and organized social life) in which a "formulation and pursuit" of interests common to a group or class may take place and hegemonic norms may be opposed (335). The existence of such forms of political life by itself does not, of course, constitute a proletarian "culture" or "subculture." The first prerequisite of a proletarian culture, according to Tenfelde (1979a), is that the "manifestations of a proletarian group existence" "reflect the special nature of the group and exhibit characteristics which are repeatable and capable of abstraction and as such may form a tradition" (37). On this level of cultural organization, Langewiesche and others distinguish several degrees of independence from hegemonic norms. The "group culture" remains within these norms; a "subculture" is given when the social conditions of the group are fundamentally different from those of other groups and its guiding social concepts are no longer compatible with the norms of the rest of society. When a proletarian subculture becomes organized, politicized and explicitly directed against the norms of bourgeois society, it becomes a "counterculture" (Langewiesche 1979, 40-41). According to Schwendter, the socialist labor movement fulfilled all conditions for a subculture, among them a significant deviation from hegemonic social norms (solidarity) and cultural self-organization (Schwendter 1973, 164-65). Historians do not agree whether the organizational culture of the Social-Democratic movement is a group, sub- or counterculture; any attempt to decide the question in favor of any of these concepts, it seems to me, would return to the discussion a classificatory rigidity which the serious study of proletarian culture was designed to subvert.

It is the lack of a revolutionary concept of culture which placed the Social-Democratic subculture under the verdict of *embourgeoisement* by scholars who emphasized, exclusively, its theoretical content. The question, what theoretical alternatives to bourgeois culture were available to the movement and, if any existed, what their concrete possibilities of implementation were within a hostile bourgeois cultural and political environment, can be answered only speculatively. Still in 1930, Rühle finds the proletarian enmeshed, "in every hour of his existence, in the web of bourgeois culture" (25); instead of realizing a revolutionary agenda of "transforming culture according to a new principle," the relationship of proletarian to bourgeois culture is one of "emulation and revolt" (30). As Tenfelde (1982) has argued, new cultural forms develop in imitation of hegemonic ones (121). Processes of organizational emancipation within bourgeois society necessarily involve processes of reintegration (Saldern 1977, 469-70). Negt and Kluge (1972, 107) have shown that in the attempt to protect the proletariat from the bourgeois way of life, the mechanisms of the bourgeois public sphere are unintentionally reproduced. These facts do not mean, however, that the cultural experiences of the bourgeoisie and those of the organized proletariat were identical. The *Verein* provided a substitute for political activity and a structure in which workers learned basic democratic processes (Tenfelde 1982, 120-21). Here bourgeois values were not merely "imitated" but became a form of protest against the socially restrictive nature of bourgeois culture. On the ground of that culture a contest for equality with the bourgeois class took place (Bausinger 1973, 29, 33). This contest was, and was perceived to be on both sides, a political one.

Implicit in the dismissal of proletarian culture as a mere adjunct to bourgeois culture is an assumption of the homogeneity of both classes and their social and cultural experiences. Historically this assumption is not warranted; and a number of theoretical and empirical distinctions in our conception of the working class are especially necessary in order to understand organized proletarian culture as a complex system of ideological functions. Kuczynski employs a quasi-Hegelian scheme to distinguish between the working class as an empirical category (the "class by itself"), as a category of consciousness (the "class for itself," aware of its historical identity) and as a category of action (the "class by and for itself," conscious, and in pursuit, of its historical mission) (1982, 86). What in this Marxist teleology appears as stages of a (necessary) evolution in reality are diverse aspects of the ideological disposition of the class which existed simultaneously during this period. These aspects reflect various causes, most important among them a number of contrasts and oppositions internal to a working class which was not homogenous but stratified and hierarchical. Rühle (1930, 258-95) discusses some of the faultlines that divided the class. Skilled workers, for instance, in contrast to unskilled ones, not only made up the leading element in the movement but also constituted a "moment of [political] inertia" (268). According to Kuczynski, this "worker aristocracy," "bribed" by its privileged economic position, provided as much of a conduit of bourgeois ideology as did the bureaucracy of party and unions (1982, 102-06). A variant of this particular contrast between skilled and unskilled workers is that between those already socialized in an urban-industrial environment and those newly arrived from the country (and abroad). The latter's responses to the demands of the industrial age were largely shaped by pre-industrial folk culture (Kramer 1973, 116). And around the turn of the century a profound generation gap becomes apparent in the movement in the relationship between autonomous and radical youth organizations and the Social-Democratic establishment which attempted to dismantle or depoliticize them.

The most important contrast within the German working class of the period is that between the male and female segments of the proletariat, of their actual and perceived social and cultural roles. Bebel's *Women and Socialism* (1891) presents a passionate and detailed picture of the double exploitation of women in the domestic and professional spheres (110-11) and their exclusion from public and political life. In this canonical text of the movement, the position of women is treated as paradigmatic of capitalist society as a system of exploitation (7). But the fact that Bebel's proposal to include the demand for the women's franchise in the party program of 1871 was turned down is an indication that the political aspects of the "women's question" were obscured, in the labor movement as much as in the bourgeois world, by inherited role models. The first form in which this "question" was recognized in the movement was the massive influx of women into the workforce, displacing higher-paid male workers and, according to Clara Zetkin, necessitating new, more democratic relations within the proletarian marriage (*PPT* 1906, 350). This phenomenon was not viewed as an economically initiated change in the social role of women whose positive and negative consequences needed to be understood and "administered" according to the "scientific" historicism of the official ideology. It was, rather, denounced as a sign of bourgeois immorality. Party leaders were thrown back upon traditional conceptions of the "nature" of woman, her sensibilities and moral purity; and it is these positions, and the language that encodes them, which not only persisted in the "anti-feminist" bias of the party (see here Popp's autobiography, 1909) but also helped shape — at times in subtle ways, as we will see in Mehring's case — the discourse of art and culture.

It is not possible to provide here a detailed reconstruction of the heterogeneous make-up of the working class around the turn of the century or of its everyday life and cultural experience. Suffice it to emphasize again that the ideological and social functions of organized proletarian culture should not be seen exclusively in terms of a lower-class version of bourgeois culture but also as the attempt, on the part of a heterogeneous and socially marginalized class, to facilitate the formation of a collective identity within bourgeois culture (Tenfelde 1982, 110). The voluntary associations (*Vereine*) became the chief vehicle of this process: "They were the institutions that nurtured and consolidated labor movement culture; socialist drama, poetry, and music all reached working-class audiences through the mediation of these associations" (Lidtke 1985, 22). With its essentially democratic structure, the *Verein* provided *both* a substitute for political activity *and* a form of socialization not determined by the class structure of society at large.

Unlike the bourgeois political parties which confined themselves to political agitation, Social Democracy represented a constituency which possessed little or no political tradition and experience. Political awareness had to be carried into the masses by means of organizational, subcultural structures. It is understandable that within these structures, political intentionality and theoretical focus became diffused by the interior ideologies of organizations devoted to culture, education or leisure activities or to social projects shared with other classes (such as prohibitionism or anti-religious campaigns). Proletarian culture in the form of an organizational culture is, first of all, a segregationist response to the social, economic and cultural segregation practiced by the bourgeoisie. The form of class awareness afforded here is that of a culturally neglected class fighting for its equality with, even superiority to, the bourgeoisie in guarding and cultivating culture. This awareness did not include, as Groschopp (1985, 154) has noted a sense of its own creative potential. Proletarian cultural organizations made it possible to "share cultural and social middle-class activities without being subject to middle-class control" (Roth 1963, 221). Regardless of their content, however, they were persecuted by the authorities and opposed by powerful bourgeois counter-organizations; and this pressure in turn led to a further politicization of segregationist attitudes (Saldern 1977, 483). Just as conservative propaganda perpetuated the notion of Social Democracy's revolutionary intentions and thereby reenforced its verbal radicalism, so the militant bourgeois response to socialist organizational culture enforced the political nature of its countercultural stance.

The associated *Vereine* and the activities sponsored by them were either ignored by the party or viewed as pure entertainment. They were seen not only as obstacles to the proper political (*PPT* 1907, 99) but also esthetic (*PPT* 1912, 49) *Bildung* of workers. In 1900 Friedrich Bosse complained that the party accepted the services of the associations without concern for their well-being (Schäfers 1961, 26). They were considered useful for purposes of socialization (and as a source of revenue) but politically irrelevant. This attitude ignored that the "organizational process of the working class itself constitutes a cultural process" and is at the same time "an element of proletarian culture" and represents "conditions of social existence produced by the class" (Groschopp 1985, 6-7). The "social-cultural milieu" of the movement, as Lidtke prefers to call it, "was held together by a number of interacting elements — occupational identification, class awareness, secular rituals, symbolisms, the hostility of non-socialist German society, a broad and diffuse sense of ideology" (1985, 6).

The last phase of the development of Social-Democratic associational culture begins with the expiration of the anti-socialist law (1891) and is, as Lidtke (1985) shows, one of enormous growth, centralization and specialization. Although most of the specialized associations were dwarfed by their bourgeois counterparts, membership figures prior to World War I indicate that they were large enough to maintain a countercultural sphere of socialization on a national scale. The athletic federation of the movement had 187,000 members, choral societies 165,000, cyclists 168,000. At this time, the journal of the cyclists was published in an edition of 168,000 copies, that of the athletes in one of 119,000. The process of centralization and specialization which accompanied this rapid development diminished the importance of the pre-political and pre-industrial origins of much of the associational culture of the movement. As Rühle (1930, 261) remarks, some of the emblems of the Social-Democratic associations reflect the traditions of the crafts and other occupational organizations; and some of its forms of communication, especially the festivals, go back to customs rooted in the community and occupational sphere. To the extent that modern associational culture became based on special interests (hiking, short-hand, singing), however, traditional group orientations became obliterated (Langewiesche 1979, 42). Separated especially from the workplace and the immediacy of its social and political significances, the "politics" of the organizational culture of Social Democracy appears, at least in a sense, functionally disembodied and abstract. Two tendencies co-existed within these organizational structures: the political one, an "extrovert" tendency still present in their subcultural segregation, their formal ties with the movement and the use of socialist symbols; and an introversion or internalization of the political impetus into formalized rituals by which a specific form of social communication and the cultivation of a social space apart from society at large was sustained and legitimated. These two tendencies were mediated and "contained" by the interior ideology (*Binnenideologie*) specific to the agenda of the association (singing, education, sports).

Research on socialist associations is rare and has focused on the early educational clubs, with special attention given to the Leipzig *Verein* in which Roßmäßler and Bebel were active and which in later years was run by the proletarian dramatist Friedrich Bosse (Schröder 1972). In this research, the educational clubs are analyzed as disseminators of the Marxist *Weltanschauung*, and their political and social functions are dissociated. Since they had to maintain political neutrality in order to remain legal, and since they subscribed, without exception, to a version of the knowledge-is-power ideology, the result of this research, as Birker (1973) shows, merely confirms that the content of their educational efforts (as revealed in their lectures and courses) is the same as that of the party's approach to *Bildung*: a politically neutral, encyclopedic concept of knowledge derived from the popular science of the day. Heinrich Lange, in his "festival proclamation" (*Festaufruf*) for the Leipzig association in 1890 summarizes the Lassallean ideology of these education associations: "Our sword, free speech,/ is our protection and sanctuary;/ our armor is our conviction,/ our shield is science" (in Ritter and Kocka 1974, 406).

The scholarly concentration on the educational clubs of the movement tends to obscure a system of cultural functions common to the associational culture as a whole. Lidtke has defined these functions as follows: 1. "pleasure in performance" (exhibition of skills, e.g., dancing or singing); 2. sociability (the association as vehicle for social communication); 3. symbolizing beliefs or ideologies ("ideological symbolism"); 4. providing services (e.g., the paramedical services of the *Arbeiter-Samariterbund*); 5. educational; often one can "discern tensions between several functions, tensions that reveal much about the precise nature of the ambiguities embedded in the movement's social-cultural milieu" (1985, 24-25).

A Culture of Celebration

Among the functions of the cultural life of the German labor movement mentioned by Lidtke, sociability is of special importance for a study of socialist literature since it shaped much of socialist literary communication (through poetry, drama, recitation and song). This is true particularly of one special form of sociability crucial to the movement's cultural life: celebration.

The socialist movement is heir to a rich German tradition of festivals — religious, seasonal, historical, occupational and personal. Before the age of mass-media entertainment, festivals afforded rare occasions for pre-political sociability and public representation of groups. There are, of course, distinct differences among many bourgeois and socialist festivals. As Dowe (1979, 137-38) has pointed out, the movement did not, for instance, celebrate the national and military anniversaries so popular with the bourgeoisie — bourgeois festivals, in Heinrich Schulz' phrase (1910, 137), looked to the past, those of the working class to the future. However, both classes cherished seasonal festivals and their naturalizing metaphoricism as well as the "founder's day" celebrations (*Stiftungsfest*) which ritualized and ceremonialized life in the individual associations. In line with the privileging of theoretical propriety which rules so much of the history of the movement, views of socialist celebrations tend to either accent their political, agitatory function or their value as petit-bourgeois recreation. Tenfelde (1979b, 232) points to the heavy emphasis, in Social-Democratic festivals, on the word, on speeches and slogans as vehicles of opposition, satire and parody. Schulz (1910, 138), on the other hand, stresses the *Fest* as a respite from the class struggle where merriment, satire and "noble pathos" are freely combined. Eisner (1904, 140), in his short history of festivals, finds that the ambiguous relationship of political and natural freedoms, both of which are celebrated in the socialist May Festival, produces an unsettled style of celebration; perhaps only in the emancipated society of the future may the class express its *Weltanschauung* adequately in its festivals.

Socialist festivals were important punctuating events in the life of the movement. While many of them were originally conceived as mere fundraisers, in due time they became central to Social-Democratic cultural practice. Eventually the party published handbooks on how to organize them according to a fixed sequence of events: choral presentation, athletic performance, sketch or recitation by the drama club, games and dance in the evening (Groschopp 1985, 35-37). Festivals celebrated by individual associations should be distinguished from mass festivals. Among the latter are the public part of the May Festival or spontaneous events occasioned by the visit or the death of a labor leader. In 1879, during the worst phase of the anti-socialist suppression, 30,000 workers assembled in Hamburg for the funeral of August Geib. Tenfelde (1979b, 232) points to Lassalle's triumphant visits to the Rhineland, with their elaborate rituals of reception and send-off, as one of the sources of demonstrative mass celebrations. These processions, in faint echo of certain religious ones, constituted a ritualized microcosm of the movement and featured representations of various regional and occupational groups, the symbolic colors of the movement and other symbolic and mythical representations (goddess of freedom). They were "an aesthetically pleasing and comprehensive image of the labor movement milieu. Beauty, youth, the arts, recreation, work, occupations, trade unions, the party, and ideology were symbolically integrated through secular ritual" (Lidtke 1985, 91). Associational and mass festivals exemplify two basic types of socialist sociability. The former strengthens the internal bonds and organizational identity of the individual association, confirms and celebrates its separateness from bourgeois society as well as the special nature of its interior ideology. The latter is primarily a public representation and demonstration of organized socialist culture before an antagonistic world. As such, the mass festival is more expressly political than the associational festival. Both, however, represent sites of social identity for the members of the movement.

What all of these celebratory events of the movement have in common is their reliance on ritual as a synthesizing agency. Lidtke recognizes that they "took place according to patterns that were repeated regularly [...] and they embodied signs and symbols that signified the values and ideals of the labor movement," but he opposes the contention of some critics of Social-Democratic culture — Emig, for instance, speaks of socialism as a "substitute religion" (1980, 94-103) — that these rituals were religious in nature. Lidtke prefers the term "secular ritual" (1985, 76). Neither term, religious or secular, is adequate in denoting the ritual aspect of the celebratory life of the movement. Its metaphorical discourse and its rituals feed on religious and mythological traditions; and this process of appropriation does not merely represent the secularization of a non-secular cultural vocabulary but draws its energy from a dialectical relationship between religious and mythical beliefs and political and scientific attitudes. The former continue to reverberate in the latter. Lassalle's own rhetoric as well as the discourse of his followers was obviously shaped by religious symbols and phrases. His idea of the movement as the *ecclesia militans* became invoked regularly on ceremonial occasions. The podium at party congresses was decorated with the laurel-draped busts of Lassalle, Marx (and later others as well). Among the slogans still displayed at the 1899 congress was Lassalle's oft-repeated saying: "The workers are the rock upon which the church of the present era will be built" (*PPT* 1899, 70).

The ambiguity of secularized religious and mythological symbols and rituals can be seen in the *Maifest-Zeitungen*, the brochures published by the party on the occasion of the May Festivals, the most important socialist festival. These came in large editions; the 1892 version was published in an edition of 500,000 (*PPT* 1892, 45). We can see here the extent to which the movement's iconography relied on mythical and religious models — of redemption, for instance, rather than conquest (see Achten 1979a & 1980). In these festival newspapers, political editorials by party leaders (Zetkin, Korn) stand side by side with mythological representations which synthesize the ideologemes of the movement in a typically Lassallean, liberal gesture. Thus a bare-breasted goddess of freedom hands the proletariat a sword (the "sword of knowledge") whose handle is surrounded by the inscription: "Knowledge is Power"; her feet rest on a stack of three books: Marx, Darwin, Lassalle (Achten 1980, 74-75). In these and other images, the passive determinism and "attentism" of Social-Democratic Marxism is contained not only in symbols of redemption and grace but also in a symbolism which undergirds all of the May Festival discourse: that of spring as natural redemption. In these quasi-religious symbols and rituals, the movement couches its class awareness, sense of mission and hope for the future in a mythical narrative in which, to put it in Hegelian terms, it objectifies itself and consumes itself with pleasure. In this sense, the celebratory side of Social-Democratic culture also represents an estheticization of its ideology; here, in Blos' telling phrase, "the class-conscious proletarian [...] finds his main enjoyment in the spiritual content of his festivals" (1914-19, vol. 1, 202).

Lidtke, who has recognized the importance of the ceremonial aspect of Social-Democratic culture more than any other historian, contrasts two aspects of this culture: ritual and rational discourse. Ritual provides cohesion for secular ceremonies; it is "presentational. It presents something, for acceptance and approval, not for discussion, debate, and resolution." Lidtke contrasts this ritual presentation at festivals with party and union congresses where, "the assumption prevailed that delegates were gathered to [...] reach resolutions through a rational process." It is this process which, according to Lidtke, determined the public image of the movement as "highly theoretical, devoted to Marxist ideology, rational and deliberative, and instrumentalist in method." He adds with great justice that the "festival environment suggests strongly that we should modify that image by incorporating as well those dimensions that were ceremonial, emotional, and evocative" (Lidtke 1985, 77). It would indeed be tempting to follow up on these suggestions and to modify Lidtke's perception of two contrasting discourses (and their complementarity in Social-Democratic culture) to a view of their strong resemblance. Any reading of the minutes of party congresses, especially those engaged in prolonged debates (on revisionism, for instance, or the role of intellectuals in the party), suggests that they were exercises in devotional hermeneutics as much as rational and deliberative processes, an aspect particularly symptomatic in the oft-lamented punitive rhetoric of the guardians of theory. Here a ceremonialized hermeneutics is present in the presentational, ritualistic invocations of a text ("correct theory") which, ironically, is rarely explicitly present. From this point of view, the most appropriate discursive environment of Social-Democratic theory was not that of deliberation but rather of ritualistic invocations of eschatological certainties.

However, as far as the literary life of the movement is concerned, there is a more important aspect of the relationship of theory and associational culture. As our discussion of the cultural theory of the party has already shown, art, including literature, is excluded from the realm of political deliberation and revolutionary action and is left to the milieu of sociability. Since this sociability is dominated by the social functions of presentation, of a celebration of future certainties rather than a cognitive approach to the challenges of the present, it should be clear that the historical meaning of socialist literature cannot be sought, exclusively or even primarily, as its later reception has done, in its theoretical content.

4: Literature: Theory, Criticism and Dissemination

IN SOCIAL-DEMOCRATIC CULTURAL THEORY, various forms of cultural practice are severed from each other: learning and enjoyment, cognition and taste, action and celebration. The culture of philosophical and scientific learning for the advancement of the class is privileged in the movement to the point of appearing at times synonymous with culture itself. Esthetic culture is either ignored or viewed as a secondary battleground of the class struggle upon which ownership of the high-cultural heritage is contested between the bourgeoisie and the proletariat. While articulations of systematic notions of esthetic culture are rare in the movement, and while neglect of this culture is truly systemic, its segregation from the political life of Social Democracy and from the movement's materialist view of history is indicative of some important functions which art and literature had within its ideological discourse. Theoretical considerations about art and literature are implicated in this process of segregation: not only is esthetic practice placed outside the realm of political intentionality and action but also is, through the privileging of bourgeois high-cultural traditions, placed in opposition to the dissemination and consumption of literature prevalent within the movement.

Literature is the one form of artistic production to receive fairly continuous attention. Since Franz Mehring's writings on literary theory, criticism and history constitute the only comprehensive and theoretically grounded statement before 1914, Mehring provides the primary access to this aspect of the cultural life of the movement and of the performance of its ideological discourse — and he does so not only because of the breadth and level of his articulation but also because his guiding metaphors and rhetorical moves are echoed by his contemporaries, proponents and opponents alike.

Franz Mehring

The assessment of the way in which Marx' work was appropriated by turn-of-the-century socialist literary critics, theorists and historians tends to be dominated by a tone of fundamentalist rigor, a tone exemplified by Georg Lukács' writings in the 1930s. Again in compliance with the hermeneutic posture of the party and many of its historians, a distinct historical discourse — that of late 19th-century socialist literary theory, history and criticism — is often separated from the larger ideological discourse of which it is, in this period, only a minor strain, and is granted a degree of autonomy which obscures some of its historical functions. The two main (and conflicting) results of this approach are, once again, the construction of an evolutionary line connecting early socialism with the literary and political agenda of the GDR or the identification of a series of formal "mistakes" by readers (and non-readers) of Marx, rather than the description of the literary discourse of the labor movement as a complex system of ideological functions and rhetorical strategies. The language of literary theory and criticism developed in an interactive relationship with the political discourse of the party and assisted in the ideological performance of that discourse. Isolating the literary discourse from this context imposes notions of discursive consistency which it did not possess and obscures its dominant (but not exclusive) functions: enacting and affirming, through a metaphoricism and rhetorical figuration of its own, a political, social and ideological reconciliation with bourgeois values which subverted the verbal radicalism of the movement's Marxist revolutionism.

As was indicated in the first chapter, during the first phase of German Social Democracy, the core of the classical bourgeois literary canon was appropriated and certain perceptions of the social location and functions of literature were canonized. Despite later attempts to problematize this canonical structure, it exhibited a remarkable resistance to the socio-political changes of subsequent decades. The argument seems historically supportable that both the socialist and bourgeois canons converge, at least partially, in the recognition of timeless values manifest in great literature, an argument advanced by Marxist and non-Marxist critics alike. A study of early socialist theorizing about literature (Mehring's and others') shows an additional motivation for the retention of a bourgeois canon of texts and functions: the need to posit a realm outside historical change, to isolate artistic and esthetic practice from a changing social praxis (or one to be changed), to depoliticize the esthetic sphere, and to preserve it as a refuge for a kind of Kantian, disinterested mimesis and contemplation undisturbed by political desire, and, finally, a need for an ideological space in which assured ethical and esthetic values could be claimed, celebrated and protected without revolutionary struggle.

The case of Franz Mehring is typical of these ideological strategies of the literary discourse of the movement. He is the founder of a formally "coherent" (Buck 1973, 20) and theoretically self-reflexive literary criticism and historiography. He practiced both as forms of *Parteiarbeit* (party work), using them as polemical weapons in the daily struggle against Prussian hegemony, bourgeois "decadence" and "revisionist" tendencies in the movement. This double orientation (the formulation of a Marxist literary theory and the use of criticism as a means of "administering" the party discourse) reproduced, within an "ideological aggregate" of Marxian, Darwinian and Kantian components (Demetz 1959, 240), the dualism of theory and practice present in the party discourse, and it generated certain fundamental forms of closure, evasion and resolution which reflected, articulated and advanced particular political and cultural aims of the party.

Much of Mehring's critical writing can be seen as pieces of a history of German literature in which the early *Lessing-Legende* (The Lessing Legend, 1891-93) stands out as a paradigmatic and singularly influential example. This fragmentary history is notable for its absences (e.g., German literature before the neo-classical period and after Naturalism) and for its reduction to a biologically conceived evolution of bourgeois revolutionary ideology, its emergence and decay. Mehring's treatment of this period (from Lessing to Hauptmann) represents a first application of the principles of historical (not dialectical) materialism to German literature; but this strategy is often at odds with his intention to destroy bourgeois "legends." His particular target is a literary history which dehistoricizes the neo-classical period in order to assimilate it into a "decadent" ideology, which writes the present back into the past, and, specifically, views the present (the Bismarckian second *Reich*) as the implementation of the will of the classical German authors. According to this thesis, the classical writers built a "spiritual empire" which Prussia's unification of Germany implemented in the political present. In Mehring's polemic against this appropriation of the classics by the current bourgeoisie, the corpus of classical texts (as canonized by the bourgeoisie itself) appears as a property claimed by false heirs; it is the task of Marxist critics to identify the rightful heir and to specify the proper uses of this "property."

Against this bourgeois appropriation of the classics Mehring pits a form of historiography which inverts the former's idealism. He rehistoricizes the neo-classical period by instituting a historical relativism radical in its time. Lessing, Schiller, even Goethe, are viewed as representatives of their class (an ascendant bourgeoisie) and much of their work as documents of a struggle against what he considers the feudal aristocracy of the day. In explicit contrast to a literary history which seeks to extract from literature timeless articulations of the human condition and consequently dehistoricizes both content and form, Mehring attempts to reconstruct the unique conditions of production and reception prevailing in a context shaped by class struggle. He reconstructs the revolutionary tone, the combative posture of Germany's classical authors and texts. He traces, in the development of German literature from Lessing to the later Schiller, the demise of the Enlightenment project, the frustration of the political impulse and its necessary sublimation into idealism and estheticism. This historical separation of political and esthetic cultures can be overcome, according to Mehring, only in a society in which all class separations are also overcome. To undo this separation, then, is a fundamental aspect of the heritage of the classics, the historical obligation that ties it to its rightful heir, the ascendant proletariat.

The formal opposition between certain kinds of bourgeois *Geistesgeschichte* and Mehring's version of historical materialism, however, is undercut by certain homogenizations and omissions reflecting basic rhetorical moves of the literary discourse which point to its relationship to the party discourse. The first of these is rooted in Mehring's undialectical application of the Marxian base-superstructure model that allows only a move from the former to the latter, establishes a tight homology between them and results in a peculiar homogenization of authors, works and their relationship to their class and society. He considers evidence which supports the notion of an author fundamentally at odds with his society to be primary. Evidence of his accommodation to this society is considered secondary and is dismissed, quite dramatically in the case of Lessing, as inevitably and excusably caused by prevailing conditions. Certain contradictions and tensions in author and work have thus been dissolved; they have been de-individualized and their function as representatives of a revolutionary and combative class has been extracted. This representative function (Bohnen 1981) is the key to Mehring's claim on the classics. And this representativeness is not the comprehensive documentary value an Hippolyte Taine looked for, nor the exemplification of complex psychological types of Diltheyan *Geistesgeschichte*, but rather a representativeness without the structure and texture of living discourse, one narrowed to the idea of struggle, to a combative gesture freed of all specificity. On this level of abstraction, for example, the question of what Schiller fought for or against becomes a secondary aspect of his reception. What he represents for the proletariat is a temperament characterized by opposition and love of freedom. Strictly speaking, then, Mehring's Schiller or Lessing no longer "represent" anything "historical": the level of abstraction on which they may be appreciated and serve as literary models for the proletariat transcends not only the specificity of textual form and content, but any historical specificity per se. Of Schiller's *Wilhelm Tell* he writes: "And we, who are far beyond the political moods and discordances which were evoked by this drama, can enjoy it unreservedly as a world-picture full of colors and figures" (1909, 265). The interaction with history in the process of literary reception here offers "vague analogies to the present" rather than a "precise dialectical challenge" (Benjamin 1937, 479). Despite his historical materialism, then, the historicity of a classical text was for Mehring a negative quality: these texts had passed the "test of time," time had washed all traces of contingency out of them and left their essence bare. History pushes art beyond its own domain: "The flood of time washes out the error, and mankind inherits the imperishable rest"

(Mehring 1893a, 69). The sense of historical relativity which Mehring was intent on introducing into literary historiography had been shown only to be annulled. The deconstruction of one legend had given birth to another.

This literary discourse which promulgates a radical relativism and at the same time contains it in an elaboration of timeless ideals (an unmediated juxtaposition of "materialist analysis and 'idealistic' hymns to the proletariat," Trommler 1976, 165) supports an ideological agenda concretized in Mehring's version of German literary history. German social and cultural history since the 18th century is divided into two distinct phases: that of an ascendant revolutionary bourgeoisie and its philosophy and literature, which Mehring sees as informed by a struggle against the aristocracy; and a second phase in which the bourgeoisie allies itself with the aristocracy and loses its revolutionary identity. The metaphorical structure of a discourse promulgating this view reveals its ideological functions. Since Mehring generally separates classes from the specific, complex and changing conditions of production they "represent" and treats them as autonomous historical structures (Kumpmann 1966, 116), they emerge as actors on a historical stage whose agonistic realm is ethical and philosophical rather than economic. He arrives at a cast of characters in the contemporary political drama which represents the unique Prussian-German situation: the simultaneous presence of the aristocratic *Junker* class, a bourgeois class which has lost its ideological identity — and the new protagonist as youthful hero, the proletariat. For Mehring, as for Kautsky, there is a strong affinity between drama and revolution (Kautsky 1904-05, 150-51). Since we have here another manifestation of a historiography which writes the present back into the past, the 18th-century revolutionary bourgeoisie and the modern proletariat become identified by virtue of the role they have in common: the fight against the aristocracy and its allies. This equating of two historically distinct classes, couched in a dramaturgical rhetoric, provides one of the metaphorical nodes of a literary discourse which describes and delimits the proletariat's cultural stature and range of activity and blurs its "post-bourgeois" identity.

The identification of two classes, central to socialist literary history and cultural policy, is also performed within another metaphorical structure, that of organicism, in which the biologism of German *Geistesgeschichte* and the movement's Darwinism converge. We have here the evocation of a cyclical notion of the growth and decay of the bourgeois revolution and its rebirth in the proletarian movement. Where this metaphor suggests the inevitability of another decline, however, the metaphor of evolution takes over. Both of these metaphoric spaces are limited by Mehring's ethicism which portrays the decay of bourgeois culture as a perversion, as a willful deviation from ethical and esthetic norms. The later bourgeois phase, then, is not viewed as post-classical but, in both ethical and cyclical terms, as anti-classical. Therefore none of its artistic forms, for instance, may be appropriated by the proletariat, even if they are informed, as much of German Naturalism was, by social protest, anti-capitalism and an attempted articulation of proletarian experience: these forms were seen as anti-classical, therefore anti-proletarian.

The repercussions of Mehring's biological metaphoricism vibrate through the very texture of his prose, reenforcing the central metaphors. Certain subsidiary clusters can be identified. One of these is the contrasting of the nature of the male (clear, action-oriented and combative) and that of the female (complex, passive and self-reflexive), a distinction sometimes used in veiled analogy to such pairs as optimistic-pessimistic, healthy-decadent, content-oriented and form-oriented. These pairs usually do not describe literary works in their totality but dramatic characters (a privileging of drama as genre which reflects its use as metaphor for history); and the central characters in literary texts are seen as emanations of an author's biography, more specifically of his biological structure. The validation of characters as "genuine" often takes the form, repeated stereotypically throughout Mehring's work, of relating them to the author by way of starkly biological metaphors: they have in their veins the author's "life-blood" (1903, 152). This biographism not only serves to overcome the limitations of a narrow derivation of superstructure phenomena from the base, as Lukács (1933, 374-75) suggests, resulting in a mere addition of mechanical sociology and biographical psychology; it also provides a strong ideological link between the literary discourse and the evolutionary attentism of the party discourse. A related biologistic metaphorization of creative processes is the notion of *Volk* as a pre-historical soil in which all great art is rooted (e.g., 1900, 136 & 1910, 141).

Mehring's identification of the 18th-century bourgeoisie and the modern proletariat, of course, can be taken to suggest that the proletariat must create its own forms of artistic expression and cultural praxis, just as the former had done. However, the infrequent attempts to formulate principles and forms of a proletarian counterculture, or to "misdirect" revolutionary fervor to artistic forms (Mehring 1913, 239-40), were seen as destabilizing the narrow class base (skilled workers) of the movement and opening it up to the masses, to a spontaneous generation of forms and practices potentially destructive of classical bourgeois culture. These attempts were renounced as "tendentious," as bourgeois radicalism, even as nihilism and *Kitsch*. The rhetorical move to resist this urge toward innovation and its political implications, within Mehring's narrative of German literary history based on the identification of two classes, consisted in recuperating, rather than rejecting, the separation of political and esthetic cultures of the 18th century. Since the classical writers were denied, Mehring argued, an opportunity for political action, they "escaped" into an idealistic art. The proletariat, which does have (some) such opportunities, does not need (and cannot afford) its own production of this art (1896, 139). For the bourgeois revolutionary writers of the mid-19th century, socialism was a hope and as such capable of energizing their imagination; as soon as socialism was understood to be a historical necessity, the old truth was confirmed that "in combat the muses are silent" (1914, 421).

The proletariat is pronounced to be a class without a literature and culture of its own — its courtship of art, as Schlaikjer (1895-96, 71) put it, is a "Platonic" one. It is a class that will have to wait until the Golden Age of all culture, the classless society, to participate creatively in the cultural life. By then, of course, the proletariat will have ceased to exist as a separate class. In Mehring's version of cultural history, then, the proletariat appears as a class of administrators of the classical heritage that will leave no heritage of its own. The impression of a deep suspicion, on the part of bourgeois-educated party intellectuals, of the cultural legitimacy of their adopted class is difficult to dispel.

The ideological work performed by the literary discourse as exemplified by Mehring can be seen as a reconciliation of historicizing and de-historicizing tendencies, the mutual subversion of two rhetorical stances and — as will be shown — as the containment of its conceptual ambiguity in an evocation of nostalgia, hope and consolation. To perform this task consistently throughout a vast body of literary history, criticism and cultural-political statements, Mehring had to duplicate this essential ambiguity and its pacification on a number of levels. One of these is the theory of esthetics which underpins his critical judgments. While proclaiming formally the historical relativity and social dependence of taste, of artistic forms and their reception, he at the same time points to the literature of the classical bourgeois canon and the esthetics of German idealism, especially Kant's, as normative for the proletariat: nowhere can the "laws of esthetic judgment" be studied better (1898, 175). With this privileging of a Kantian interest-free art of the ideal (and his decided sympathy for Schiller's dictum that esthetic form "consumes" content), a number of assumptions enter into the discourse: the esthetic capacity is a human property which — while manifesting itself only historically and socially — is pre-social in nature, "an originary capacity of mankind and as such subject only to its own laws" (1902, 36); while never free, especially in times of historical crisis, from the encroachments of desire, morality or philosophy, it is generically separate from these. "Pure art" is never possible in times of class struggle but it remains an ideal inherent in all art. Therefore, art and politics are discrete spheres whose interactions are of no particular theoretical interest (Hermand 1968, 107). Since the proletariat, as a class, is defined essentially by its political and social desires, its historical temperament is fundamentally unesthetic.

The critical normatism implied in this stance becomes clear, for instance, in Mehring's rare attempts to assess the socialist and proletarian writers of his day. These assessments tend to measure the extent to which the political "tendency" of these writers violated the laws of esthetics. Although he praises the novelist Robert Schweichel for his *engagement* in the labor movement, special praise is reserved for the fact that he never forgot, in Mehring's stereotypically recurring terms, that in the political arena "the muses may accompany but not lead" (1887, 456). Not all socialist and proletarian writers, however, placed traditional esthetic norms above political intention. In Minna Kautsky's case, the political "tendency" "ruptured the esthetic structure" (1912, 452), in Müller-Jahnke's, the "political fighter took the laurel from the poet" (1908a, 487). Mehring does not read these "ruptures" of traditional standards as politically motivated challenges to a bourgeois esthetics of disinterested representation. He is willing to forgive them as "transgressions" and temporarily suspend esthetic judgment (1893b, 477) since in the literature of an ascendant class, "knowledge and the will" will always accompany (and deform) esthetic intention (1908b, 489).

Mehring's unwillingness to entertain the idea of an agitatory art has its conceptual basis in a non-dialectical view of the relationship of base and superstructure: in this form of historical materialism, literature appears as a product of socio-economic conditions but not as an ideological construct which also may act upon those conditions — with the possible exception of such hybrid forms as political caricature (1904, 182). Although Marx had pointed to the complicated nature of this relationship as exemplified in the continued reception of classical art (Marx 1857, 640-42), Engels, in his evaluation of Mehring's *Lessing-Legende*, blames himself and Marx for having neglected the autonomy of ideological structures (1893, 96). He criticizes "the vulgar, undialectical notion of cause and effect as totally opposed poles, the absolute ignoring of the fact of mutual causality," of the fact "that a historical phenomenon, as soon as it has come into existence through other (ultimately economic) causes, now reacts to its environment and may act upon its very own causes" (98).

From Mehring's perspective of classical esthetics, history consists of a series of social structures which impair the realization of a pure, interest-free esthetic capacity. Only the classless society will bring, once and for all, the full reign of the classical canon of taste and forms: "Then the artistic soul which resides in every real person will stretch jubilantly, and Goethe's name will appear in its full radiance in the sky of German culture" (1899, 89). Implied in Mehring's separation of the esthetic realm from the social dialectic is an estheticization of the classless future; and the present uses of art for the proletariat are those of reprieve, consolation, celebration, anticipation and escape — uses intended to locate the cultural life of the class in a dehistoricized zone between a classical promise and its future fulfillment. And of these uses celebration, as a pre-enactment of an esthetically conceived future, may well be the dominant value of art. The modern proletariat, according to Mehring, does not want to see in art "dirt and dust" but, "in Schlaikjer's excellent phrase, 'the festive glow of candles' in accordance with the natural, i.e. historically given mood of a class sure of its victory and joyful about its future" (1898, 223).

No explicit canonization of Mehring's literary-theoretical orientations took place in the movement, nor any form of problematization (Füllberth 1972, 68), since alternative models did not exist and Mehring's writings, in *Neue Zeit*, *Volksbühne* and other party-affiliated journals, dominated the literary discourse. Between the World Wars, his influence (perpetuated, for instance, in Gertrud Alexander's contributions to the communist daily *Rote Fahne*) persisted in the Social-Democratic as well as the Communist Party. Despite Mehring's rather mechanistic form of historical materialism, Thalheimer (1929) endorses his prescription of an "idealizing" art, his rejection of a "decadent" contemporary bourgeois art, and the appropriation by the proletariat of the classical heritage for the purpose of acquiring the esthetic taste necessary to create its own art — after the final victory. Lukács' detailed critique, written in 1933 and published in 1954, represents the first comprehensive assessment of Mehring's theoretical positions and their historical context and defines the frame of reference for later critics, both for West German investigators of Social-Democratic *embourgeoisement* and for East German attempts to use Mehring to legitimate the official literary-political positions of the 50s and 60s. Lukács' essay originally supported Stalin's attacks on certain German leftists in the early 30s; its publication in 1954, along with its punitive rejection by Koch (1959), reflects East German cultural politics of the 50s, marked by de-Stalinization, the end of Lukács' reign as chief literary legislator and a subsequent "pompous rehabilitation" (Trommler 1976b, 27) of Mehring initiated by Ernst Engelbert (Kumpmann 1966, 9-10). Lukács makes it clear that a properly Marxist literary theory and history will not be possible until Mehring's ideological mistakes are recognized and overcome (403). These mistakes are historically conditioned and typical for the German intellectuals of bourgeois origin of the Second International, especially their Lassallean (and Kantian) idealism, German provincialism and simplistic view of capitalist development (352), together with an underrating of the mimetic power of literature and an "uncritical" appropriation of the bourgeois literary classics — the basis of a "German Trotzkyism" which denies the possibility of a proletarian-revolutionary literature (319). These mistakes — this is the tenor of Lukács' essay — can only be overcome by a conscientious return to Marxist hermeneutics.

Koch's rehabilitation of Mehring revolves around two issues raised by Lukács which were central to the literary politics of the GDR: the bourgeois literary heritage and Mehring's failure to develop a theory of realism. In order to establish Mehring as the ancestral source of modern GDR literary theory, the charge of un-Marxist approaches on both counts had to be disproven. Koch's attempt to show that Mehring's appropriation of the classics was a critical one merely repeats Mehring's own abstract assertions about the value to the proletariat of everything noble, progressive and revolutionary in the literary classics (1959, 133), assertions which marked the GDR's own claim to the German "cultural property" (*Kulturbesitz*). Lukács' charge that Mehring's Kantian estheticism prevented the development of a realist theory of literature is denied by Koch who not only views Mehring as an early theoretician of realism but, specifically (although implicitly), as one who developed preliminary versions of those central concepts (typicality and totality) which are associated with Lukács' own theory of socialist realism.

While Koch's (and Girnus', 1971) view of Mehring's work as an important first phase in the evolution of Marxist literary theory did not significantly affect the later reception of Mehring, Lukács' essay became the primary intertext of much of the later scholarship (e.g., Keller 1972). In that scholarship, echoing Lukács, Mehring's failure to provide a dialectical nexus between literature and politics is elaborated (Kumpmann 1966, Füllberth 1972) and the reasons for this failure are sought in the bourgeois origins of his political ideology (Kumpmann); frequently the emphasis is on the unique biography of a democratic moralist and polemicist (Raddatz 1979). A special aspect of Mehring's later reception is his appropriation of the classics. Western critics like Lützeler (1971) emphasize the differences as much as the continuities between Mehring and Lukács in this regard; Bohnen (1981) points to the legitimating function Lessing has for both (Bohnen 1981). Gille (1982) pleads for a recognition of Mehring's radical (though partial) historicization of the classics.

Some Debates

Mehring's dominant position in historical and literary matters and the subsequent attention paid him by Lukács and others tend to obscure the fact that the ideological performance of Mehring's literary discourse (a balancing of historical relativism and esthetic essentialism) is also discernible in the literary debates which took place in the movement during the period under discussion, debates both formal and informal — and is discernible on both sides of the disputes. Whatever positions are taken, they reflect, as Füllberth has remarked (1972, 124-26), highly restrictive concepts of politics (parliamentarianism) and literature (preservation of classical standards). Both W. Liebknecht's contention that art and politics, "lyre and sword," do not mix and that a combative class has no time to compose poetry (1890-91, 710) and Bernstein's statement of an "incongruity" of art and the current political struggle (1892-93, 267) echo basic Mehringian positions, as does Rühle's conception of art as a property withheld from the proletariat (1907, 10-11).

Even in attempts to diminish the "esthetic distance" between literature and politics (which usually took the form of attempting to distinguish legitimate and illegitimate forms and degrees of "tendency" in literature), the basic positions encoded in Mehring are affirmed. Rosa Luxemburg, for instance, acknowledged that all literature is "tendentious" (as did Zetkin and others) but she rejected a conscious and agitatory use of this characteristic (Serebrow 1961), as her critique of Gorky's *The Mother* shows (Schiller 1977, 360). She confirms Tolstoy's conception of art as an important historical form of social communication (1908, 251), praises his demand for a synthesis of artistic expression and the social sensibilities of workers (252) and agrees with his assertion that the art of the higher classes can never be valid for the entire nation (253). However, these arguments do not lead her to call for a literature indigenous to the class and sustained by its unifying *Weltanschauung*. On the contrary, the proletariat is pronounced incapable of producing its own art under present conditions (1903, 367). It should, instead, turn to Tolstoy's later works (1912-13, 189-90) and "guard bourgeois culture against the vandalism of the bourgeois reaction" (1908, 367).

The party intellectual who most consistently supported proletarian writing — by Müller-Jahnke, Krille, Märten — and other forms of proletarian cultural practice (Kliche 1976, 45), and who came closest to a theoretically grounded advocacy of proletarian literature, was Clara Zetkin. She rejected the "esthetic defamation" of all tendency in literature as a bourgeois ideological ploy (1910, 73) and emphasized the revolutionary and educational value of progressive writers such as Ibsen (1906a, 42). In the literary section of the woman's journal *Gleichheit*, she attempted to build thematic bridges between political actuality and literature (Reutershan 1985, 133-48). In her preface to Krille's *Aus engen Gassen* (1904b), Zetkin views the proletariat as producer of new cultural values rather than as mere recipient (5) and defines Krille's political tendency as an "inner necessity of his poems which irresistibly seeks its own form" (4). This emphasis on an emotional and vitalistic conception of proletarian art (Trommler 1976a, 267) clearly distinguishes her attitude from the prevailing fear of proletarian *Kitsch*. In this essay, Zetkin does not defer indefinitely the realization of proletarian art; the seeds of its "renaissance" are already planted (1904b, 5). In her letter to Mehring concerning Krille's poetry (Mehring 1904a, 596), she protests against the "bourgeoisifying" cultural trends in the movement. The proletarian concern with culture, she maintains, should not be confined to the mere absorption and perpetuation of bourgeois culture but must begin the process of a "revaluation of all values." A few years later, however, Zetkin's optimism has waned to a point where her basic positions are no longer distinguishable from those of Mehring and others. She praises Lu Märten's play *Bergarbeiter* (Miners, 1909) for the fact that it avoids overt politics and instead concretizes the "new spiritual and ethical powers" of the movement (1912, 63). And in her essay "Kunst und Proletariat" (Art and the Proletariat, 1911), Zetkin has come to accept the view of Mehring, Kautsky, Luxemburg and many others that a specifically proletarian culture may not be produced under the conditions of capitalism and that socialist cultural activity must have recourse to the classical models of bourgeois literature. The idea of socialist art has dwindled to the notion of the renaissance of a socially and historically disembodied esthetic sensibility on that "isle of the blessed, the socialist society" (504).

The incongruence of an affirmation of the political nature of all culture and the attempt to preserve art as a transcendent sphere informs not only the literary discourse of party intellectuals of bourgeois training and background but is also passed on to the first generation of party leaders and poets of proletarian origin. Zetkin's protégé Otto Krille, for instance, derides a cultural policy which attempts to carry art to the masses by way of a complex and ideologically indifferent bourgeois art that can only kill the proletariat's awakening literary interest. The art that would invigorate that interest, according to Krille, would have to be of its own *Weltanschauung* (1904-05, 460). He, too, however, ends up severing "true art" from politics: not only will the golden age of art have to wait until the classless society (1905-06, 534), but even within the reality of class struggle, the ultimate aim of art is to "understand the innermost harmony of the soul and the pure edification of the heart" (1904-05, 460). The young poet writes in his autobiography that he had finally begun to "breathe that free human air in the gardens of poetry so seldom found in the sultry atmosphere of political strife" (1914, 117). There is a consensus among party-affiliated intellectuals that "proper" art either has no purpose at all (J. H. 1892-93, 247-48) or may realize its functions only in the classless society of the future ("Die Kunst und der Sozialismus" 1895, 60). This latter postponement of socialist art — which we have already encountered in Mehring, Zetkin and Krille — is not dictated by political pragmatics alone. It also is, as Bebel's invocation of a future "era of art and science as the world has never beheld before" (1891, 326) suggests, a utopian deferral of "true art," of an art free of desire and therefore of disappointment. In this context, art represents the consolation of an existence beyond history.

There were few attempts to problematize the agenda of depoliticizing art and appropriating the bourgeois classics; and none of these developed a viable basis for a proletarian cultural production. Horn (1913) suggests a kind of literary "counter-canon" based on a dehistoricized notion of progressive politics. Lu Märten's aphorisms "Kunst, Klasse und Sozialismus" (Art, Class and Socialism, 1906) do not constitute a coherent approach to the topic but they do point to the important difference between a "classical" art of the emancipated society of the future and a "proletarian," i.e., politically combative art. Korn (1908) presents a comprehensive critique of the party's Lassallean concept of *Bildung* and a politics of appropriating the classics based on that concept. But Korn does not reject the primacy of the cultural heritage over proletarian cultural production; rather he wishes to change the practice of appropriation. Instead of a process by which knowledge is acquired, it should be one directed toward contemporary life and action (415). It is precisely this "utilitarian" reading of the classics (which implies a spontaneous dissolution of literature's historicity in the consciousness of the present) which Mehring, Luxemburg and others had attacked in the so-called Schiller Debate of 1905.

This debate is seen by orthodox Marxist historians as an occasion which facilitated a substantial advance in Marxist literary theory (Jonas 1988b, xviii). During the centennial of Schiller's death, Social-Democratic intellectuals not only attempted to destroy the "idolatrous image [of Schiller] which the bourgeoisie had erected" but also to greet "in grateful humility this towering ancestral figure of the proletarian fight for emancipation" (Mehring 1905a, 97), i.e., to develop a form of appropriating Schiller commensurate with the movement's historic mission. In contrast to the indeterminate, ahistorical and abstract reception by the bourgeoisie, the working class, so Mehring, reads Schiller historically, critically and concretely (1905b, 278-79). Some of the Social-Democratic essays written on this occasion, however, seemed to belie this latter assumption, especially a volume on Schiller published by the party's own Vorwärts publishing house whose contributors (Stampfer, Lily Braun, Eisner, Schikowski, David and Molkenbuhr) belonged the "revisionist" wing of the party. Here, according to Luxemburg, a "peculiar process of assimilating" Schiller typical for the proletariat becomes visible. Schiller is not received in his historical complexity and totality, but aspects of his revolutionary thought are appropriated into the current revolutionary ideology (1904-05, 533-34). Instead of dehistoricizing cultural phenomena, Luxemburg urges, they must be shown in their "objective socio-historical contexts," as Mehring had done in his Schiller monograph for workers (534).

Since the leaders of both "factions" of the party were involved in this attempt to claim Schiller as a legitimate property of the movement, historians have reconstructed this exceptional journalistic effusion as a reflection of the ideological division of the working class (Münchow 1981, 177), as a "controversy" between Marxist and revisionist positions (Füllberth 1972, 74; Jonas 1988b, x), between — specifically — an "ahistorical installation of Schiller as the poet of freedom per se" (Jonas 1988b, xix) on the one hand and his reception "at a critical distance" (xxii) on the other. Hagen (1977, xv) rejects this transfer of party-political positions to literary theory and insists that the veneration of Schiller was a unified ideological phenomenon in which the entire labor movement "recognized itself" (xvi). A reading of the relevant texts, including Mehring's Schiller monograph, indeed reveals that the differences between "Marxists" and "revisionists" were incidental rather than central; and not only did this massive encounter with the problem of the classical heritage not lead beyond Mehring's positions described above, but it ended up confirming the classics as a source of transcendental norms.

Except for Molkenbuhr's naive importation of Schiller's idealism into the movement (1905, 147), the "revisionists" struggle as much with Schiller's historical datedness as do the "Marxists." Maurenbrecher recognizes that Schiller is neither of the current age nor of the proletariat (1905-06, 9), as does Stampfer (1905, 117); and Eisner concedes that Schiller's idealism is both his greatest achievement and his greatest curse (1905, 126). Finally, there is little difference between the Schillerean values which each of the parties in this "debate" proposes to appropriate for the proletariat — nor, for that matter, are they significantly different from those celebrated by the liberal bourgeoisie: the "sublime beauty of his life's *oeuvre*" (Luxemburg 1904-05, 536), the "immortal work of genius" (Mehring 1904-05, 285), the "idea of freedom" (Mehring 1905b, 279) or the "pathos of freedom" (Mehring 1905a, 233). Most of the Marxists value Schiller as a pedagogue of the proletariat. While his political thought is obsolete, so Kautsky (1904-05, 177), he is invaluable for the "formation of political character." He teaches the "harmonic development of the whole human" (Diederich 1905, 231). He is the teacher of the "highest civic virtues" and sublime ideals (Zetkin 1909-10, 261). Bernstein's conclusion that Schiller's essential ideology was timeless and classless (1905, 194) is the logical extension of a process of appropriation which ultimately seeks the value of literature by depoliticizing it. The so-called Schiller Debate of 1905 represents a culmination and affirmation of a literary politics which — by privileging a passive cultivation of the classical heritage — not only devalued the proletariat's own cultural production but also prevented alliances with contemporary progressive literary movements. These latter two aspects of the party's Lassallean concept of *Bildung* (as knowledge rather than cultural action) were the subjects of two other debates, the "Naturalism Debate" (1891-96) and the "Tendency-Art Debate" (1910-12), both of which also confirmed the Mehringian esthetics of the movement.

The "Naturalism Debate" began after the expiration of the antisocialist law, at a time when the party was anxious to protect its legality against conservative charges of immorality and revolutionism. In some of these charges, the movement was identified with anarchism and Naturalism. Many of the radical Young Turks who challenged the politics of the leadership in 1891 were associated with the center of German Naturalism, the Friedrichshagen writers' circle (Scherer 1974). The early rejection of Naturalism, then, also must be seen in the context of a defense against accusations of esthetic and moral anarchy; and it is not surprising that some of the arguments used by party leaders against Zola and his German disciples echoed those of the conservative campaign against Naturalism. Most of these arguments, systematized by Mehring in 1896 and 1898, were already articulated in 1890-91 by Liebknecht, Kautsky and Schweichel: the incompatibility of politics and literature (Liebknecht), for instance, or the misrepresentation of the proletariat in Naturalist literature and the Naturalists' emphasis on the decadence of bourgeois society which excluded any positive perspective on the future (Kautsky 1890-1901). Schweichel, who in 1885 had blamed Zola's "artistic excesses" on his pessimistic *Weltanschauung* (362), now considers this pessimism a "declaration of philosophical bankruptcy" (1890-1901, 49). Proper proletarian literature, according to Schweichel, is marked by "ethical pathos" and enthusiasm (53) while German Naturalism, by practicing social criticism without an explicit ethical position, exists ethically on the same level as that which it depicts (48) — a logically peculiar inference for which Julius Hart takes Schweichel to task (1891, 57). These points are taken up and differentiated by Mehring in his first, and tentatively positive, assessment of Naturalism in which the Naturalistic concern for the oppressed is seen as a "reflection" of the labor movement in art (1892-93, 129). He distinguishes two forms of Naturalism: one still rooted in capitalism and one in a democratic and social orientation (1891). The latter, however, would falter unless infused with a vision of the coming emancipated society (1892-93, 131). The responses to this criticism of Naturalism within the movement, exemplified here by Landauer and Schlaikjer, indicate that the embracing of Naturalism by some social democrats implied an impatience with a depoliticized notion of art and its encoding in the normative appropriation of the classics. In 1884 Zadek had already pitted Naturalism against the literary norms of German classicism (242) as a style appropriate to an age which rejects absolutes, esthetic or otherwise (252). In contrast to the limited relevance of a contemplation of the classics to the present situation, so Landauer (1891-92, 118), Ibsen, Tolstoy and Hauptmann attempt to affect the will, to point to a goal (120). Schlaikjer (1893-94) provides the most emphatic opposition to the prevailing, historically disembodied concept of art. In direct response to the often-invoked adage *inter arma silent musae*, Schlaikjer praises Naturalism as an art of strong effects, as an art heard above the din of political battle (180).

In contrast to this first phase of the debate, which at least touched upon the possibility of a literature that would give voice to the proletarian experience and tie it to its contemporary environment (Hugo Ernst Schmidt 1896, 161), the second phase — a formal debate at the party congress of 1896 — reduced its scope to a question of decency in art. Here the debate became part of a continuing discussion of the performance of the party's entertainment journal, *Die Neue Welt*. Its literary selections had either been deplored as being of low quality (*PPT* 1892, 262) or as taxing the mental capacities of its main audience, women (*PPT* 1893, 134). After the extended debate of 1896, this discussion continued. The journal's new editor, Edgar Steiger, an ardent proponent of modern literature, was accused of turning the magazine over to literary experimentation. In an attempt to guide the discussion toward a consideration of the party's literary politics, Steiger published a series of articles in which — in a thinly veiled criticism of the hegemony of the classical canon — he advocated a shift from the "cool contemplation of a dead past" to a contemporary art to which workers could relate experientially (1896a, 188). He contended that Social Democracy, at the forefront of politics and the social sciences, lagged behind the bourgeoisie in esthetics (1896b, 203). However, the "petit-bourgeois" (Steiger 1896c, 209) charges against *Neue Welt* and its Naturalistic texts (of purveying pessimism, immorality and decadence) brought forward by Bérard (1896), Frohme and others, dominated the discussion. Neither the movement's relationship to contemporary critical realism nor the political and social functions of art were addressed. Bebel helped disarm the debate by supporting a compromise to which all parties agreed: to protect "true art," and its Social-Democratic readers (especially women), from the indelicacies and obscenities found in some modern literature. Schönlank's remark that his colleagues' eulogy of "true art" amounted to a eulogy of "the eternal truth of bourgeois society" (Rothe ed. 1986a, 225) represented a rare (and unnoticed) moment of theoretical insight. Thus, the central paradox of late 19th-century socialist literary theory, the supposed incompatibility of political and esthetic values in literary texts and their reception, which the first phase of the debate had brought to the forefront, remained unthematized here and therefore unresolved; and Singer's summary of the discussion as one which showed "the German working class at the cutting edge of intellectual progress" (Rothe ed. 1986a, 233) was adequate only in its unintended irony.

Kurt Eisner was one of those who voiced dissatisfaction with the congress debate, which he read in part as a rehash of the decade-long "art war" fought by the conservative bourgeoisie against Naturalism (1896, 246). For Eisner the most important aspect of this debate was the avoidance of the question of a properly *Social-Democratic* literature, of a "party-political" form of writing (248-49). While a need for such a literature existed, the Social-Democratic "professors" would continue to "negate the present for the sake of the future and to seek a substitute in the past" (250). Mehring, who did not attend the congress, provided a sort of afterword to the discussion whose revision of his earlier position became normative for the movement. He no longer distinguishes progressive and regressive strains but views all of Naturalism as a product of bourgeois decadence whose pessimism is in irreconcilable opposition to the optimism of the proletariat as a revolutionary and ascendant class (1896, 135). Here the various complaints against modern pessimism which dotted the debate are condensed into the simple and final antithesis of bourgeois pessimism and proletarian optimism without regard to their possible esthetic or cognitive functions or, for that matter, for the distinction Benjamin makes between an optimism of action and one, prevalent in the movement, of mere expectation (1937, 488). Some years later, Eisner pits the autonomy of art, tentatively identified by Marx in 1857, against Mehring's undialectical homologizing of a declining bourgeois class and its entire art as decadent (1913, 128, 131-32).

While for Brauneck (1974, 104) the "Naturalism Debate" is one of several articulations of the unresolvable problem of "tendency art" as posed by the movement, and Trommler (1976a, 146-63) views the debate as a special case of the movement's relationship with bourgeois intellectuals, most historians of the event (Kaiser 1950; Münchow 1964; Füllberth 1972; Scherer 1974; Rothe 1986b), despite differences in detail, tend to perpetuate the party's own assessment of Naturalism as a mere bourgeois "rebellion" and to downplay the historical possibilities of an alliance of the two. Münchow projects the struggle against "Modernism" which occupied the literary politics of the GDR in the 50s and 60s back into the Naturalism Debate as its historical source; here Mehring's opposition to Naturalism is seen as the view of the working class itself and the debate as a genuine *Volksdiskussion* (616). Despite some common ideological sources (the revolution of 1848 and popular Darwinism) (Pforte 1974, 178), Naturalism is seen by these critics as a style, as an "end in itself" rather than as a possible means to advance the ideology of the proletariat (Pforte 1974, 199). Huyssen, on the other hand, emphasizes the untapped potential of the program of the leftist opposition within the movement and the Friedrichshagen Naturalists to overcome the separation of politics and art and to experiment (especially in the popular theater, the *Volksbühne*) with the creation of a countercultural public sphere.

In the "Tendency-Art Debate" (*Tendenzkunst-Debatte*) of 1910-12, as Brauneck has pointed out (1974, 190), the positions outlined by traditionalists in the "Naturalism Debate" are restated in a new thematic context; and this happened at a time when, according to Bürgel, there was "no politically relevant group in the German labor movement which seriously considered a contemporary proletarian or socialist art either necessary or worthy of support" (Bürgel 1987b, xix). The theme here is "tendency" (*Tendenz*) which denotes a discernible attempt at political persuasion. The debate is the final phase before 1914 of the enshrinement and institutionalization of the antinomy of art and politics as the canonical center of socialist literary theory; and it offers only occasional hints of a socialist esthetics beyond this antinomy. The chief antagonist of the traditionalists here was the successful Dutch playwright Herman Heijermans who wrote for the party daily *Vorwärts* under the pseudonym Heinz Sperber. Sperber offered no theoretically coherent program; his many contributions to this debate are marked by theoretical lapses and exaggerations which made it easy for traditionalists to ignore relevant questions posed by Sperber and to sit in judgment of an "esthetics of the calloused fist," "a nonsense," according to Mehring, "equally disgusting in esthetic and moral terms" (Bürgel 1987a, 88).

Sperber belongs to a long line of critics of socialist cultural policy who insist that since all literature is an expression of historically specific and class-bound tendencies, the proletariat's literary interest should not be confined to the reception of works remote from its historical situation and class interests (1910b, 14). The "generally human," routinely invoked by traditionalists as the essence of art, can only be pursued by the artist to the limits of his class consciousness (1910c, 22). Especially in an age in which art has become completely commodified (1910a), the proletariat must produce a tendentious art freely expressive of its own values. Sperber does not propose here a radical revision of the movement's classical concept of "true art" as historically transcendent, but he does not believe that this "true art" will exist before the classless society of the future; the *present* need is to undo the incompleteness of a movement which has excluded art from its political agenda and to produce a "transitional art which alerts, an art of trenchant criticism and propaganda" (1911a, 52). Most offensive to traditionalists was Sperber's opposition to an imposing of esthetic standards "from above." His contention that workers show more understanding of drama, for instance, than the blasé bourgeois theater audience (1911c, 65) is based on the belief that in matters of art, "class instinct" should be a main source of judgment for a politically combative class — unless, he adds, "class perspective [*Klassenstandpunkt*] is just an empty phrase" (1911b, 59-60). Sperber does not, as the movement had not done, define class instinct or class awareness. Like Luxemburg, however, he assumes that it is more than a mere accumulation of historical and scientific knowledge, that it is indeed capable of spontaneous political, social and artistic production. Despite his occasional radicalism and lack of conceptual differentiation, it is clear that his criticism was directed chiefly at the exclusivity of the bourgeois literary canon and its values, at the movement's refusal to incorporate art into its political struggle and thereby problematize the exclusivity of traditional notions of art and its social functions. He had few supporters in this campaign.

The responses to Sperber's initiative ranged from the abrupt dismissal by Mehring to Märten's attempt to shift the theoretical concern to a new focus by changing the content-oriented question of art and politics to one which considers the changing dialectic of forms, media and functions as well as content (1911-12). The majority of these responses represents a final collective articulation of the literary politics of pre-war Social Democracy. Their tenor, in disregard of some of Sperber's ideas, is to condemn any attempt to posit political and esthetic values as mutually constitutive. The norms of taste are more durable than political orientations (Franz 1910, 15). It is understandable, so Ströbel, that the worker does not seek in art a "deep and clear representation of life as it is" but rather a "means to instruction and improvement of life, i.e., tendency, tangible tendency" (1910-11, 45). But he must be taught that the value of an art work resides in its objective characteristics, to be ascertained by knowledgeable experts rather than in the subjective reactions of amateurs (41) — which Grötzsch (1911-12, 112) ranks particularly low in the case of workers. As far as bourgeois art is concerned, he must be taught how to separate "the poetic power from an objectionable [political] tendency and to assimilate only what is compatible with his *Weltanschauung*" (Ströbel 1911-12, 94). Sperber's supposed insistence that class instinct be made the exclusive measure of esthetic excellence elicits the response from Stampfer: "poor art! Poor proletariat!" (1911b, 63). The successful artist is not primarily a social democrat or political fighter — but an artist (Ströbel 1910, 30). As a socialist, in Stampfer's phrase, the proletarian poet is ours, as a poet, he belongs to mankind (1911, 57). Most of these responses are filled with an indignation at a supposed form of cultural vulgarization and iconoclasm; instead of a discussion of the possibilities of a proletarian or socialist art, of a literary revolution as part of the political one, we find the dominance of the Mehringian positions to have become complete and rigid. And once again it is Bernstein (1912) who carries these positions unapologetically to their logical extremes. He rejects the idea of a tendentious socialist literature on theoretical as well as historical grounds. The laws of art are not those of party or class (141); "art and tendency are mutually exclusive categories" (137): the latter may provide material to art but never adds to esthetic value (137-38). Bernstein makes a distinction with a finality which most of the other contributions to the debate merely imply, namely that there are two kinds of tendency: tendency "in the grand, ethical sense" (which informs all great art) and the tendency of political utilitarianism (which "poisons" art) (139). As far as the historical possibilities of a socialist art are concerned, Bernstein finds that the movement's "decided rationalism and objectivism" mitigates against it (140). In Bernstein's essay the dispute of the early 1840s between Freiligrath and Herwegh concerning the viability of a party-political poetry, so often invoked in the movement, had finally lost its power of precedence.

During the "Naturalism Debate" the party's policy of isolating the proletariat from contemporary culture was confirmed, but so was — in the compromise resolution of the party congress of 1896 — the legitimacy of a plurality of tastes and theoretical orientations in literary matters. The tone and outcome of the "Tendency-Art Debate," by contrast, indicate that in the waning years of Wilhelminian Germany, the movement in its entirety — from "revisionists" to "radicals" — had absolutized the antinomy of "disinterested" art and utilitarian politics and thereby conceded the impossibility of a contemporary socialist art. In the assessments of this debate, as the culminating phase of a theoretical impasse, historians from East and West are in agreement. Füllberth was the first to analyze the relevant documents. For him the common front of Marxists and "revisionists" against Sperber, and the Marxists' inability to "develop the political relevance of Sperber's position," are not so much the result of the latter's conceptual inadequacies as they are an expression of an indifference to problems of art in particular and contemporary political problems in general (1972, 149). Brauneck (1974, 176-94) shows the extent to which the debate was embedded, terminologically and conceptually, in the discussion of art and tendency conducted by contemporary liberal critics; and Bürgel, the GDR editor of the documents of this debate, demonstrates that the party's resistance to the introduction of political motivations to cultural activity was not the result of specific revisionist or reformist forces but rather of an axiomatic attitude of the entire movement (1987b, xxxviii).

Another area of cultural activity which the movement exempted from politics is the education of children and juveniles. Radical youth organizations which had grown rapidly, especially under the leadership of Karl Liebknecht and Ludwig Frank, were either abolished by the party or depoliticized under the threat of the new law of association of 1908. Zetkin was the only party leader to advocate forcefully a conception of socialism which did not merely consist of political and economic measures but rather comprised a comprehensive *Weltanschauung* which shaped all relations, including those of parents and children. In opposition to K. Bl. (1903-04, 157) who feared that exposure to socialist ideas at an early age might breed a mindless herd of followers, Zetkin insisted that the emotional and intellectual foundation of socialism should be laid as early as possible (1906b, 1). It is Zetkin who supported the idea of a socialist literature for children and youth, especially (since 1909) in the children's supplement of *Gleichheit*, edited primarily by Käte Duncker. In her campaign for a socialist youth literature, Zetkin was assisted — despite his official position on juvenile literature — by Heinrich Schulz (under the pseudonym Ernst Almsroth), and later by Edwin Hoernle (Trommler 1976a, 266). However, her conviction that a "growing demand for socialist children's literature" proved that the fighting proletariat "needed new tools for new tasks" (1906b, 2) was not shared by any faction within the party.

Demands for the creation of a socialist literature for juveniles were raised occasionally at party congresses (accepted, for instance, at the congress of 1894, and rejected in 1895), but the axiom of the incompatibility of political and artistic motivations was reinforced in this context by the idea of the "golden naivete and innocence" of youth which needed to be protected — so Schulz in his official statement (1900-01, 172). Schulz endorses Ferdinand Avenarius' distinction between an inferior literature written for a particular public and genuine *Dichtung* which is seen as the expression of the poet's innermost needs (176). Once the concept of a socialist juvenile literature was rejected with arguments developed in the discussion of "adult" literature, the issue of juvenile reading was reduced to a campaign against literature harmful to young people. Here Schulz recommends that the movement support liberal efforts to protect the young from literary "trash." The form of Schulz' argumentation (replacing the need for a socialist juvenile literature with the need to fight literary "trash") is repeated in most essays on the subject. Bär (1903-04, 128) insists on a need to educate the young to enjoy "true art." Both he and K. Bl. (1903-04, 154) agree with the liberal reformer Heinrich Wolgast that the chief requirement of good juvenile literature is that it be "genuine art." Besides, according to Fendrich (1905, 323), political agitation is antithetical to the imagination of the young.

A particular aspect of the fight against *Kitsch* (substandard art) is the campaign against *Schundliteratur* (literary trash) waged since the 1870s. During the early stages of the movement, the term, or its cognates, referred to most entertainment fiction published commercially; by the time *Schund* is debated again prior to World War I, Social-Democratic cultural politicians and librarians have joined the campaign of bourgeois liberal educators against "literary poison," a concept defined by Ernst Schultze as a literary substance which corrupts the soul and leads to crime and suicide (1909). Crime fiction, for instance, is acceptable to Schultze only if the description of crime is "framed by deep and beautiful thoughts" (1910, 157). Unlike the debate over a possible socialist juvenile literature which ended in the mere restatement of classical esthetic norms, however, in this debate about the possible ill effects on juveniles of certain kinds of popular literature, some specifically proletarian aspects of literary consumption are touched upon, albeit lightly. Döring acknowledges the vulnerability of undereducated young proletarians to a literature which deflects from social reality (1910, 366) — while R. H. (1911, 339) recognizes the special needs of workers for distraction and freedom of the imagination. Hanauer (1910), points to the growing influence of the entertainment industry (movies, music, advertisements) on workers and their inability to read high-literary texts (113-14). In contrast to the preceding literary debates, this confrontation with "pulp" fiction in the 1910s not only deplored the existence of "bad" literature but also recognized that the socially and historically disembodied process of high-literary reading stipulated by traditional hermeneutics did not reflect the reality of proletarian reading and the needs it met. These ideas, however, remained marginal to the literary discourse of the movement.

The various instances chronicled here of theorizing about literature and its uses, about the literary heritage and the possibilities of a proletarian or socialist literary production demonstrate the exclusivity and tenacity of a literary politics, systematized by Mehring, which privileges the understanding and enjoyment of the "true" literature of German classicism as an activity of *Bildung* and cultural emancipation. Its tenacity extends into the cultural politics of the GDR, as Mehring's rehabilitation indicates. It is this traditionalism of socialist literary politics which provides the historical auspices under which much of the recent discussion in East and West took place: the criticism and defense of contemporary East German literary politics. Trommler (1976b), Brückner and Ricke (1974) and others have analyzed this traditionalism. In Burggraf's rebuttal of these critiques (1978), Mehring's rejection of a contemporary socialist literature and his advocacy of an appropriation of the pathos of the bourgeois classics is seen both as the inevitable result of capitalist-imperialist circumstances and, curiously, as a model for a "factually existing" socialism. The conflict between a search for past or present forms of a revolutionary literary culture and the defense of a newly-inscribed cultural conservatism provided the post-war discussion of early socialist literature and literary theory with an urgency which now — with the sudden demise of the GDR — is largely lost. This loss may well result in an ideologically less restrictive approach to the literary life of early German socialism.

Literary Dissemination and Consumption

The literary debates conducted in the movement, the official endorsements of high-literary texts and the stipulations of proper hermeneutic behavior rarely touched upon the *actual* literary life of organized workers — except in occasional condemnations of "bad taste" and "harmful literature." Mehring's theorizing about proletarian uses of the classics and the workers' supposed immunity to the temptations of popular literature (1896, 134-35) took place in a utopian vacuum. Its remoteness from the social and cultural reality of 10-hour workdays and minimal educational preparation, as well as the realities of distribution and consumption of literary products within the subculture of Social Democracy, is duplicated by attempts of later critics to establish a corpus of proletarian literature in terms of the "proper" theoretical content of selected texts. Despite sobering reports by Social-Democratic librarians on the reading habits of organized workers (many of which appeared in the cultural section, edited by Mehring, of *Die Neue Zeit*), the notion of the party as "pedagogical province" (Eisner 1908, 18) and of the worker who sits down after a 9- or 10-hour workday to study Marx' *Kapital* (Langewiesche and Schönhoven 1976, 198) or the literary classics persisted as the high-cultural norm persisted to such an extent that many of the librarians' reports express surprised disappointment with the workers' actual avoidance of all reading which "requires intensive thinking" (Nitschke 1913, 367).

Workers' libraries (run by party groups, educational associations or union locals) started out as collections of political texts for the education of functionaries of the movement; as the party's aspiration to become a "cultural movement" took hold, they were converted into general libraries to guide workers from the "light" reading of entertainment fiction to the "serious" reading of the literary and political classics, a form of *Emporlesen* (reading one's way up) widely propagated in the movement. However, the "transitional reader" (Reißmann 1913-14, 550) frequently never made the transition to the high-literary texts; and even when a proletarian reader made an effort to acquire the ability to "distinguish between good and bad" literature (H. Holek 1911, 361) by reading large quantities of sanctioned texts, this effort, as H. Holek's account of his reading shows, often remained in mimicry of unreflected bourgeois notions of *Bildung* and served primarily to enhance the reader's social status. Early user statistics of workers' libraries register a weak demand for the party's political pamphlets (J. S. and E. F. 1894-95, 154) and for the literary and political classics but a strong interest in fiction (Advocatus 1895-96, 632-33 and 1894-95, 815). These "unhealthy" facts are confirmed 15 years later by Kliche (1910, 295) whose example from the transport workers' library in Berlin (779 readers of Dumas vs. 12 of Goethe) indicate a continuing decline of "serious" reading. As the statistics of the Berlin woodworkers' library for the years 1891-1911 suggest, not only did readers' interest shift from political and scientific texts to literary ones, even within *belles-lettres* a rapid decline in the popularity of non-narrative genres took place. While borrowings of poetry and drama decreased from 12.6% (of total borrowings) to 4.3%, those of fiction rose from 14.6% to 70.4% (Langewiesche and Schönhoven 1976, 170-71). It must be remembered in this context that the librarians of the movement, "rigorous purists" according to Langewiesche and Schönhoven (194), subjected "light reading" to a "particularly strict censorship" (J. G. 1898-99, 89), and some felt that the problem of an "excessive" consumption of entertainment literature could be solved by removing "literary poisoners" like Karl May from the shelves (Bär 1906-07, 719). Most of them, however, realized that if the popular authors of the day (Marlitt, Eschstruth) were available in Social-Democratic libraries, their proletarian readership would be large indeed (Kliche 1911, 316). In these critical accounts of an excessive use of entertainment literature (especially on the part of women) and a corresponding neglect of "instructional" texts, the simple polarity and valuation of these two readerly motivations (entertainment and instruction) was not questioned. Since the original purpose of workers' libraries (political instruction) had been lost and entertainment had become their chief service, so Mehlich (1913-14, 66), their mission could well be performed by the country's public libraries (68) — a cooperation with bourgeois cultural institutions which, according to Siemering (1911, 59), had already been accomplished in Vienna. Only Nitschke (1913, 369-70) proposed to go beyond the traditional condemnations of entertainment literature for its esthetic and psychological defects and to use it to enhance the workers' social understanding. This challenge to the exclusivity of classical esthetic standards, however, is quickly contained by Nitschke's own rejection of all "tendency" (370).

Steinberg (1967, 129-50), the first among modern scholars to evaluate some of these user statistics, sees in them a confirmation of his thesis of the discrepancy of revolutionary discourse and cultural practice within the movement and of a "disappearance of the theoretical sense among workers" (142); Füllberth (1972, 114), in line with his criticism of revisionist practices in the party, relates the "intellectual apathy" evident in the reading habits of organized workers to the loss of the party's mission of mobilizing the masses. Both these historians of the political and cultural development of Social Democracy retain the high expectations of theoretical educability of workers characteristic of Social-Democratic cultural policy and of the early assessments of proletarian reading habits. Their inclusive verdict of a Social-Democratic *embourgeoisement* does not, as Gebauer (1972) charges, rest entirely on the testimony of "revisionist" sources but it does obscure the need to problematize both the party's expectations and the validity of its concept of literary entertainment. Langewiesche and Schönhoven (1976), in their comprehensive analysis of workers' reading habits, challenge these judgments in view of the social, economic and cultural deprivation of the proletariat (135-42) and the fact that its preferences of entertainment literature, despite these cultural handicaps, corresponded precisely to the international average of readers of all classes (182). They also question a condemnation of workers' reading habits based upon an undifferentiated understanding of entertainment and instruction and point to such didactic characteristics as social criticism in some of the fiction favored by workers, especially Zola, their second favorite author (195). These tentative distinctions are crucial to Hoffmann (1975, 506-60) whose analysis of the statistics leads to conclusions radically different from those of Steinberg, Füllberth and the early socialist librarians. The fact that 8 of the 10 most favored writers are social critics, for instance, indicates an interest in the informational, emancipatory and social-critical aspects of literature (517-26). The continued preference for certain kinds of light reading, Hoffmann maintains, is not a symptom of intellectual inertia but rather the result of the failed literary politics of the party. Socialist authors such as M. Kautsky, Otto-Walster, Ernst Preczang and A. Ger were readily accepted by proletarian readers, but the party encouraged neither the critical reception of contemporary bourgeois literature nor the development (or reception) of a socialist literature as such (559).

If, by the movement's own standards, the workers' libraries had failed to guide their users to a "serious" hermeneutic encounter with classical literary texts, how did Social Democracy succeed in implementing its literary politics in its critical reception and dissemination of literary texts? Any attempt to answer this question necessitates a look at the socialist press so essential to the constitution of a socialist countercultural sphere of communication. Perhaps the least important aspect of the party's dissemination of literature are the book publications of its three publishing houses. Hoffmann (1975, 423) estimates that 15-20% of their monograph publications were devoted to *belles-lettres*. Hottingen-Zürich and Vorwärts were especially active in the dissemination of the literary classics and the work of the "freedom poets" but also served as publishing outlets for socialist writers. While Hottingen was particularly effective in providing educational associations with socialist plays and song-books during the era of the anti-socialist law, Vorwärts, since 1912-13, made a number of socialist fiction writers available in inexpensive editions (Ger, Preczang, Andersen Nexø), issued such semi-official poetry collections as *Buch der Freiheit* (ed. Karl Henckell, 1893-94) and *Von unten auf* (ed. Franz Diederich, 1910-11) and published 18 socialist plays in its series "Sozialistische Theaterstücke." The literary publications of the Dietz-Verlag were devoted almost entirely to socialist authors: 5 poetry collections and 5 additional volumes introducing the work of Hasenclever, Frohme, Lepp, Audorf, Lavant, Kegel and Scheu, novels by M. Kautsky and Schweichel, plays by Stern and Märten as well as autobiographies of Social-Democratic leaders (Bebel, Belli, Popp). Although these works of socialist writers issued by party-affiliated publishers constituted a representative (rather than inclusive) dissemination of the (publishable) literary production within the movement, the effect of this form of distribution on the literary sensibilities of organized workers was not considerable. Workers rarely purchased books (or borrowed them from libraries); their chief access to literature, fiction in particular, came through periodical publications (newspapers, party calendars and entertainment and fiction magazines).

The party-affiliated press played a decisive role in the constitution and development of the movement. In its early years, the forms of public communication of the lower classes changed dramatically. The occasional use of the printed word (the Bible, catechism, calendars) of the mostly rural lower classes was replaced by the regular use of printed materials by an industrial proletariat. The rapid change of social life created a cognitive deficit which Social-Democratic newspapers and pamphlets attempted to address (Loreck 1977, 95). The press, as an instrument of agitation and information, was "to enlighten workers and raise their class awareness" (I. Auer, *PPT* 1890, 231) as well as provide a "protective wall" (R. Fischer, *PPT* 1892, 88) to isolate organized workers from bourgeois influences. The socialist press grew rapidly. By the time the anti-socialist law suppressed it in 1878, the movement possessed 42 party-run and 14 union-run newspapers with a combined readership of approximately 165,000 (Bebel, *PPT* 1890, 35). By 1914, Social-Democratic newspapers were published in a total edition of 2 million copies (Fricke 1987, vol. 1, 539). Such absolute figures, however, do not properly express the relative appeal of the socialist press in Germany where, at the turn of the century, 3,500 newspapers competed for 17.5 million readers (Fricke, ibid.). As important as the press was for a movement which subscribed to a "knowledge-is-power" ideology, the discrepancy between the percentage of Social-Democratic voters (34.8% in 1912) and the percentage of Social-Democratic newspapers (2.2% in the same year) (Kantorowicz 1922, 31) indicates a severely limited appeal of the party's newspapers among non-affiliated sympathizers. A major reason, according to Kantorowicz (36), is the "party-theoretical" character of this press which he attributes in part to the fact that the roles of party functionary and journalist were commingled: most of the editors also occupied positions in the party leadership and sat in parliaments and other elected bodies (103). This close association of party bureaucracy and press helped create a style suited only to a homogenous constituency with clearly-defined ideological attachments.

The newspaper sections on culture, entertainment and literature (*Feuilleton*) tended to be neglected and were usually run by underqualified or part-time editors. In order to enhance the appeal of the party's national daily, *Vorwärts*, for instance, the party congress of 1896 resolved to enhance and enlarge its *Feuilleton*. Since the *Feuilleton* was to help recruit new readers (and party members) from among the politically indifferent (and especially women), it was to be kept relatively free of political "tendency." As far as the dissemination and criticism of literature in newspapers is concerned, then, the movement's apolitical conception of art here intersected with the party's need to appeal to the politically indifferent. If we follow the debate on form and function of the socialist *Feuilleton* conducted between 1911 and 1914 in the newsletter of the "Workers' Press Association" (*Mitteilungen des Vereins Arbeiterpresse*), it becomes clear that the chief function of the *Feuilleton* was to compete for readers with the vastly successful bourgeois press and that the serialized novel was of "immeasurable importance" (Franke 1913, 4) in that endeavor. Haenisch's suggestion that a commission pre-select these novels to weed out unsuitable material (1911, 9) initiated a debate in which a number of characteristics of the "right" novel were put forth, none of them even remotely suggestive of the idea of a socialist or agitatory literature. Kliche (1914a) stressed the record of socialist papers in fighting literary "trash" and publishing only "known and cherished" authors (1914b, 5). According to Franke (1913, 5), the serial novel must combine three qualities: artistic merit, promotional power and an absence of "tendency." What, in the absence of "tendency," is to be promoted would appear to be Social Democracy as a primarily cultural, rather than political, movement. Rabold (1913, 2) makes clear that, while instruction, entertainment and the improving of workers' cultural competence remains the formal purpose of the *Feuilleton,* the fiction published in a socialist newspaper should be commensurate with its readership's disinterest in form: "The *Feuilleton* of the party press should never become literary."

Despite the fact that the Social-Democratic newspaper *Feuilleton* was one of the important institutional spaces provided by the movement for the dissemination and criticism of literature, it has attracted little scholarly attention. This is especially true for its literary criticism. Feddersen's dissertation of 1923 retains the traditional separation of politics and art and is based on an idea of the *Feuilleton* as a specific esthetic genre which may not be invaded by "party politics": politics — in the "larger" sense — may be presented here only in "esthetically conceived contributions" (53). Feddersen measures the extent to which Social-Democratic *Feuilletons* overcame their "petit-bourgeois" values almost entirely by their propagation of "progressive literature," i.e., Critical Realism and Naturalism. His position, in 1923, is essentially identical with Edgar Steiger's during the Naturalism Debate of the early 1890s. According to Hoffmann (1975), the critical reception of literature in the socialist periodical press evolved from an attempt to develop a specifically socialist point of view and vocabulary to the application of generally accepted standards of excellence; he registers a change in orientation from educating readers "through art" to educating them "for art" (324). The reception of the Critical Realism of the 19th and 20th centuries was extensive; it is not, however, motivated by a sense of ideological kinship but rather by a curiosity about bourgeois society (380). While the *Feuilleton* of *Vorwärts* perpetuated a "classical normative esthetics," the left-leaning *Leipziger Volkszeitung* represented, during the period 1894-1902, a progressive concern not only with Critical Realism but also with contemporary art, literature and music (Feddersen 1923, 169) and socialist literature, especially Russian and Scandinavian (Fricke 1987, vol. 1, 553). Although the Social-Democratic press published socialist authors regularly, especially their poetry, its occasional reviewing of their work was tied to received esthetic norms and therefore did not, as the reviews of the early *Sozialdemokrat* (1879-1890) had done, highlight its specific utility for the working class (Hoffmann 1975, 414).

The most important vehicles of literary dissemination (especially of poetry and fiction) were the party's newspapers, journals and annual calendars. The calendar was a form of reading which, especially in its 18th-century form, combined entertainment and enlightenment. Its popularity was considerable: Engelsing (1973, 119) estimates that the total edition of calendars in 1853 amounted to 1 million. As early as the 1870s, both socialist parties utilized the calendar for purposes of political agitation. In addition to a number of regional calendars, *Der arme Conrad* served as national party calendar until 1878 when it was published in an edition of 60,000 (*Lexikon*, 267); from 1883 until 1933, the *Neue-Welt-Kalender* served the same function. The literary form favored by early socialist calendars was the short story with a strong didactic bent. Since in the first decades of the movement practically every socialist writer (including Otto-Walster, Schweichel and M. Kautsky) contributed to them (C. Friedrich 1975, xxii) and the texts published were often commissioned to assist the party's propaganda, the *Lexikon* sees in these "occasional" forms of literature "building blocks for a broad development of socialist literature in the 19th century" (269). According to the same source, however, the Social-Democratic calendars soon followed the development of such socialist entertainment magazines as *Neue Welt* and became indistinguishable from *Gartenlaube* and other bourgeois family magazines.

Since the movement recognized early on that newspaper *Feuilletons* and calendars offered only a limited scope for socialist literary activity, the Lassalleans' *Social-politische Blätter* and the "Eisenach" party's *Volksstaat-Erzähler*, were established, both in 1873, to advance a socialist view of literature. The latter, for instance, published poetry of Social-Democratic writers (Rhenanus, Kegel) alongside that of progressive bourgeois poets and introduced its readers to two socialist writers, Otto-Walster and Lübeck. With the creation of *Neue Welt* (first as an independent magazine, then as a free supplement to Social-Democratic newspapers), however, and the later fiction magazine *In Freien Stunden*, the emphasis shifted from opposing a socialist literature to the petit-bourgeois fiction of the *Gartenlaube* to using the latter's appeal to the masses to attract new voters to the party. The double motivation which guided the party's dissemination of fiction — to improve the workers' literary taste and to attract the politically "indifferent" to the party — caused regular confrontations at party congresses even before the Naturalism Debate of 1896. Baake, the editor of *Neue Welt*, in response to complaints about the quality of its fiction (*PPT* 1892, 262), points to the fact that since the magazine is supposed to advance the party's cause even in remote rural areas, higher literary standards would be counterproductive (263). Fuchs' biting comparison of *Neue Welt* with his own *Süddeutscher Postillon* (*PPT* 1893, 112) is undercut by Eichhorn's reminder that the "intellectual capacity of women" should not be overloaded (134). These arguments can be heard with reference to all periodical publications of literary texts. It should not be forgotten, however, that Kliche's assessment of the quality of fiction in the party press (1914b) was essentially correct: it was considerably above the quality of fiction published in small bourgeois newspapers and it was free of features offensive to the working class and to accepted public taste. Neither should the political implications of this fact be overlooked: as readers of Social-Democratic publications, organized workers felt assured that *they*, in contrast to the bourgeois, petit-bourgeois and politically indifferent lower-class segments of society, upheld not only the highest artistic standards and traditions but also a progressive social ethics. This social, countercultural function of fiction-reading of organized workers cannot be fully ascertained by quantitative analyses of the fictional content of socialist periodicals.

However, the studies which have been made of the literary content of *Neue Welt, Gleichheit* and *Arbeiter-Jugend* (Hoffmann 1975), *Neue Welt, In Freien Stunden* and *Vorwärts* (Zerges 1982), and *Neue Welt* and *Gartenlaube* (Seybold 1986) not only shed light on the quantitative aspect of the dissemination of socialist literature in these periodicals but also show the extent to which the intertextual environment of these journals discouraged the recognition of socialist literature as distinct from other forms of "acceptable" literature. Hoffmann's content analysis attempts to measure the proportions of non-political and "politicizing" literature, the latter category comprising texts advocating a socialist or democratic transformation of society as well as social criticism. It is doubtful that many readers of *Neue Welt*, for instance, were capable of making such distinctions. To them the fact that a text appeared in a Social-Democratic publication sufficiently signalled its compatibility with socialist taste and ideology. However, Hoffmann's statistics confirm the thesis of a progressive de-politicization of literary texts published: in the case of *Neue Welt*, during the period of 1876 to 1913 the percentage of "politicizing" literature declined from 49% to 16%, in the case of *Gleichheit*, between 1892 and 1913, it declined from 81% to 61%. The proportions in *Arbeiter-Jugend* are similar to those of *Gleichheit*. According to Zerges' analyses, most of the authors published in the socialist press belonged to the bourgeois literary canon. This is particularly true for the party daily *Vorwärts*, two-thirds of whose authors belonged to the "world-literary" canon. Least dependent on this body of sanctioned texts was *Neue Welt* which regularly published socialist authors (Preczang, M. Kautsky, Ger) as well as contemporary regional literature (*Heimatliteratur*). Seybold finds many of the ideologemes of the movement represented in the narratives of the latter journal: the biological decadence of the bourgeoisie, the depiction of political aspirations in terms of expectation rather than political action, the lack of specificity of the class struggle. Since the "catalogue of virtues" of *Neue Welt* and *Gartenlaube* are essentially identical (industriousness, decency, courage and honesty), the depiction of actions deviating from bourgeois behavioral norms is hardly possible. The thematic emphasis on class struggle in the early issues of *Neue Welt* disappears. Especially after 1905 — a time in the history of the party marked by the Russian revolution and the mass-strike debate — regional art (with its evocation of timeless rural life and celebration of timeless human virtues) dominates *Neue Welt*. The beginnings of a materialist approach to class relations in the early fiction of the journal here appears transformed into timeless "idealistic" struggles (Seybold 1986, 286).

In studies of socialist literature primarily based on textual content, forms and context of literary dissemination are understandably neglected. Similarly neglected, however, is a periodical form of literary publication specially designed to express and support the political views of the movement: the two satiric journals, *Süddeutscher Postillon* (independent since 1883, 40,000 subscribers in 1894) and *Der wahre Jacob* (since 1879, 371,000 subscribers in 1913). Both were closely affiliated with the party and were run as extensions of its political work. As magazines of humor and political satire, they developed or appropriated a repertory of short, and politically pointed, literary forms which, immune from a Mehringian esthetic verdict, combined traditional literary qualities (narrative, drama, symbol, allegory, etc.) with political utilitarianism. These dialogues and sketches, letters and satiric reports, stories and various forms of topical poetry (Völkerling 1969, 58) were examples of what Eduard Fuchs, editor of *Süddeutscher Postillon*, called "genuine party art." Its motifs were taken from the daily political struggle and shaped into literary weapons (1898a, 79). The journals offer an opportunity to test the thesis of the *embourgeoisement* of the movement's literary life. A comparison with bourgeois satirical journals (*Simplicissimus, Kladderadatsch*) may well reveal a broad range of significant similarities: a predominance of "freedom" as satiric standard (rather than class struggle) and of historically "obsolete" satiric targets (*Junker* rather than industrialists), a tendency of the humor to become satirically "non-referential," of "satirizing without attacking," as Fuchs put it (1894a, 7). Of particular interest, however, are the utilitarian literary forms peculiar to these journals and the "symbiotic" relationship discernible in them between three levels of the Social-Democratic discourse: the political rhetoric of the party (closely reflected especially in the semi-official *Der wahre Jacob*), the metaphoricism of socialist poetry and the iconography of illustrations. Here, where the three levels co-exist in a "democratic" constellation, their correspondences and exchanges become visible. An example is the unmediated juxtaposition, in the party discourse, of social criticism and the evocation of an idyllic future which is closely paralleled in the poetry (which frequently couches the notion of political change in the metaphor of an inevitable spring) and in the iconography of an unmediated juxtaposition of the worker as victim and as laureled hero of freedom — the latter, in the opinion of an early critic, an example of socialist allegory as "direct epigone of ancient art" (ch. 1896, 327). This unique institutional space — in which utilitarian and non-utilitarian artistic expressions co-exist and interact — remains largely unexplored. The validity of Knilli's contention that here we have an example of a class-conscious iconography, "with its own syntax, semantics and pragmatics, with its own allegorical and emblematic language" (1970, 12) still needs to be demonstrated.

After 1890, the two satirical journals became increasingly literary; and since they also published literary criticism and appreciations regularly, they became, in Völkerling's words, "organizational centers of early socialist literature" (1969, 170). Especially important is the fact that a large percentage of the movement's poetry was published here, poetry which reached its readers in a context of political agitation. Some of the major socialist poets of the time were closely associated with these journals: Fuchs, Klaar, Schönlank (with *Süddeutscher Postillon*), Kegel, Lavant, Müller-Jahnke (with *Der wahre Jacob*), Seidel (with both). While some selections from these journals have been made available (Häckel 1959, Schütz 1977, Achten 1979b), their evaluation as factors in the literary life of the movement to this date is at best preliminary. GDR critics (Häckel, Völkerling, Knilli, Piltz 1979a) tend to emphasize the extent to which these journals "reflect" the growth of "opportunism" or "revisionism" in the party. Western critics like Hollweck (1973, 81) measure them against "objective" artistic standards represented by their more famous competitors. In both cases, the unique role these journals played in the literary and ideological life of the movement is neglected. They lived by the short literary and graphic gesture, the aphorism, joke, caricature, poem; here the socialist *Weltanschauung* is not explained, differentiated, historicized or even narrativized but used as a "natural," general and self-evident satiric standard. These literary gestures are punitive (not persuasive) satire whose efficacy depended in part on the simplicity and self-evidence of its targets (fat industrial bosses, degenerate aristocrats, duplicitous clergy, brutal military officers). The diffuseness of this standard has to do with the economy of popular satire; the fact that it may have corresponded to some extent to the diffuseness of the movement's revolutionism should not move us to reduce these journals to mere reflectors of party politics, but rather to widen the scope of our investigation of the complex system of socialist political rhetoric and its metaphorizations.

5: The Literary Genres

THE EXCLUSIVE USE OF received forms of valuation which characterizes the literary theory and criticism of German Social Democracy is appropriated into the literary politics of the early GDR. Here a continuity is posited which brackets out the era between the wars and specifically the debates on Expressionism and on the possibilities of proletarian-revolutionary literature which took place during that period. This partial occlusion of internal traditions is not unusual in the movement. These debates, for example, took very little notice of the socialist literary production prior to World War I. The war had propelled into the foreground an Expressionist "worker's literature" (identified with such celebrated poets as Lersch, Engelke and Bröger) which became synonymous with proletarian literature, as Martini's definition of 1956 still shows. To the critical concern with this new phenomenon, the literary production of pre-war Social Democracy appeared as a prelude at best (Ecks 1924, Loeb 1932) or is dismissed for its formal dependence on bourgeois models (Bab 1929). Early Social-Democratic poetry is absent from v. Wiese's analysis of recent political literature (1931) and from Strasser's sociological and formal definitions of *Arbeiterdichtung* (1930). In the National-Socialist view of workers' poetry, finally, Social-Democratic political poetry appears as a Jewish-inspired form of fragmenting national cohesion and identity into antagonistic classes (Jelken 1938, 9). Even for Hermes (1926), who is concerned with the cultural life of organized workers, the esthetic sensibilities of the proletariat are deformed by low-quality literary products to such an extent that it lacks all creative impulse; artistically, the class remains "mute despite the fact that its attitude toward life is far from passive" (230). Even Kürbisch's anthology of workers' poetry (1969) acknowledges only Greulich, Jacoby, Kämpchen and Scheu as "precursors." By the early years of the Weimar Republic, then, as Witte (1977a) has noted, the literary production of the movement had become a historical event without a tradition, without a living context of reception either in scholarship or in the cultural life of the movement (7), without "theoretical mediation" (10), without, we should add, a "hermeneutic" memory to guide the critical concern which arose, hesitantly, in the two parts of post-World-War-II Germany.

This modern concern, as we have seen, begins with interrogations of individual texts. In the GDR, their theoretical content is analyzed and their possible function as precursors of present literary models are tested. The normative model for this kind of analysis is given in the "Sketch of a History of German National Literature" etc. ("Skizze," 1964) which served as the basis of the semi-official history of German literature (Kaufmann 1974, Böttcher 1975) and other literary-historical projects in the GDR. Since early socialist literature is tested here for the theoretical accuracy of its "reflection" (the foundational concept of Socialist Realism) of socio-political realities, the approach favors thematic, rather than formal or functional, interests and results in a rather abstract assertion of its ancestral relationship to present-day Socialist Realism. In West Germany, a search is conducted for formally as well as politically revolutionary properties of individual texts. In both cases, there is a distinct tendency to discredit the majority of texts and to assimilate whatever noble exceptions are found into a present (GDR) or historically "lost" canon of properly socialist literature. In both instances, we also witness a tendency to homologize closely the content of texts with the perceived ideological development of the movement and to classify texts and authors in terms of revisionism, opportunism, *embourgeoisement*, etc. This concentration on formal textual properties obscured what, from a different methodological angle, can be seen to make this literature — *functionally* — "socialist": the system of social functions which constituted the literary life of the movement (solidary sociability, celebration, *Bildung* as knowledge, consolation, deferral of political goals).

While both of these scholarly orientations persisted into the 1980s, they were complemented since the 1970s, both in the GDR and in West Germany, by an interdisciplinary interest in the *Lebensweise* of the proletariat, its social experience, and the roles literature played in the totality of social and cultural relations which made up the counterculture of early Social Democracy. In GDR studies of culture and proletarian *Lebensweise* (exemplified by Jacobeit and Mohrmann 1973; Groschopp 1983, 1985; and Mühlberg and Rosenberg 1983), the impetus came not only from English social historians (Raymond Williams, Richard Hoggart, Edward P. Thompson) (Mühlberg 1983, 34-35) but also from Naumann's insistence on viewing literary reception in the context of the social praxis of everyday life (29-30). In this approach to early socialist literature (which Lidtke 1985 best exemplifies in the West), literature is viewed "functionally" (Mühlberg and Rosenberg 1983b, 7), with special emphasis on its "organizing function" within proletarian communication (15). Rosenberg (1983) combines the description of this functional concept with a critique of attempts in the GDR to place the literary production of early socialism within an evolutionary (and normative) line of literary realism extending from the classical period to Socialist Realism — attempts which often led to a half-hearted and unconvincing defense of the realist quality of this literature (47). Rosenberg stresses the advantage of abandoning the idea of a narrow intertextual line of tradition in favor of considerations of the "social uses of literature" within the Social-Democratic system of literary communication. This system was neither homogeneous nor completely independent from the bourgeois system it opposed.

Bourgeois literature circulated within that system (64), products of socialist writers were distributed by bourgeois publishers (63), and in the case of its popular theater organizations, access was provided to bourgeois cultural institutions. This is a "relatively independent" system (71) which by 1918 had lost most of its countercultural functions (69-70). Rosenberg's description of the literary system of early socialism also demonstrates the problematic nature of any attempt to separate the literary production of Social-Democratic writers from the context in which they were received. While it may well be impossible to reconstruct that context in its entirety, the fact has to be borne in mind that "socialist" literature constituted only one component of this system which shaped its reception. As the following accounts of the reception of early socialist literature will demonstrate, the implementation of a functional approach to this literature, despite its theoretical appeal, is conspicuous by its absence. It is remarkable in this context that Trommler's comprehensive study of 1976 remained relatively unnoticed. His detailed reconstruction of a dialectic of autonomy and dependence which existed between the socialist literary politics and production and the bourgeois cultural system which surrounded it offered a number of possibilities of overcoming an exclusively content-based approach to early socialist literature.

It is traditional in scholarship on early socialist literature to attend to the development of individual genres. In studies conducted in the GDR (which constitute the vast majority of scholarship in the field), this approach is usually indebted to Mehring's classical notion of genre as a fixed and enduring ensemble of textual properties. Here the special interest is in the appropriation, by the proletariat, of a formal tradition and the cultural competence of its writers to "administer" this heritage. In addition to esthetic and ideological deficiencies, violations of generic propriety are noted. Since both the standards of ideological accuracy and of generic propriety in this criticism are seen as constant, the distinctions made between the genres tended to be formal rather than reflective of different social functions. The recent interest in the proletarian *Lebensweise* inaugurates a different approach to genre in early socialist literature. Here genre is seen as a social institution, as an ensemble not only of textual properties but of functions as well, of special ways of "organizing" proletarian communication. The text is not separated from its uses, its reception. The singers of songs, the readers of novels, the amateur actors in socialist plays do not represent identical generic constituencies. Within the genres, further distinctions are in order: the mass song of protest, for example, functions differently from a poem celebrating utopian certainties; Schweitzer's dramatizations of *Kapital* are to be distinguished from a Founder's Day performance by an educational association or a Naturalist play by Preczang; and, finally, fictional depictions of urban proletarians represent a form of "politicizing" quite distinct from Otto-Walster's humorous caricatures of duplicitous liberals. In the following accounts of the reception of the main genres of early socialist literature, the difference between formal and social conceptions of genre should be kept in mind.

Poetry

Poetry — as a literature to be read and as a literature to be recited and sung — represents the paradigmatic form of literary communication in early German socialism. The fact that the tradition of revolutionary literature in Germany was a lyrical one (Freiligrath, Herwegh, Heine, Weerth) accounts for this primacy of poetry to some extent. Other reasons can be found in the proletarian experience itself: the only knowledge of literature which most workers brought to the movement consisted of poems memorized at school (some of them political in the sense that they were patriotic) and of popular songs sung in church and at private and public celebrations, including songs of political protest and satire. In this minimal exposure to literary culture, rhythm and rhyme were combined with celebratory sociability and political expression. These facts suggest that the principles of traditional literary criticism and of a literary history based on formal traditions are only partially adequate in assessing the nature of early socialist poetry. The notion of a culturally "competent" reader communing with a conceptually complex literary text in an intimate relationship circumscribed by the hermeneutic moment does not indicate the dominant social habitat of this poetry. Its consumption and expression is not primarily intimate and individual but communal and public. While much of the early poetry acquainted workers with the political ideals of the movement (freedom, justice, equality), and in that sense had a cognitive function, the conceptual and metaphoric vocabulary remained essentially unchanged in subsequent decades and therefore lost most of its referential quality: increasingly the cognitive function was replaced by that of celebrating the timeless ideals of the movement.

This is true for the rich repertory of party songs as well as for much of the revolutionary poetry which — in its allegories of inevitable spring, for instance — tends to celebrate certainties rather than represent or analyze realities. It is texts such as these that make up the canon of socialist poetry of the time, a canon perpetuated in the official and semi-official anthologies of the movement and its allied organizations and inherited by later historians. This is a canon of texts of political optimism whose limited arsenal of concepts, metaphors and emotional gestures accounts for its continuing capacity to invoke, "tune" and celebrate a sense of solidarity and community. What does not appear in this canon are poetic texts written to intervene in specific political situations either by calling for particular actions (as in the case of strike songs) or by satiric attack. Since most of these "operative" texts did not survive their specific occasions, they were kept on the margins of the canon — individually and generically. Their historical importance can be gauged by Kaiser's anthology of poems on the Paris Commune (1958), Völkerling's collection of poetic responses to the strike of textile workers in Crimmitschau (1962) or the collection of "social poems" from *Süddeutscher Postillon* (Fuchs 1894b) re-issued by Völkerling. It is important to note here that the official canonizing of poetic texts in the movement (by way of anthologizing and reviewing) is a process of Social-Democratic cultural self-representation which favors values marginal to the literary life of organized workers: authorship, textual autonomy, poetic individuality, innovation, historical antecedents. Since both reviewers and anthologists selected texts or books for their "literary quality" and general appeal rather than their social or political functions, their valuations reflect the perspective of cultural functionaries rather than of the "users" of poetic texts. Lavant's anthology *Vorwärts* (1884), emphasizes agitatory texts and Dietz' 5-volume collection *Deutsche Arbeiterdichtung* (1893) is devoted entirely to poets of the movement (Hasenclever, Frohme, Audorf, Lavant, Kegel, Scheu). But only half of the selections in Kegel's *Sozialdemokratisches Liederbuch*, published in the year of the Erfurt Congress (1891), are songs of socialist writers. Henckell's collection *Buch der Freiheit* (1893) assimilates socialist poetry into a European context of freedom poetry; and, finally, most of the authors represented in Diederich's *Von unten auf* (1911) belong to the contemporary bourgeois canon (Pforte 1979, 54-55 and 1969).

The occasional reviewing of early socialist poetry in the contemporary Social-Democratic press rarely departed from the norms Mehring had set. Whoever appeared to come up to the standard of bourgeois revolutionary poetry (for Mehring the only form of "socialist" poetry imaginable), was canonized, as was Leopold Jacoby. Operative forms were ignored as "tendentious" and much of the poetry of proletarian writers was tolerated only as a literary activity which did not necessitate (or deserve) esthetic considerations. There is a particular discourse of reviewing at work whose basic vocabulary can be found in Mehring's stereotypical reiterations of certain epithets which extol abstract virtues (health, courage, honesty, simplicity, joy, freedom) rather than concrete political representation or activity. This vocabulary can be encountered in baroque density in some of Zetkin's reviews; its reigning term is "freedom." Zetkin's call for a proletarian literature (1904a) remained an isolated and abstract gesture, as was Kreowski's hope of a socialist esthetics to reevaluate the function of tendency (1903, 131) or Wagner's lament that there was nothing specifically proletarian in the emotional make-up of socialist poetry (1910, 295). Most of Zetkin's reviewing is exemplified by her appreciation of Müller-Jahnke (1899) which stresses the rich inner biography of a writer who avoids all "intentional tendentiousness" (61). Even in the case of authors who regularly produced operative political texts, reviewers highlighted such aspects of their work as their fight for truth (A. G., on Seidel, 1896, 130). Klaar, in his obituary of Kegel, the most prolific of all early "operative" poets, emphasizes the latter's proletarian origin and fight for freedom rather than his poetic interventions in the daily political struggle (1902, 139).

If there is a development in the reviewing practice in Social-Democratic periodicals, it is the reverse of the charge of *embourgeoisement* which dominates so much of the later reception of this poetry. Diederich considers the "militant didactic poetry of attack, derision and proclamation" of the first decades of the movement only a preliminary phase of socialist poetry. In the work of Seidel, Scävola, Müller-Jahnke, Klaar, Preczang and Lessen, for instance, this poetry has deepened to include all personal emotions and all aspects of human existence (1907, 292). As his analysis of poets like Kämpchen and Petzold illustrates, this new attribute of socialist poetry, emotional wealth, is no longer a class-specific one; and the poetic function of political intervention has receded into historical memory. Düvell's account of the evolution of socialist poetry (1909) parallels Diederich's: originally an "accusatory" genre, it now testifies to the fact that the "soul of the proletariat" has grown richer, has gained new cultural values. Its fuller range of expressions is a measure of its maturity (329). Franz (1910-11), finally, wants to dissociate socialist poetry from its tradition of military metaphor since a language of battle and victory seems "anachronistic," even "barbaric" (343), for a political movement characterized by "disciplined patience" (i.e., reformism). Satire (Franz' own forte as a poet) will engender the same political passions today as did the military metaphors of the past (344). Here, at the end of pre-war Social Democracy, bourgeois and socialist notions of the essence of their respective forms of poetry have almost merged. And, again, in this reviewing practice, non-cognitive functions — sociability, celebration — were not recognized; Mehring's appropriation of elitist norms would only have allowed for these functions to be described as "entertainment" — a concept which denoted a trivial mimicry of hermeneutic propriety.

This is why little attention was paid, in the literary criticism of the time (or of later periods, for that matter) to singing as the most important use of poetry in the formation and maintenance of a Social-Democratic countercultural identity. The National Association of Workers' Glee Clubs (*Arbeitersängerbund*), for instance, which had a membership of 200,000 in 1914, was ignored by the party leadership (Dowe 1979, 125). In these clubs, too, a growing trend is evident to abandon a tradition of singing as a form of political proclamation, agitation and solidarity-building and to rival bourgeois repertoires and standards of performance. Schult (1914, 110) praises Hamburg's clubs for progressing from the singing of "tendentious songs to the comprehensive cultivation of choral music," as Bernstein praises those in Berlin for attempting to "ennoble political content with art rather than replace the demands of art with those of politics" (1907-10, vol. 3, 399). There were some attempts to defend the *Tendenzlied* against its Social-Democratic detractors (Wurm 1907, 111-13; Noack 1909, 113), to preserve the revolutionary song as a response to contemporary socio-political reality (Schauder 1907, 117-18) and proletarian singing as a politicizing and class-integrating event (Duncker 1902, 110-11). However, these challenges to a depoliticized cultivation of musical culture remained as tentative, and as unheard, as the demands for a proletarian literature.

What distinguishes the pre-1914 reception of Social-Democratic poetry within the movement from its reception after World War II is the total absence in the former of "ideological correctness" as a standard of evaluation. While lyrical texts were measured against traditional generic standards, they were not judged by their representational performance but rather by the freshness and fullness of their rejection of a decadent bourgeois society and their endorsement of political optimism, by the energy with which they utilized a fixed set of general ideologemes and poetic gestures. The consistent and insistent privileging of ideological content over the tone, uses and functions of early socialist poetry, which shapes most of its later reception in East and West, then, is a critical stance that may derive to some extent from the political discourse of the early movement but not from its literary life. The first comprehensive study of this body of literature was conducted in the GDR (W. Friedrich 1964) and appeared at the same time as the *Skizze*. Both articulate and implement a content-oriented methodology which not only shaped subsequent research in the GDR but also set some parameters for early Western scholarship. Although Friedrich concedes — apologetically — that many early poems were meant to "excrcisc thc function of poetry in public" (182), their social functions are not thematized; instead, socialist literature, including poetry, is treated as a medium of reflection and articulation which accompanies the evolution, the intellectual unfolding of Marxist thought, a historical process which is also read as the development of a mostly unembodied notion of "realism." When this tight homologizing of the (presumed) maturing of Marxism and Social-Democratic poetry fails, as indeed it often does, Friedrich is forced to resort to explanations which undermine the logical premises of his approach: some writers lagged behind the party's development, some adhered to erroneous Lassallean notions, some were unfamiliar with proletarian life, etc. The attempt to identify the literature of the early movement as one of the links between a classical "realism" and modern Socialist Realism entails a retrospective imposition of representational and ideological responsibilities which few of the texts, least of all poems and songs, can meet; the result of this sorting process of ideologically "correct" and "incorrect" texts creates a canon of early socialist literature more ideal than real.

The blueprint of the *Skizze*, which Friedrich's study endorses, and the semi-official literary history (Kaufmann 1974, Böttcher 1975) represent a norm perceptible in most studies in the GDR, among them a number of dissertations on various aspects of early socialist literature and the highly meritorious series of text editions (*Textausgaben*). This party-sanctioned standard, however, undergoes some differentiation. In the literary history (Kaufmann 1974) we still encounter the unmediated juxtaposition of descriptions of selected texts and stereotypical assertions of their role in the ideological growth of the movement: the early poetry is seen as "a synthesizing of theoretical knowledge and practical experience of the class struggle into the unity of lyrical expression" (172) and as a "mirror of the action and passion of a class which has become an active molder of history" (173). This standard, however, not only is complemented since the early 70s by studies of the everyday life of the proletariat (*Lebensweise*), it is also differentiated significantly within its own theoretical parameters, as Münchow's study of the relationship of the labor movement and literature (1981) shows. Münchow still sorts the first generation of socialist poets according to their Lassallean or Marxist leanings (32-55) and applies a standard of realist reflection by inquiring of a later generation of writers "to what extent they studied scientific socialism and how much this study enabled them to reflect lyrically new aspects of an increasingly complex reality" (379). However, the homogeneity of this traditional standard is broken up by a serious concern for the individuality of tone, style and intention of poets, for the difference in function of various poetic genres (the operative-topical texts of Audorf and Kegel, for instance, or Lepp's chansons). And, at least in passing, Münchow acknowledges the uses of certain types of text in a "proletarian culture of celebration" (114). Her book confirms the need to modify traditional standards of textual content in the evaluation of early socialist literature and to view that literature as part of a "second, proletarian culture" (377); but it also raises doubts about the ability of a theory of literature rooted in the notion of reflection to carry out that task.

In contrast to a reception of early socialist poetry which is committed to an agenda of constructing an evolutionary "pre-history" of Socialist Realism, Western reception tends to view this poetry as indicative of an arrested or disrupted development which might have taken it from its early hybridization of an agitatory content and inherited poetic structures to the creation of a proletarian or socialist poetics. The possibility of such a new poetics is often (and usually implicitly) deduced from its palpable absence in the early poetry or, as in the case of Stieg (1973), it is seen to exist in the worker's poetry of the Weimar era. While in GDR criticism the reliance on the formal and thematic repertoire of the classical age and the freedom poets is construed as an "independent extension of the best literary traditions of political poetry in Germany" (Kaufmann 1974, 174), to Western critics this traditionalism is a sign of *embourgeoisement* (Ludwig 1976, 18), an orientation which prevents the development of esthetic "authenticity" (Hohendahl 1978, 229) or betrays an unwillingness to confront contemporary reality in poetically adequate ways (27). Trommler points out that in a literary epoch fixated "epigonally" on the classics, socialist traditionalism was not unique (1976, 217) and that its function for the movement was not the same as for the bourgeoisie. While to the latter the classics represented a greatness lost, the socialist viewed it as the promise of a better future — "undoubtedly a very specific form of politicization" (218). To a number of critics, an important feature of socialist poetry is its use of allegory (religious, military, seasonal) which, according to Witte (1977a, 32-33), circumvents contemporary political and social realities and is symptomatic for what Vaßen calls a "discrepancy between literary rhetoric and the worker's everyday experience" (1980, 125). Not all critics, however, see this "mimetic refusal" as a weakness. With "allegory as the essential form of proletarian poetry, reality is shown as alterable. Contemporary life is not represented but rather transfigured in an optimistic view of the future" (Heid, Vinschen and Heid 1989, 236). For Bollenbeck and Riha (1978, 236), finally, the use of seasonal allegory is quite compatible with the Social-Democratic concept of history as a "self-moving," natural process; and the mimetic and activist concern with contemporary reality is to be found in the less accessible ballads, satires, parodies and aphorisms (238).

Little attention has been paid by historians of early socialist literature to the songs of the movement as a special vehicle of poetry. If the 225-page file on Social-Democratic song-books in the Berlin police department of 1896 (Lammel 1971, 10) is any indication, the Prussian authorities took songs quite seriously as instruments of agitation. Where this tradition of political singing is recognized, songs are usually stripped of their musical attributes and their function in communal performance. Reduced to their lyrics, they are categorized, formally and historically, according to their manifest ideological content. Lammel (1962), for instance, distinguishes between songs that depict social conditions and political situations and those which proclaim political ideals; her history of the worker's song is that of the rise and decline of a medium of ideological reflection. It is Lidtke (1973, 1985) who insists on the importance of organized singing to the literary and cultural life of the movement and its typicality as a literary-cultural activity. The content of songs proved even more impervious to real or perceived changes in the party's political philosophy than purely verbal literature. As a body of texts and tunes, the movement's repertoire of songs represents a fairly stable system of texts, images, emotions and poetic and musical gestures which is tied in many ways to bourgeois revolutionism but also to other traditions of the German *Lied* (patriotism, idealization of nature). Since most of the songs used traditional familiar tunes which represented different ideological contexts and messages, organized singing often constituted a complex ideological interplay between the manifest content of the song, the ideological associations of the "borrowed" tune (sometimes resisted parodically, sometimes not, see Lidtke 1973) and the specific occasion of its performance. The political messages are often abstract, if not trivial; these songs must be seen as a "mixed blend of evocative symbols and general labor movement notions" (Lidtke 1985, 114). With the exception of strike songs which "project a sense of immediacy, of time and place" (128), the vision of the movement's songs is of the "optimistic future" rather than the past or present (122). The importance of political songs and singing to the character and cohesiveness of Social Democracy as a countercultural movement remains largely unrecognized, partly because Social-Democratic musical culture, in its "texts," does not always differ significantly from its bourgeois counterpart. However, in their use of "borrowed" texts and cultural practices for the purposes of a politically charged countercultural solidarity, the singing associations enacted their own version of the complex dialectic of integrationist and revolutionary moments which informed the political and cultural discourse of the movement.

Drama

The development of theatrical activity in the Social-Democratic movement can be divided into three relatively distinct phases. Before the imposition of the anti-socialist law, a number of agitatory comedies were written by officials of the Lassallean and the "Eisenach" parties and performed by amateurs at party functions. These farces were operative forms which expounded points of political theory or tactic or exposed political opponents to ridicule through the use of caricature and polemical dialogues between class antagonists. Their didactic intentions and satiric targets were quite specific. *Der Schlingel* (The Rascal, 1867) and *Die Gans* (The Goose, 1869) by Schweitzer, Lassalle's successor as president of the ADAV, skillfully enliven an explication of Marx' *Kapital* with elements of low comedy. Otto-Walster's *Ein verunglückter Agitator* (An Agitator's Mishap, 1875) explicates Liebknecht's pamphlet on landed property in a tumultuous farce of considerable formal complexity. August Kapell's *Dr. Max Hirschkuh* (1872) and Kegel's *Press-Prozesse* (Trials of the Press,

1876) satirize liberal unions and the suppression of the socialist press respectively. In these plays, no attempt was made to emulate the bourgeois theater of the time; rather, play-acting, political enlightenment, proletarian self-representation and satiric destruction of opponents were part of a larger celebratory context which combined "politics and agitation with celebration and entertainment" (Ludwig 1976, 21). Thus Kapell's *Hirschkuh* was the highlight of a program which also featured classical music, political song, poetry recitation, pantomime and a ball in the evening (Knilli and Münchow 1970, 156-57).

The further evolution of this operative genre — in which esthetic pleasure, political enlightenment and class-oriented socialization were not separate but mutually constitutive elements — was halted by the anti-socialist law of 1878, which forbade all political activity of the workers' associations. It was not until the late 1880s that a regular production of political plays was resumed in the Leipzig educational association under the leadership of Friedrich Bosse, the most productive of early socialist dramatists. The form of these plays was largely (but not exclusively) dictated by the threat of censorship. *Demos und Libertas* (1876, by an unknown author) expresses the movement's agenda in term of an allegorical defeat of "Parasitus" by a coalition of the figures of the title. Wittich's *Ulrich von Hutten* (1887) and Bosse's own *Die Alten und die Neuen* (The Old and the New, 1888) use figures from German history to represent Social-Democratic ideals. In both of these evasions of censorship, the mythicizing allegory and the historical parallel, contemporary political ideas are deprived of their agitatory specificity and transformed into timeless ideals (freedom, justice). In contrast to the agitatory plays of the first phase, a tradition begins here of amateur plays celebrating abstract ideals and an assured utopian future rather than participating in the political struggles of the day — a tradition very much pre-formed in the poetry of the movement.

The expiration of the anti-socialist law (1890) coincided with the founding of the *Freie Volksbühne* (Popular Theater Association) in Berlin, which institutionalized the party's rejection of the idea of a socialist theater and drama in favor of gaining access to public theaters and their repertoire. The association contracted with existing theaters to hold special low-priced performances for its subscribers. It was founded by a group of radicals and proponents of Naturalism, most of whom were expelled from the party the following year. The association split into two branches, the larger run by Mehring. Despite initial differences in the programs of the two associations, in the long run neither was able to influence the selection of the plays offered by its host theaters. Mehring's branch concentrated on introducing the classics to its members. Here, as in other cities, the proletarian theater associations eventually became mere matinee additions to the local theater programs. This development heralds a decisive change in the role drama played in the movement's counterculture. In its first phase, amateur theater — made, performed and received within a closed proletarian cultural circuit — represented a rare case of agitatory art, of an art which participated in the various political struggles of the movement. During the party's period of rapid growth, amateur theater became expelled from party respectability and left to wither on the vine of associational sociability. It continued to grow in terms of organizations, publishers and texts but, scorned by the party, it degenerated into "dry ritual" and "petit-bourgeois entertainment" (Rector 1980, 240). The rejection of indigenous theater was quite explicit: the winter program of the party's educational associations for 1908-09 warned that amateur performances contaminated taste (Knilli and Münchow 1970, 422); and the National Association of Workers' Theaters, an organization consistently snubbed by party and unions, reported official recommendations to oppose the amateur theater clubs (1913) and to consider them harmful to the movement (1915) (Rüden 1973, 190). In conjunction with the development of a literary politics exemplified by Mehring, the party's interest in drama had been reduced to the propagation of traditional bourgeois dramatic culture. This official position is the reverse of an iconoclastic anonymous attack in the *Volksstaat* of 1875 on bourgeois theaters as cultural "brothels" ("Über die Schaubühne" 1875, May 7, 1) and on a historical body of dramas which had lost its canonical authority (May 9, 1). Revolutionary challenges to the textual canon or the institution of bourgeois theater had become anachronisms.

In the third phase recognized by historians, socialist drama is no longer identified by its utilitarian functions within the movement but by its content. It is a full-length play written for the bourgeois stage; it is written not by party functionaries as part of their agitatory work but by would-be full-time artists primarily intent on depicting proletarian existence for a bourgeois audience. This type of play makes its first appearance with Bosse's "strike drama" *Im Kampf* (In the Battle, 1892) and is further exemplified by Preczang's *Töchter der Arbeit* (Daughters of Labor, 1898) and *Im Hinterhause* (Proletarian Quarters, 1903), Rosenow's *Die im Schatten leben* (Life in the Shadows, 1899) and *Kater Lampe* (The Tomcat, 1902), Starosson and Nespital's *Tutenhusen* (1912) and *Verflucht sei der Acker* (Cursed be the Land, 1913) as well as Märten's *Bergarbeiter* (Miners, 1909). Despite the official rejection of Naturalism, dramatists like Hauptmann, Sudermann, Ibsen and Tolstoy provided the only form of "social" drama socialist writers could appropriate. With this form came an obligation to represent truthfully the contemporary conditions of proletarian life: the comic-optimistic tone of the early agitatory plays is frequently replaced by the tragic sensibility of the Naturalist stage.

This latter development is clearly reflected in the criticism of socialist drama in the party-affiliated press. There is no interest in a socialist theory of drama (Schröder 1965, 74); reviewers did not provide a set of evaluative standards (Wendemuth 1913-14, 638); and there is no recognition of an earlier, agitatory tradition. According to Diederich (1913-14, 952), "worker's drama" began as an "episode of bourgeois drama," then became a liberal drama of social compromise from which Naturalism saved it. The current form is termed "Proletarian Naturalism" (956). Most reviews vary the formula of Mehring's rare responses to socialist drama (Bader, Starosson/Nespital, Märten) which consisted of praise for the "natural" and typical depiction of the proletariat and other social classes and for the absence of tendentiousness, together with a determination of the degree to which an optimistic perspective is present in the work. Given the sway that the Naturalist style and classic notions of form held in the Social-Democratic *Feuilleton* of the time, it is not surprising that an author like Rosenow, whose work came closest to the celebrated forms of Naturalistic comedy and tragedy, attracted special attention. In his early work, so Wendel (1911-12, 644), content and form were "raped" by tendentiousness. Both he and Roland agree that Rosenow's later work had overcome that weakness and reached the level of "pure art" (Roland 1914, 75): here tendency enters the heart of the audience "unnoticed" (Sommer 1912, 470). However, what many of these plays do not yet provide is the depiction of the class-conscious, politically active and optimistic proletarian (Wendel 1911-12, 646; Roland 1914, 75). This complete application of Mehringian critical principles, and the endorsement of the form of bourgeois social drama and of the context in which it was received (the professional theater), is accompanied by an aversion to theatrical amateurism. Such activity "may lead straight to the alcoholized dramatic club" where artistic standards are replaced with "loud tendentiousness and dripping sentimentality" ("Theater" 1913, 404-05). If young people *must* play theater, Poensgen-Alberty advises them to perform Hans Sachs' 16th-century farces or some harmless self-made skit (1913, 239).

The modern reception of early socialist drama began in the GDR in the 1960s and is indebted to the work of Ursula Münchow. The texts published in Münchow 1964, 1965, 1972, and in Knilli and Münchow 1970, illustrate most phases and formal aspects of the genre. Her critical accounts between 1963 and 1981 show few substantial changes and are representative of the reception of early socialist drama in the GDR. In the case of poetry, the imposition by GDR critics of an evolutionary trend toward Socialist Realism was possible only by privileging representational texts or the representational function of texts. In the case of drama and narrative, however, the historians' agenda of reconstructing a pre-history of that realism is carried out with few apologies and reservations. Although Münchow regrets that in the development of early socialist drama the "aggressive experimentalism" (1972, ix) and agitatory and non-Aristotelian forms (1981, 440) of the first phase were lost, this loss is considered necessary: "In drama, too, the process of an artistic appropriation of reality by the combative proletariat led to the formulation of socialist-realist positions" (1972, viii). In this account of the development of socialist drama, Prezcang's, Rosenow's and Märten's Naturalist plays represent the "transition from social to socialist drama" (1972, ix).

Schröder's assessments echo Münchow's historicizing procedures. His dissertation of 1965 carefully distinguishes the various genres of the early production (comedy, farce, dialogue, allegory, tragedy) without allowing for the variety of social functions these represented. Similarly, in his accounts of Bosse's dramatic club in Leipzig (1966, 1972), Schröder concentrates on the ideological content of the plays produced there and explains the diffuseness of their political notions and ideals as the result of backwardness and censorship. Little attention is given to the fact that in the festive sociability of these associations, a celebration of justice, truth, freedom, etc. appropriated these abstract liberal ideals as weapons and ideological attributes of an emancipatory class. The fundamental test applied to the early texts is Engels' notion of the "unity of the individual and social-typical" (1965, 349) which is at the heart of Socialist Realism. Since only the Naturalist plays of socialist writers with their differentiated characters meet this standard, they signal a decisive change in the development of socialist drama: it "leaves the realm of pre-literary forms [...] and begins to enrich national literature with its best works" (1965, 256-57).

One of the stereotypes of the criticism of early socialist drama in the GDR — one symptomatic of a persistent unresolved conceptual ambiguity — is the lament that the improvement in artistic quality was accompanied by a weakening of its political content and a loss of its topicality (Schröder 1965, 358-60). Knilli rejects this stereotype: the "antagonism" of political progressiveness and artistic stagnation, and of artistic progressiveness and political stagnation, reflects not historical reality but rather a dominant scheme of literary valuation which posits that there is a development of literary quality independent of political progression or stagnation (1970, 52). This kind of criticism, according to Knilli, ignores the specific contexts in which early socialist drama functioned: the agitatory plays were part of the political struggle and belonged to the countercultural sphere of the movement, while Preczang's *Im Hinterhause*, for instance, was part of the dominant bourgeois public sphere (52-53). Knilli's challenge to the undialectical dualism of politics and esthetics, fundamental to socialist literary politics, is a rare moment of self-reflection.

Much of West German criticism of early socialist drama reflects the canon of texts and the vocabulary of GDR scholars; and the description which Münchow and Schröder give of a progressive depoliticization of this drama was readily absorbed into the reigning notion of West German criticism, *embourgeoisement*. On the other hand, Western critics were more apt than their Eastern counterparts to herald the first phase of this drama as a lost indigenous tradition of operative or properly realist drama. Witte (1977, 23-24) views the agitatory theatrical practice of the 1860s and 1870s as an anticipation of Brecht's theater of political learning and practice; and Pehlke (1971) defends Bosse's *Im Kampf* (1892) against both Western and Eastern interpretations as an example of the kind of realism which Marx and Engels had propagated.

Western historians of early socialist drama devote particular attention to the causes and consequences of its transition from agitation and intervention to realist representation. Rüden (1973) traces the development of a theater of *Bildung* caused by the movement's political attentism, by its exclusive concern with politics and economics and a rapid growth in membership which brought new social groups and their petit-bourgeois sensibilities into the movement (216). Trommler (1976a, 236) balances the losses and gains of this transition: Preczang, for instance, overcomes the party allegories and stereotypical socialist heroes of the past by developing "tendency" from the dramatic action; and while this may prevent a "ritualization of political theses," it also carries the risk of depoliticizing and trivializing class struggle. The most comprehensive and detailed study of the early dramatic production of the movement is Trempenau's (1979) which restates and differentiates basic findings of his predecessors. There is a fundamental tension in socialist drama, according to Trempenau, between form and content: while the "classical form of drama" which socialist dramatists appropriate encodes a reconciliation with reality as it is, socialism is a *Weltanschauung* based on the changeability of that reality (64). The tension which derives from that contradiction is perpetuated by the dualism of politics and art in socialist cultural politics (64-65). Trempenau goes beyond this statement of a basic dualism, however, and analyzes the ways in which content may bend form to its purposes. He demonstrates the rich variety of expressions of the radical and integrationist strains in socialist drama. He explores a corpus of texts which substantially exceeds the canon formulated by GDR critics and inherited in the West: especially by including works which do not meet the standards of realism and ideological correctness prescribed by GDR literary politics, Trempenau's study resists the stereotypicality inherent in much of the criticism of early socialist drama (dualism of bourgeois form and socialist content, of revolutionism and revisionism, of realism and trivial idealization) and attempts to present the whole range of dramas performed and published in the movement as a wide spectrum of formally mediated responses to perceived social and political realities.

Fiction

In the criticism and literary debates of the movement, poetry and drama are readily recognized as forms appropriate for political purposes, sanctioned by traditions which the party claimed as its own: the drama of German classicism and the lyrics of the German freedom poets. While poetry is seen as the proper vehicle of celebration and exhortation, drama — especially in its Schillerean form of an ethical contestation — is seen to give form to the moral essence of class struggle. There is little theoretical recognition, on the other hand, of the generic peculiarity of prose fiction and its functions, the novel in particular. This is so not despite the fact that the novel enjoyed wide popularity among the lower classes but to a large extent because it did so. Whatever conception there is of prose fiction in the early phases of the movement, it is embedded in the discussions of entertainment literature (in the party congress portion of the Naturalism Debate, for instance, or the discussions of the role of the *Feuilleton*), in which "entertainment" frequently served as a codeword for fiction. The novel was not seen as a form ennobled by classical example but rather as an essentially formless kind of literature which served several purposes in the party press: the recruitment and cultivation of new members (women in particular) and the fight against literary "trash" and political enlightenment. It was also a valued source of revenue. It is this disparate collection of functions which helped prevent a discussion of the possibilities of socialist fiction. Left theoretically unattended by the movement, its practitioners had to orient themselves by two models: the social novel of the Naturalists and the immensely successful commercial entertainment novel, which they were expected to "preempt." Kautsky's assessment of fiction is symptomatic for the reasons why the genre was neglected by party intellectuals: "Fiction was published in the party press only for the wives of party members who — because of their intellectual limitations — wanted such reading and had to be offered something to make the paper attractive to them" (1960, 299-300). (Kautsky, incidentally, was the son of the most prolific of early socialist novelists). Considering, then, that the novel in the press was, to use Trommler's term, a "necessary evil" (1976a, 224) for the party, neither its political content nor its literary quality was of preeminent concern. Important was that "women expect that something happens that touches their hearts" (Franke 1913-14, 25). According to Fuchs, a fiction weekly like *In Freien Stunden* had to meet the following expectations to fight substandard literature effectively: the texts had to be "good and interesting," the illustrations popular but artistic; and the print and the paper were to be of good quality (1898b).

Another reason for the neglect of fiction as genre is the fact that — in contrast to poetry and drama, which frequently provided occasions of a public and communal reception of literature — fiction was consumed privately and had no comparable institutional presence in the movement. The fact that fiction did not provide a means of Social-Democratic socialization does not mean, however, as some critics seem to assume, that the ideological functions of fiction written in the movement derived exclusively from its manifest ideology. Here too the reception of literature does not consist entirely of a readerly realization of ideological content unmediated by any conditions of reception: the fact that it appeared in party-sanctioned publications, framed by informational and political material, legitimated this fiction as enlightening and ennobling and as such strengthened the reader's sense of countercultural identity.

An indirect debate of the novel as form can be detected in reviews which deal with the "social," i.e., Naturalist novel. Zola's immense popularity among proletarian readers (confirmed by practically every library statistic of the period) seemed to indicate the validity of a form which disclosed "the inner workings of society" (Blos 1886, 425) and depicted "the laboring populace" (Carpin 1896, 326). However, Zola's German disciples do not fare well at the hands of socialist critics: they lack his spirit and often use the social aspect as an excuse for "smuttiness" (Blos 1886, 424-25); they also tend to foist a party-flag upon the story, as Otto-Walster, according to Carpin (1896, 326), was "childish" and "naive" enough to do in his *Am Webstuhl der Zeit* (The Loom of Time, 1873). With all their concern for the life of a disenfranchised class, social novelists are not to ignore the purpose of art to provide a "gateway to beauty" (Blos 1886, 425). As tendentious works, social novels are merely "documents of the will barely touched by the imagination," "imitations of the real far removed from esthetic effect" (Hochdorf 1911, 1568).

Not all reviewers, however, are content to preserve art from the encroachments of "tendency" without recognizing the special historical position of the novel in modern times and its possible uses by socialist authors. Wittner, in his discussion of "The Novel of the Proletariat" (1913), marks the change that Naturalism brought to the genre. Originally a bourgeois vehicle to explore individuality, the novel turned to the depiction of the social environment and its effects. In Andersen Nexø's *Pelle, the Conqueror* the working class had found its own voice (89). The new proletarian novel now represents one form of a proletarian self-realization in art (90). Lenzner (1913, 642) criticizes the fact that the traditional bourgeois underrating of narrative prose is still alive in the socialist movement; socialist critics need to realize that not all novels are mere entertainment: with Naturalism the genre has become "art," and its special strength is its ability to depict social totality. Wittner's and Lenzner's reviews are indications of a continued advocacy of an indigenous poetics of the novel and a realism of social totality to replace, or at least complement, the movement's privileging of esthetic considerations, inherited forms and ethical idealism. These views were either drowned (Naturalism Debate) or, as in the case of Wittner and Lenzner, came on the eve of a new era of socialist art (1913) — in any case, their canon was foreign (Zola, Gorky, Andersen Nexø), not German.

Social-Democratic authors of fiction (Schweichel, Otto-Walster, M. Kautsky, Ger, Preczang) were reviewed only sporadically in the party-affiliated press and rarely did their reviewers depart from traditional and vague notions of "well-made" and non-tendentious art. Mehring's appreciations of Schweichel and Kautsky are representative of the reception within the movement of writers some of whom attempted to instrumentalize fiction for the purposes of political enlightenment and class solidarity: they were primarily judged by their ability to depict the lower classes as morally superior to the bourgeoisie, as imbued with the political idealism which the latter had betrayed, and by the degree to which politics was assimilated into character and plot. Mehring concentrates on those of Schweichel's works which deal with historical periods and social settings remote from proletarian existence and affirms Schweichel's notion of the rural *Volk* as a source of moral renewal (1887, 456-57). His works are praised as formally perfect novellas and modern epics. Mehring ignores Schweichel's attempts in the 1870s to popularize Social-Democratic cultural policy and to depict the intellectual and political emancipation of proletarians in short prose texts written for party calendars. It is not a participation of art in the political struggle which Mehring values in Schweichel, but rather the fact that he offered workers the "salvation of beauty" (1901, 464) and "transfigured" their struggles and sufferings (1906, 466). These reviews of Mehring's confirm Schweichel's own view that the ideology of the party is a "very limited substance from which a writer could draw" (in Liebknecht 1973, 496). Minna Kautsky, on the other hand, viewed her fiction as a contribution to the class struggle inspired by Marx (1909, 23-24); the result of this combative attitude is, according to Mehring, that the political fighter prevails over the artist (1912, 451).

In the Social-Democratic *Feuilleton*, Schweichel appears as a practical example of the appropriation of the literary heritage propagated in the movement: "classical" are his use of form, his language and his "healthy realism coupled with idealism" (Kunert 1906, 212); and by giving the proletariat fictional access to the great freedom movements of the past — especially in *Der Falkner von St. Vigil* (The Falkners of St. Vigil, 1881) and in his vast fictionalization of the German peasant wars, *Um die Freiheit* (For Freedom, 1898) — Schweichel continues the radical-democratic tradition of guarding the "flame of freedom" (Kreowski 1907, 5408). In the reception of Schweichel's work, the critical vocabulary is inspired by his perceived proximity to classical literary models and liberal idealism. Minna Kautsky's proximity to petit-bourgeois entertainment fiction, on the other hand (apparent, for instance, in idealizations of proletarian heroes criticized by Engels and others), causes reviewers to weigh, as Mehring does, her cliches of character and plot against her Social-Democratic convictions and intentions: after all, it is not easy, says Julie Zadek in her review of *Die Alten und die Neuen* (The Old and the New, 1884), to avoid tendentiousness in a "tendency novel" (1884, 155). As far as the cliches Kautsky "borrows" from the dime novel of her time are concerned, it is not clear from this criticism what better conventions she could have used to provide access to the Social-Democratic *Weltanschauung* for a barely literate class. In any case, these "formal" weaknesses are more than compensated for, in the opinion of critics, by her ability to "draw poetic figures from today's social conditions" and to demonstrate the moral superiority of the lower classes over a degenerate bourgeoisie (Review of *Victoria* 1889, 236), to show the proletariat in its ascendancy (Carpin 1896, 338), and by her love of everything that is progressive, strong and healthy (Kunert 1907, 182).

The implied standard of this criticism of early socialist fiction — an undefined aggregate of descriptive realism and ethical idealism — prevented the continued reception of two agitatory works which stand at the very beginning of socialist fiction in Germany: Schweitzer's *Lucinde oder Capital und Arbeit* (Lucinde or: Capital and Labor, 1863-64) and Otto-Walster's *Am Webstuhl der Zeit* (1873). Neither the one (which mixes a helter-skelter melodramatic plot reminiscent of Eugène Sue and the penny-dreadfuls with political lectures and lengthy quotations from Lassalle), nor the other (which blends satire, comedy and narrative irony with agitatory demonstrations of every possible form of revolutionary and democratic organization) (Mathes 1987, 55), conformed to the normative standards of a dignified realism — nor did their descriptions of proletarian revolution fit into the reformist temper of a later age.

The historical location of early socialist fiction — between the "social novel" of Naturalism and popular petit-bourgeois fiction — generated in its contemporary reception an unthematized and unresolved conceptual dualism of what in modern parlance would be called realism and *Kitsch*. This dualism can be traced into the reception of this fiction in the GDR and, to some extent, in West Germany. There is in the early criticism a submerged tendency to judge socialist fiction by expectations characteristic of a realist poetics: the unity of the individual and historical-typical (Carpin 1896), the typifying relationship of characters with social issues (Wittner 1913), the depiction of social totality (Lenzner 1913). However, the realist orientation of this criticism (inspired by Zola's Rougon-Macquardt series more than Balzac's *Comédie Humaine*) is always tempered by traditional Social-Democratic notions of formal and behavioral propriety and political-ethical idealism. The fact that later critics used Engels' definition of realism as a standard "teleologically" inherent in early socialist fiction itself can be explained in part by the fact that Engels developed this standard in response to contemporary socialist novels by Kautsky and Harkness. The "truthful reproduction of typical characters under typical circumstances" (in Engels' original English, 1888, 157) and his admonition that tendency must emerge from "situation and action" (1885, 156) have become yardsticks of modern criticism of early Social-Democratic fiction. These private communications of Engels', however, did not become known and imbued with normative authority until much later; to project their ideas back into the literary life of early Social Democracy either indicates a belief in the historical teleology of Socialist Realism or it imposes on the early movement a Marxist hermeneutic obligation which — as we have attempted to demonstrate in previous chapters — was fully suspended in its cultural life. The problematic nature of such a retroactive imposition of realist standards becomes apparent in Engels' opinion that solutions to social problems need not be indicated in literature (1885, 156) and in his condemnation of M. Kautsky's *Helene* (1894) — an explicitly agitatory novel — as a "bad imitation" of sensationalist fiction (1894, 323): here all agitatory literature is banned as unartistic. What is not readily remembered in this context is that Engels had a literate bourgeois readership in mind rather than organized workers whose associational culture was one of explicit invocation and celebration of the "tendency" which made up their political identity. In terms of the unresolved dualism of realism and *Kitsch* which the criticism of early socialist fiction perpetuates, texts which do not conform to realist expectations tend to fall under the verdict of *Kitsch* or are seen as unstable textual amalgams of progressive and regressive, "revolutionary" and petit-bourgeois orientations. The specific conditions of reception of this literature (the readers' literary competence and expectations, for instance, or the emancipatory function of an appropriation of bourgeois novelistic conventions into a literature of proletarian heroes) is rarely considered.

In GDR criticism, Engels' judgments of Kautsky were imported directly into the *Lexikon* (1964, 279) and the semi-official history of German literature (Böttcher 1975, 783-84) — and, of course, perpetuated in the assessments of Kautsky's work (C. Friedrich 1965, xiii) — and served as the basis for a realist standard which the early socialist writers could not possibly meet. Among the requirements were the reproduction of the "complexity and contradictoriness of historical processes" and the inclusion of "all factors relevant to their unfolding." Works which did not meet these expectations were likely to suffer from "schematism" and a mere "declamation of tendency" (Böttcher 1975, 784). In the opinion of the *Lexikon*, Kautsky's "illusory reformism" obstructed her progress "to an inclusive, realistic reflection of German society" (280).

The concept of realism operative in these judgments, of course, does not denote a phenomenological approach to historical detail but is tied to a prescribed teleological reading of historical reality. Failure to implement this particular realist "episteme," therefore, signifies ideological shortcomings. Examples are writers of fiction who still concentrated on a depiction of proletarian suffering while the party had already gone "from triumph to triumph" (W. Friedrich 1964, vol. 1, 254). Rare praise is reserved for historical narratives which extend the genealogy of the socialist revolution back into the past — Otto-Walster's *Braunschweiger Tage* (Brunswick Days, 1874) and "Eine mittelalterliche Internationale" (A Medieval International, 1875) and Schweichel's monumental fictionalization of the peasant wars, *Um die Freiheit* (1898). The latter's realism consists in its use of historical events to demonstrate "the justice and necessity of proletarian struggle against the ruling classes" (Böttcher 1975, 952); by "viewing the proletariat as advocate and heir of the revolutionary peasants, [Schweichel] was able to understand and depict the latter's demands as [...] historically justified" (Pick 1964, xvi).

In cases where the narrow historical mimeticism of this realist standard is clearly not intended by the author, tentative exceptions of its applicability are made, but these do not serve to problematize the standard itself. Otto-Walster's satiric *tour de force* in *Am Webstuhl der Zeit* is criticized because, "for the sake of comic effect, he weakens the conflict and even trivializes the proletarian struggle" (*Lexikon* 1964, 392) — but the same agitatory element is also seen to give the work its vitality (Münchow 1981, 289). In the case of this early socialist novel (whose long-lived popularity Reinelt 1967 traces) and most of Kautsky's fiction, a need is felt in GDR criticism (palpable but usually unacknowledged) to explain the relationship between their lack of realism and their popularity with proletarian readers, to problematize and differentiate, in other words, the implied identification of non-realism and *Kitsch*, of the legitimacy of primarily agitatory rather than mimetic uses of literature. Münchow, for instance, realizes that Kautsky's use of the conventions of entertainment fiction contributed to her singular success among workers but does not investigate the agitatory efficacy of this use in the propagation of socialist ideas and the socialist ethic. Rather, in her extensive discussion of *Helene* (a defense of sorts against Engels' summary condemnation of this work), the degree of its realism is elaborated in some detail (1981, 305-12). Not even Bürgel (1983), who analyzes some instances of "political agitation cloaked in the conventions of trivial literature" (182) of the 1870s, is able to overcome the dualism of agitation and literary cliche — as if literary cliche could not be, or have been, a most efficacious means of agitation among certain segments of the population or, for that matter, as if "cliche" were an objective and class-transcendent state of representational "untruth" (as untrue and "compensatory" for the proletarian as for the educated bourgeois). Despite the call for a "functional concept" of socialist literature made by the volume in which Bürgel's essay appeared (Mühlberg and Rosenberg 1983), the author only manages to reiterate the unreflected binarism of the "objective contradiction of an attempt to combine narrative structures of bourgeois entertainment literature with a politically agitatory content" (175).

In West German accounts of early socialist literature, fiction is usually passed over as a genre "trapped in inherited traditions" (Vaßen 1980, 131) which, underdeveloped to begin with, came to a "complete standstill" in the 1890s (Rector 1980, 244). In its mixing of "elements of the dime novel and political agitation," it appears to scholars as a "particularly unattractive form of ideologically colored trivial literature" (Witte 1977, 35). Conceived as a competition to the bourgeois entertainment literature of the *Gartenlaube* variety, it became shaped by its competitor (Rector 1980, 245). The dualism of petit-bourgeois form and progressive content, and the essentially bourgeois and elitist charge of triviality are as pronounced here as they are in the criticism of GDR scholars. And the same standard prevails: while Vaßen insists on the historical context of Engels' concept of realism (the 19th-century novel and its bourgeois readership), he offers no "proletarian" alternative to this standard (1980, 135). Ludwig (1976, 25), by discussing only one fictional text (Kautsky's *Die Alten und die Neuen*) ("because it provoked a poetological remark from Friedrich Engels"), indirectly affirms the legitimacy of Engels' concept of realism. In view of Schweichel's regionalism and Kautsky's inability to depict all social classes and her dependence on conventions of bourgeois entertainment literature, Trommler (1976a, 231) announces a kind of retroactive agenda for early socialist fiction: "what was lacking was a realist tradition, a journalistic and literary familiarity with the existential conditions of a rapidly changing environment." The implementation of this agenda would undoubtedly have "raised" socialist fiction to a level of representational actuality, accuracy and totality favored by liberal bourgeois intellectuals, but just as surely it would have eliminated that fiction from the social and cultural circuits in which it circulated.

Two studies in the 1980s attempt to replace the dominant approach to early socialist fiction as "autonomous" art with an analysis of its functions within the movement (Quatember 1988, 25) and to appeal the verdict of triviality. However, in the case of Quatember's study of Austrian socialist fiction between 1867 and 1914, the concept of "function" is narrowed to notions of reflection and "realism" appropriated directly from Engels and Lukács, and these become, once again, the exclusive measure of "esthetic" worth (75-76). With the upholding of the realist standard, the traditional dualism of content and form is restored:

"That Social-Democratic authors used [...] elements of trivial literature cannot be justified from a literary point of view. It was a didactic necessity [...]" (145). A more substantial problematization of the verdict of triviality is Köppen's study of 1982. In his opinion, this verdict is based on unexamined concepts (trivial, *Kolportage*) which are seen in unmediable opposition to socialist ideology (60-61). Köppen attempts to overcome this dualism by showing the appropriateness of the plot and character structures of this fiction to the changing, *actual* ideology of the movement. The Social Democrat as a man of science, truth and higher morality and as a leader of the proletariat, as we find him in Kautsky, for instance, represents the values which constituted a counter-reality to society at large, i.e., Social-Democratic culture as a form of internal realization of socialism. Socialist fiction had a controlling function: it took the rebelliousness out of political dreaming by directing it to the "disciplining" context of Social-Democratic culture (326). Content and form here appear as incommensurable only if the former is taken to be informed by revolutionary intention. Köppen's perception of early socialist fiction as a mechanism which guided perception and emotion within the value system of the Social-Democratic subculture represents one of the few examples of a description of this literature as fulfilling, rather than perverting, important functions. But even Köppen is uncomfortable in the presence of a literature which "restricts perception to the mere affirmation of that which is already known" (341): once again a modern esthetic principle, that of innovation, of cognitive displacement, casts its trivializing shadow over a party-literature of socialization, celebration and invocation of certainties.

The Proletarian Autobiography

Modern criticism of the literary production of the early socialist movement tends to entail a search for two qualities of this literature: "realism" (especially in the GDR) and proletarian (or revolutionary) "authenticity" (especially in Western criticism). Within the sphere of socialist literary communication — marked by classical standards and high-literary expectations, on the one hand, and a dependence on "petit-bourgeois" conventions in production and consumption, on the other — few texts circulated which exhibited these qualities in more than marginal ways; and later critics had to hypothesize traces of either with little regard to the ways in which literary texts functioned in the cultural sphere of the movement. Some of the proletarian autobiographies which appeared between 1903 and 1914, however, seemed to offer these qualities as constitutive generic characteristics: an unapologetically realistic description of typical collective processes (social and cognitive) as well as a style, motivation and world-view generated in and by the proletarian experience itself. Here the literature of social compassion of the Naturalists and other bourgeois sympathizers of the working class seemed suddenly superseded by a form of proletarian "literary self-realization" (Vaßen 1980, 249). By becoming a narrating subject, the proletariat was seen to have overcome the traditional dualism of content and form of socialist literature in a unity of individual and class experiences and an indigenous form of expression. The spectacular success of the first volume of Karl Fischer's memoirs (1903) indeed seems to confirm the arrival of a new style or genre. The irony of this modern perception of the proletarian autobiography of the turn of the century, however, is that, with very few exceptions, the contemporary distribution and reception of this genre took place outside Social-Democratic cultural life and remained without influence on the literary texts and literary practices of the movement. The proletarian autobiography as an authentic form of socialist literature is a later construction based on perceived textual qualities rather than on its functions within Social-Democratic culture. As a *literary* phenomenon, it had a more marked impact on the bourgeois public than on the Social-Democratic one, as the contemporary reception indicates.

The group of texts which is generally seen to embody the prototypical proletarian autobiography (K. Fischer, 1903, 1904, 1905; Bromme, 1905; W. Holek, 1909; Rehbein, 1911) was written for a bourgeois readership and made public in expensive editions by the Social-Democratic theologian Paul Göhre who, in his editorial interventions in the texts and in his introductions to the volumes, de-emphasized their political aspects and highlighted their value as documentations of lower-class life — an editorial practice already condemned by Mehring (1909b). These publications, together with F. Fischer's autobiography (1909, edited by Friedrich Naumann) and Levenstein's collections of proletarian letters, autobiographical sketches and literary texts (1909a, 1909b), constitute a corpus of autobiographical writings by workers of various degrees of political awareness and, in some cases, of socialist orientation, which has been canonized as the first phase of the genre's evolution. The second stage represents either an advance or a deterioration, depending on the critical perspective: the "how-I-became-a-Social Democrat" life-story of functionaries of the movement already preformed in Bromme's autobiography and best exemplified by Adelheid Popp's widely-read *Jugendgeschichte einer Arbeiterin* (The Early Years of a Female Laborer, 1909). In contrast to the first phase, in which — with emphatic claims to authenticity and truth — typical proletarian experiences are described for the enlightenment of the bourgeoisie, this type of proletarian autobiography closely resembles the shape and ideology of the classical German *Bildungsroman* (Witte, in Stieg and Witte, 1973, 62-63; Vogtmeier 1984, 249), with its emphasis on an "inner" biography of education and cognition which results in the protagonist's successful socialization — not in bourgeois society, in this case, but in the organizational culture of the movement. A third type generally recognized by critics, the autobiography of socialist writers (Märten, 1909; Petzold, 1913; Krille, 1914), finally, conforms fully to the model of the *Künstlerautobiographie*: the account of the formation of an esthetic consciousness.

This perceived evolution of a *socialist literary genre* is based on a narrow formalistic teleology flatly contradicted by the actual reception of this kind of autobiographical literature in the bourgeois and Social-Democratic cultural circuits. The autobiographies of class-conscious and politically motivated workers make up only a small part of a veritable avalanche of memoirs and confessions by members of the lower classes (including maid-servants, prostitutes and vagabonds) published at the time. As some critics have shown, its general reception was shaped by a number of ideological interests, among them an agenda of reintegrating the lower classes into the "organic whole" of the *Volk* (Hermand 1971) and a vitalistic philosophy of life which validates the kind of raw subjective experience which Karl Fischer, for instance, seemed to express as the primary "organon of cognition" (Bollenbeck 1976, 239). While a sociologist like Max Weber doubted that these writings expressed a "unique, individual [...] emotional life that searches for its own, new cultural values" (Trommler 1976a, 352), there is in this reception, in addition to a recognition of its documentary aspect, an anti-intellectual (and, in some instances, anti-Naturalistic) hope for a cultural rejuvenation deriving from, in Hegeler's terms, the "power of [the common people's] unprejudiced perception" (Trommler 1976a, 343-44). In contrast to the Social-Democratic reception, many of these autobiographical texts were read as a kind of new "folk art" (Bollenbeck 1976, 239). Their reception as art is also an indication of a general avoidance of their documentary content and their intended social appeal (Vogtmeier 1984, 315).

The Social-Democratic press did not develop its own approach to the proletarian autobiography as literature. The texts of the first "type" were reviewed only sporadically and were read, not as literary products *of* the proletariat, but as documents *about* the "situation of workers" (Mehring 1907, 494, on W. Holek), as works which provided access to the "soul of workers" (Review of Levenstein 1909a, 1909, 479) and are "rather interesting in terms of cultural history" (Lessen 1913-14, 904, on Dikreiter's memoirs of 1914). The autobiographies of party functionaries, on the other hand, while ignored as literary documents, were widely discussed and promoted in the socialist press as valuable vehicles of agitation. They were seen as sources of ideological inspiration at a time when the idea of proletarian revolution was under siege (Kautsky 1908-09, 316, on Popp), as providing models for the typical Social-Democratic ascent from "the depth of human misery to the sublime heights of knowledge" (Kette 1909, 40, on Popp). The advent of a celebrated *Arbeiterliteratur* in the

Weimar Republic, however, overshadowed these proletarian narratives and they remained practically forgotten until the 1970s. Strasser (1930, 54) echoes Weber's contention that they were informed by a slightly modified petit-bourgeois ideology (Trommler 1976a, 352); and Trunz' dissertation of 1934, apparently the only post-World War I treatment of the subject, privileges those works not yet "tainted" by a divisive politics of class struggle as works of folk literature which exude a sense of the tragic (38) — a term, incidentally, already used by Göhre in his introduction to W. Holek's work and roundly condemned by Mehring (1909b, 499).

With Hermand's article of 1971 and Münchow's book of 1973 (1973a), the proletarian autobiography of the turn of the century becomes a catalyst in the search for predecessors of Socialist Realism and for specimens of a forgotten proletarian literary authenticity. In GDR criticism, the canon of autobiographical texts is narrowed to conform to the idea of a tight evolutionary pattern: K. Fischer, W. Holek (pt. 1), Bromme, Rehbein, Popp and Bebel (Kaufmann 1974, 171). On the basis of this corpus, the proletarian autobiography is seen to develop in an ascendant line from the first stirrings of the narrative voice of the proletariat (K. Fischer) to the vita of model party functionaries (Popp) to the paradigmatic synthesis of individual life and party history in Bebel's memoirs. By separating this body of texts from its original contexts of production, distribution and reception and from its native intertextual environment of bourgeois and petit-bourgeois literary conventions, the idea becomes plausible that at least these texts did not evolve from existing forms (as socialist fiction had) but constituted a new beginning, a form of narrative sui generis: "something indigenous, unique and appropriate to the class which these autobiographies represented and which could not have been achieved in any other way" (Kaufmann 1974, 165). The semi-official history of German literature thus stresses the "fundamental significance" of this new beginning (a narrative synthesis of individual, class and social history) for 20th-century socialist fiction (Kaufmann 1974, 170-71) while at the same time admitting that later proletarian-revolutionary writers were hardly aware of their "predecessors" (171).

It is Münchow who repairs this curiously broken teleology by shifting from the perception of a distinct proletarian genre to the notion of a literary phenomenon whose chief importance lies in its contributions to various aspects of socialist literary activity. The proletarian autobiography provided an impetus for the development of a socialist form of the autobiographical novel (1973a, 45), the "proletarian novel of development" (1981, 557); it opened new thematic areas for socialist literature and furthered the "development of a socialist image of man in German literature" (1973a, 99); and — at a time marked by a "bourgeois crisis of narration" — it initiated a "renaissance of narrative" (175). The semi-official history of German literature presented the proletarian autobiography as a form of spontaneous proletarian creation beyond the influence of inherited models which evokes the notion of "proletcult" viewed with suspicion by socialist literary politicians from Mehring to Lenin to Ulbricht. Münchow, on the other hand, restores the inclusive teleology of Socialist Realism as the creative appropriation of classical models by integrating the proletarian autobiography into inherited generic contexts: the European autobiographical novel and the development of Socialist Realism, to which it contributed new areas of realistic depiction and a new narrative optimism.

In West German accounts of the proletarian autobiography, the question of proletarian authenticity was more persistent than it was in the GDR. Hermand, in the article which inaugurated this discussion (1971), argues against Göhre's strategy of presenting K. Fischer to a bourgeois readership as a "naive" writer. Hermand replaces this concept of naivete with the notion of "authenticity," which he pits not only against a cognitively inert naivete but also against a literature imbued with party politics and designed to influence readers: Fischer's is a critical and emancipatory realism, an authenticity of the "naked truth" (105-06). From the perspective of most critics of this genre who are searching for an authentic *socialist*, i.e., politically conscious, literature, however, Hermand's implication that the latter is somehow unauthentic is hardly acceptable. Witte comes closest to Hermand's valuation of Fischer and other early autobiographers: they are authentic because they depict the reality of a struggle in a capitalist world in which the individual is defeated (1973, 46); the later autobiographies are unauthentic by comparison — not, however, because they are politically conscious but because, as approximations of the bourgeois *Bildungsroman*, their subject-oriented personal histories obscure rather than illuminate class struggle and reflect the socialist movement's deviation from a revolutionary class perspective (43). This assessment of the autobiographies of party functionaries and socialist writers is shared by other critics: Scharrer, for instance, reads Bromme's *Life* as a tale of *embourgeoisement* which reflects the reformist development of the party itself (1976, 38); and Ritter reads the autobiographies of party officials as Social-Democratic versions of the Horatio Alger success story (1959, 225-26).

Hermand and Witte represent an approach which validates the early autobiographies for their raw documentary realism and empirical authenticity. Emmerich (1974) and Bollenbeck (1976), on the other hand, offer three classes of proletarian autobiography, two of which tend to be *ideologically* unauthentic: the self-description of the politically unaware victim of the capitalistic system (K. Fischer, W. Holek) and the life-story of the Social-Democratic artist who no longer lives *for* the party but *by* it (Krille, Preczang and Petzold). The third type (exemplified by Bromme,

Popp and Rehbein) narrates the evolution of the party-leader from proletarian victim to class-conscious fighter; this form of the proletarian autobiography was valuable to the movement since it offered exempla of class-conscious conduct and inspired optimism in the membership (Emmerich, 24). Bollenbeck also applies a stringent standard of Socialist Realism derived from Engels and Lukács to these texts. None of the autobiographies match this standard, of course: neither the first type, whose "spontaneous materialism" and documentary precision (153) he admires, nor Bromme, Dikreiter and W. Holek, whose trenchant social criticism is unmatched by a radical perspective of scientific socialism (186). Only Rehbein, despite a disproportion of subjective and objective aspects of the work (339), approximates the standard of Socialist Realism not only because of his conscious realism but also because he attempted to destroy the false idyllicisms which proletarian literature had inherited from its bourgeois counterpart (336).

Most of the critics cited so far assess the authenticity of the proletarian autobiography — as unreflected realism, as Socialist Realism or as "party literature" — on the basis of its textual properties. But just as Köppen (1982) and Quatember (1988) attempted, with varying degrees of success, to replace essentialist approaches to socialist fiction with functional analyses, so Vogtmeier (1984) expands Trommler's emphasis on the contemporary published reception of these texts to an analysis of both the ideological intentions of these autobiographies and the realization of these intentions in that reception. Vogtmeier finds that the reception in the Social-Democratic press of the autobiographies canonized by later critics is, on the whole, quite "adequate" to their ideological intentions. None of them are written from the perspective of revolutionary class struggle; even in Popp's memoirs, contrary to Bollenbeck's and Münchow's readings, the emphasis — both in Bebel's preface and in the text itself — is on the emancipation of the individual (229) and on the education of women rather than on a revolutionary class confrontation. In the Social-Democratic reception, their empirical realism and social criticism are recognized and confirmed, as are their reformist orientations. The autobiography of socialist poets, finally, stresses individual processes over collective ones even more than other forms of the proletarian autobiography, a fact which is positively received in the socialist press (255-58). Vogtmeier's analysis of the ideological intentions and Social-Democratic reception of these texts suggests that they constitute neither an independent genre nor simply a badly-written version of the bourgeois high-literary autobiography. There are a number of types. While the "social proletarian autobiography" (K. Fischer, Rehbein) shows a certain generic independence whose authentic voice is heard by some contemporary critics, the other types, in their emphasis on the ascent and socialization of individuals, increasingly fall under the auspices of the conventions of the bourgeois *Bildungsroman* and are received in terms of these conventions. Vogtmeier's attempt to problematize radically the traditional textual analysis of the proletarian autobiography, of course, merely expands, in a sense, the range of textual investigation by adding reviews to the primary texts. Most Social-Democratic writers and reviewers belonged to the same circle of culturally "competent" party intellectuals, so that it is not surprising that Vogtmeier's results confirm much of what textual critics had already ascertained.

The criticism of the fourth genre of socialist literature, the proletarian autobiography, highlights the difficulties of defining forms of socialist literature of this period on the basis of textual qualities not shared with the dominant bourgeois literary culture in substantial formal and ideological ways. There is, textually speaking, no socialist or proletarian autobiography unless that definition pivots entirely on political content. To shift to the question of *when*, and *under what circumstances*, these texts were viewed as the unique property and expression of an ascendant class would entail more than a quantitative expansion of the textual basis of the investigation. It also would entail a challenge to the dominant philological orientations of traditional academic literary history and criticism and to that specific form of hermeneuticism which prevailed not only in the German Social-Democratic movement but also in its historiography.

Works Consulted

Abendroth, Wolfgang. 1978. *Aufstieg und Krise der deutschen Sozialdemokratie*. 4th ed. Cologne: Pahl-Rugenstein.

Achten, Udo, ed. 1979a. *Illustrierte Geschichte des 1. Mai*. Oberhausen: Asso.

—, ed. 1979b. *Süddeutscher Postillon*. Berlin and Bonn: J. H. W. Dietz Nachf.

—, ed. 1980. *Zum Lichte empor. Mai-Festzeitungen der Sozialdemokratie 1891-1914*. Berlin and Bonn: J. H. W. Dietz Nachf.

Advocatus [Paul Vogt]. 1894-95. "Was liest der deutsche Arbeiter?" *Neue Zeit* 13, 814-17.

—. 1895-96. "Ein weiterer Beitrag zur Frage: Was liest der deutsche Arbeiter?" *Neue Zeit* 14, 631-35.

Arbeiterdichtung. Analysen — Bekenntnisse — Dokumentationen. 1973. Ed. Österreichische Gesellschaft für Kulturpolitik. Wuppertal: Peter Hammer.

Arbeitshefte 15. "Forum: Musik in der DDR. Arbeiterklasse und Musik. Theoretische Positionen in der deutschen Arbeiterklasse zur Musikkultur vor 1945." Berlin: Akademie der Künste der DDR. 1974.

Arnold, Heinz Ludwig, ed. 1977. *Handbuch zur deutschen Arbeiterliteratur*. 2 vols. Munich: Edition Text + Kritik.

Bab, Julius. 1929. *Arbeiterdichtung*. New exp. ed. Berlin: Volksbühnen-Verlag.

Balser, Frolinde. 1962. *Sozial-Demokratie 1848-1863*. 2 vols. Stuttgart: Klett.

Bär, Adam. 1903-04. "Jugendliteratur und Sozialismus." *Neue Zeit* 22, 127-28.

—. 1906-07. "Die Arbeiterbibliotheken." *Neue Zeit* 25, 718-20.

Bausinger, Hermann. 1973. "Verbürgerlichung — Folgen eines Interpretaments." In *Kultureller Wandel im 19. Jahrhundert*, ed. Günter Wiegelmann. Göttingen: Vandenhoeck & Ruprecht, 24-49.

Bebel, August. 1891. *Die Frau und der Sozialismus*. Stuttgart: Dietz.

—. 1910-14. *Aus meinem Leben*. 3 vols. Reprint: Berlin: J. H. W. Dietz Nachf., 1946.

Becker, Bernhard. 1874. *Geschichte der Arbeiteragitation Ferdinand Lassalles*. Braunschweig: Bracke. Reprint: Berlin and Bonn: J. H. W. Dietz Nachf., 1978.

Benjamin, Walter. 1937. "Eduard Fuchs, der Sammler und der Historiker." In *Gesammelte Schriften*, ed. Rolf Tiedemann and Hermann Schwepphäuser, vol. 2, pt. 2. Frankfurt am Main.: Suhrkamp, 1977, 465-505.

Bérard, R. 1896. "Das arbeitende Volk und die Kunst." In Rothe, ed. 1986a, 192-95.

Bernstein, Eduard. 1892-3. "Etwas Erzählungsliteratur." *Neue Zeit* 11, 260-70.

—. 1899. *Die Voraussetzungen des Sozialismus und die Aufgaben der Sozialdemokratie*. 13th ed. Stuttgart: J. H. W. Dietz Nachf.

—. 1903. "Vorwort." In Koigen. 1903, III-XIV.

—. 1905. "Schiller und die Revolution." In Jonas, ed. 1988a, 192-99.

—. 1907-10. *Die Geschichte der Berliner Arbeiter-Bewegung. Ein Kapitel zur Geschichte der deutschen Sozialdemokratie*. 3 vols. Berlin: Vorwärts. Reprint: Glashütten/Taunus: Auvermann, 1972.

—. 1912. "Klassenromantik." In Bürgel, ed. 1987a, 132-42.

Birker, Karl. 1973. *Die deutschen Arbeiterbildungsvereine 1840-1870*. Berlin: Colloquium.

Bl., K. 1903-04. "Jugendliteratur und Erziehung zum Sozialismus." *Neue Zeit* 22, 153-57.

Blos, Wilhelm. 1886. "Der soziale Roman." *Neue Zeit* 4, 424-28.

—. 1914-19. *Denkwürdigkeiten eines Sozialdemokraten*. 2 vols. Munich: G. Birk.

Böhme, Helmut. 1969. *Prolegomena zu einer Sozial- und Wirtschaftsgeschichte Deutschlands im 19. und 20. Jahrhundert*. Frankfurt am Main: Suhrkamp.

Bohnen, Klaus. 1981. "Aspekte marxistischer Lessing-Rezeption (Mehring, Lukács, Rilla)." In *Das Bild Lessings in der Geschichte*, ed. Herbert G. Göpfert. Heidelberg: Schneider, 115-30.

Bollenbeck, Georg. 1976. *Zur Theorie und Geschichte der frühen Arbeiterlebenserinnerungen*. Kronsberg/T.: Scriptor.

— and Karl Riha. 1978. "Im deutschen Kaiserreich." In *Geschichte der politischen Lyrik in Deutschland*, ed. Walter Hinderer. Stuttgart: Philipp Reclam jun., 232-60.

Böttcher, Kurt, et al. 1975. *Geschichte der deutschen Literatur*. Vol. 8, pt. 2, *Von 1830 bis zum Ausgang des 19. Jahrhunderts*. Berlin: Volk und Wissen.

Brauneck, Manfred. 1974. *Literatur und Öffentlichkeit im ausgehenden 19. Jahrhundert. Studien zur Rezeption des naturalistischen Theaters in Deutschland*. Stuttgart: Metzler.

Brückner, Peter and Gabriele Ricke. 1974. "Über die ästhetische Erziehung des Menschen in der Arbeiterbewegung." In *Das Unvermögen der Realität: Beiträge zu einer anderen materialistischen Ästhetik*, ed. Chris Bezzel, Peter Brückner, et al. Berlin: Wagenbach, 37-68.

Brüggemeier, Franz J. and Lutz Niethammer. 1978. "Schlafgänger, Schnapskasinos und schwerindustrielle Kolonie. Aspekte der Arbeiterwohnungsfrage im Ruhrgebiet vor dem Ersten Weltkrieg." In *Fabrik, Familie, Feierabend. Beiträge zur Sozialgeschichte des Alltags im Industriezeitalter*, ed. Jürgen Reulecke and Wolfhard Weber. Wuppertal: Peter Hammer, 135-75.

Buck, Theo. 1973. *Franz Mehring: Anfänge der materialistischen Literaturbetrachtung in Deutschland*. Stuttgart: Klett.

Bürgel, Tanja. 1983. "Das Problem der Unterhaltungsliteratur in der deutschen Arbeiterpresse vor dem Sozialistengesetz." In Mühlberg and Rosenberg, eds. 1983, 163-82.

—, ed. 1987a. *Tendenzkunst-Debatte 1910-1912*. Berlin: Akademie-Verlag [= *Textausgaben*, vol. 27].

—. 1987b. "Einleitung." In Bürgel, ed. 1987a, ix-xl.

Burggraf, Uta. 1978. "Kunst und Proletariat. Zur Differenzierung einiger theoretischer Positionen am Ende des 19. Jahrhunderts." *Weimarer Beiträge* 24, 98-122.

Carpin. 1896. "Der soziale Roman." *Neue Welt*, 326-7, 338-39.

ch. 1896. "Kunstblätter." *Der sozialistische Akademiker* 2, 326-29.

Dammer, Otto, Wilhelm Fritzsche and Julius Vahlteich. 1862. [Letter to F. Lassalle, December 4, 1862.] In La'man and Harstick 1975, 352-53.

David, Eduard. 1907. *Referenten-Führer. Anleitung für sozialistische Redner*. Berlin: Buchhandlung Vorwärts Paul Singer.

de Man, Hendrik. 1926. *Die Intellektuellen und der Sozialismus*. Jena: Eugen Diederichs.

Demetz, Peter. 1959. *Marx, Engels und die Dichter. Zur Grundlagenforschung des Marxismus*. Stuttgart: Deutsche Verlagsanstalt.

Diederich, Franz. 1905. "Schillers Volkstümlichkeit." In Jonas, ed. 1988a, 223-31.

—. 1907. "Arbeiterdichtung." *Neue Welt*, 284-87, 291-94.

—. 1911. "Proletarier-Lyrik." *Vorwärts* 17 (January 25), 67-68; 18 (January 26), 70-1.

—. 1913-14. "Ein Landarbeiterdrama." *Neue Zeit* 32, 952-56.

Dokumente und Materialien zur Geschichte der deutschen Arbeiterbewegung. Ed. Institut für Marxismus-Leninismus beim Zentralkomitee der SED. Berlin: Dietz, vol. 3, 1974; vol. 4, 1975.

Döring, E. 1910. "Fort mit der Schundliteratur!" *Arbeiter-Jugend* 2, 365-66.

Döscher, Karsten Heinrich. 1911. "Die Aesthetik der schwieligen Faust." In Bürgel, ed. 1987a, 75-77.

Dowe, Dieter. 1979. "Die Arbeitersängerbewegung in Deutschland vor dem Ersten Weltkrieg: eine Kulturbewegung im Vorfeld der Sozialdemokratie." In Ritter, ed. 1979a, 122-44.

—. 1980. *Protokolle und Materialien des Allgemeinen Deutschen Arbeitervereins (inkl. Splittergruppen)*. Berlin and Bonn: J. H. W. Dietz Nachf.

Duncker, Hermann. 1902. "So, Mann der Arbeit, sollst Du Feste feiern!" In *Arbeitshefte* 15, 110-11.

Düvell, Fritz. 1909. "Arbeiterdichtungen." *Zeitgeist*, 325-30.

Ecks, Karl. 1924. *Die Arbeiterdichtung im rheinisch-westfälischen Industriegebiet*. Borna-Leipzig: Universitätsverlag Robert Noske.

Eisner, Kurt. 1896. "Parteikunst." In Rothe, ed. 1986a, 243-51.

—. 1904. "Feste." *Neue Welt*, 139-40.

—. 1905. "Über Schillers Idealismus." In Jonas, ed. 1988a, 125-38.

—. 1908. "Kommunismus des Geistes." In *Gesammelte Schriften*. Berlin: Cassirer, 1919, vol. 2, 15-26.

—. 1913. "Karl Marx' Kunstauffassung." In Bürgel, ed. 1987, 127-32.

Emig, Brigitte. 1980. *Die Veredelung des Arbeiters. Sozialdemokratie als Kulturbewegung*. Frankfurt am Main and New York: Campus.

Emmerich, Wolfgang, ed. 1974. *Proletarische Lebensläufe. Autobiographische Dokumente zur Entstehung der Zweiten Kultur in Deutschland*. Vol. 1, *Anfänge bis 1914*. Reinbek: Rowohlt.

Engels, Friedrich. 1872-73. "Zur Wohnungsfrage." In *MEW*, vol. 18, 208-87.

—. 1885. Letter to Minna Kautsky (November 26). In Marx and Engels 1967-68, vol. 1, 155-56.

—. 1888. [Sketch of letter to Margaret Harkness]. In Marx and Engels 1967-68, vol. 1, 157-59.

—. 1891. "Zur Kritik des sozialdemokratischen Programmentwurfs 1891." In *MEW*, vol. 22, 225-40.

—. 1893. Letter to Franz Mehring (July 14). In *MEW*, vol. 39, 96-100.

—. 1894. Letter to Friedrich Adolph Sorge (March 21). In Marx and Engels 1967-68, vol. 2, 323.

—. 1895. "Einleitung [zu Karl Marx' *Klassenkämpfe in Frankreich 1848 bis 1850*]." In *MEW*, vol. 22, 509-27.

Engelsing, Rolf. 1973. *Analphabetentum und Lektüre. Zur Sozialgeschichte des Lesens in Deutschland zwischen feudaler und industrieller Gesellschaft*. Stuttgart: Metzler.

Feddersen, Harald. 1923. "Das Feuilleton der sozialdemokratischen Presse Deutschlands von den Anfängen bis zum Jahre 1914." Ph.D. diss., Univ. Leipzig.

Feidel-Mertz, Hildegard. 1964. *Zur Ideologie der Arbeiterbildung*. Frankfurt am Main: Europäische Verlagsanstalt.

Fendrich, Anton. 1905. "Zur Frage der Jugendliteratur." *Sozialistische Monatshefte* 9, 321-25.

Fischer, Edmund. 1909. "Der Entwicklungsgedanke." *Sozialistische Monatshefte* 13, 576-83.

Franke, Arno. 1913. "Der Unterhaltungsteil." *Mitteilungen des Vereins Arbeiterpresse* 14, no. 118, 4-6.

—. 1913-14. "Die Parteipresse auf dem Parteitag." *Neue Zeit* 32, 22-27.

Franz, Rudolf. 1910. "Tendenzkunst und Kunsttendenz." In Bürgel, ed. 1987a, 14-17.

—. 1910-11. "Revolutionäre Lyrik." *Neue Zeit* 29, 341-44.

Fricke, Dieter. 1976. *Die deutsche Arbeiterbewegung 1869 bis 1914*. Berlin: Dietz.

—. 1987. *Handbuch zur Geschichte der deutschen Arbeiterbewegung 1869 bis 1914*. 2 vols. Berlin: Dietz.

Friedrich, Cäcilia, ed. 1964. *Aus dem Schaffen früher sozialistischer Schriftstellerinnen*. Berlin: Akademie-Verlag [= *Textausgaben*, vol. 8].

—, ed. 1965. *Minna Kautsky. Auswahl aus ihrem Werk*. Berlin: Akademie-Verlag [= *Textausgaben*, vol. 4].

—, ed. 1975. *Kalender-Geschichten*. Berlin: Akademie-Verlag [= *Textausgaben*, vol. 14].

Friedrich, Wolfgang. 1964. "Die sozialistische deutsche Literatur in der Zeit des Aufschwungs der Arbeiterbewegung während der sechziger Jahre des 19. Jahrhunderts bis zum Erlaß des Sozialistengesetzes." 2 vols. Habilitation diss. Halle-Wittenberg.

[Eduard Fuchs]. 1894a. "In eigener Sache." *Süddeutscher Postillon* 15, 7.

—, Karl Kaiser and Ernst Klaar, eds. 1894b. *Aus dem Klassenkampf*. New ed. by Klaus Völkerling. Berlin: Akademie-Verlag, 1978 [= *Textausgaben*, vol. 18].

[—]. 1898a. "Der erste Mai im Bilde." *Süddeutscher Postillon* 10, 78-80.

[—]. 1898b. "Eine Wochenschrift für das arbeitende Volk." *Süddeutscher Postillon* 10, 22.

[—]. 1900. "Kunst und Partei." *Süddeutscher Postillon* 21, 148-50.

Füllberth, Georg. 1971. "Sozialdemokratische Literaturkritik vor 1914." *Alternative* 14, 2-16.

—. 1972. *Proletarische Partei und bürgerliche Literatur. Auseinandersetzungen in der deutschen Sozialdemokratie der II. Internationale über Möglichkeiten und Grenzen einer sozialistischen Literaturpolitik.* Neuwied and Berlin: Luchterhand.

—. 1974. *Die Wandlung der deutschen Sozialdemokratie vom Erfurter Parteitag 1891 bis zum Ersten Weltkrieg.* Cologne: Pahl-Rugenstein.

A. G. 1896. Review of *Aus Kampfgewühl und Einsamkeit* by Robert Seidel. In *Der sozialistische Akademiker* 2, 130.

J. G. 1898-99. "Was lesen die Wiener Arbeiter?" *Neue Zeit* 17, 89-91.

P. G. 1902. "Das religiöse Moment der Maifeier." In Achten, ed. 1980, 113.

Gebauer, Horst. 1972. "Die Lektüre der Arbeiter vor dem ersten Weltkrieg in der gegenwärtigen bürgerlichen Historiographie." *Der Bibliothekar* 26, 596-601.

Geschichte der deutschen Arbeiterbewegung. Ed. Institut für Marxismus-Leninismus beim Zentralkomitee der SED. Berlin: Dietz. Vol. 1, *Von den Anfängen der deutschen Arbeiterbewegung bis zum Ausgang des 19. Jahrhunderts*, 1966; vol. 2, *Vom Ausgang des 19. Jahrhunderts bis 1917*, 1966; *Biographisches Lexikon*, 1970.

Gille, Klaus F. 1982. "'Nur eine wertlose Scherbe' — zur Rezeption der Weimarer Klassik bei Franz Mehring." *Neophilologus* 66, 246-58.

Girnus, Werner. 1971. "Neue bürgerliche Forschungen zum 18. Jahrhundert und Franz Mehrings *Lessing-Legende*." In *Von der kritischen zur historisch-materialistischen Literaturwissenschaft*, ed. Werner Girnus, Helmut Lethen and Friedrich Rothe. Berlin: Oberbaumverlag, 58-83.

Grötzsch, Robert. 1911-12. "Kunst und Arbeiterschaft." In Bürgel, ed. 1987a, 110-13.

Groh, Dieter. 1973. *Negative Integration und revolutionärer Attentismus. Die deutsche Sozialdemokratie am Vorabend des Ersten Weltkrieges.* Frankfurt am Main: Ullstein.

Groschopp, Horst. 1983. "Die proletarische Klassenorganisation als Kommunikationsstruktur der deutschen Arbeiter vor 1914." In Mühlberg and Rosenberg, eds. 1983, 75-107.

—. 1985. *Zwischen Bierabend und Bildungsverein. Zur Kulturarbeit in der deutschen Arbeiterbewegung vor 1914.* Berlin: Dietz.

Grote, Heiner. 1968. *Sozialdemokratie und Religion. Eine Dokumentation für die Jahre 1863 bis 1875.* Tübingen: J. C. B. Mohr (Paul Siebeck).

Gumpert, Fritz. 1923. *Die Bildungsbestrebungen der freien Gewerkschaften.* Jena: Gustav Fischer.

J. H. 1892-93. "Die bürgerliche Kunst und die besitzlosen Klassen." In *Zum Kulturprogramm des deutschen Proletariats im 19. Jahrhundert*, ed. Helmut Barth. Dresden: VEB Verlag der Kunst, 1978, 247-55.

R. H. 1911. "Detektivgeschichten, Kriminalromane, Polizei-Schwarzbücher und dergleichen." *Der Bibliothekar* 3, 338-39.

Häckel, Manfred, ed. 1959. *Der Wahre Jakob. Lyrik und Prosa 1884-1905*. Berlin: Rütten und Loening.

Haenisch, Konrad. 1911. "Eine Anregung." *Mitteilungen des Vereins Arbeiterpresse* 12, no. 102, 8-9.

Hagen, Wolfgang. 1977. *Die Schillerverehrung in der Sozialdemokratie. Zur ideologischen Formation proletarischer Kulturpolitik vor 1914*. Stuttgart: Metzler.

Hanauer. 1910. Review of *Die Schundliteratur, ihr Vordringen, ihre Folgen, ihre Bekämpfung* by Ernst Schultze. In *Der Bibliothekar* 2, 112-14.

Hart, Julius. 1891. "Ein sozialdemokratischer Angriff auf das Jüngste Deutschland." In Rothe, ed. 1986a, 54-59.

Heid, Ludger, Klaus-Dieter Vinschen and Elisabeth Heid, eds. 1989. *Wilhelm Hasenclever. Reden und Schriften*. Bonn: J. H. W. Dietz Nachf.

Hermand, Jost. 1968. *Synthetisches Interpretieren. Zur Methodik der Literaturwissenschaft*. Munich: Nymphenburger Verlagsbuchhandlung.

—. 1971. "Carl Fischer: Denkwürdigkeiten und Erinnerungen eines Arbeiters (1903-1905)." In Hermand, *Unbequeme Literatur. Eine Beispielreihe*. Heidelberg: Lothar Stiehm, 87-106.

Hermes, Gertrud. 1926. *Die geistige Gestalt des marxistischen Arbeiters und die Arbeiterbildungsfrage*. Tübingen: J. C. B. Mohr.

Hobsbawn, E. J. 1974. "Labor History and Ideology." In *Journal of Social History* 7, 371-81.

Hochdorf, Max. 1911. "Tendenzromane." *Sozialistische Monatshefte* 15, 1568-70.

Hoffmann, Dirk. 1975. "Sozialismus und Literatur. Literatur als Mittel politisierender Beeinflussung im Literaturbetrieb der sozialistisch orientierten Arbeiterklasse des deutschen Kaiserreiches 1876-1918." Ph.D. diss., Univ. Münster.

Hohendahl, Peter Uwe. 1978. "Vom Nachmärz bis zur Reichsgründung." In *Geschichte der politischen Lyrik in Deutschland*, ed. Walter Hinderer. Stuttgart: Philipp Reclam jun., 210-31.

Holek, Heinrich. 1911. "Wie ich mich emporlas." *Der Bibliothekar* 3, 357-61.

Hollweck, Ludwig. 1973. *Karikaturen. Von den Fliegenden Blättern zum Simplicissimus*. Munich: Süddeutscher Verlag.

Horn, Robert. 1913. "Tendenz-Literatur." *Der Bibliothekar* 5, 657-59, 669-71, 685-87.

Huyssen, Andreas. 1979. "Nochmals zu Naturalismus-Debatte und Linksopposition." In *Naturalismus/Ästhetizismus*, ed. Christa Bürger, Peter Bürger and Jochen Schulte-Sasse. Frankfurt am Main: Suhrkamp, 244-58.

Jacobeit, Wolfgang and Ute Mohrmann, eds. 1973a. *Kultur und Lebensweise des Proletariats. Kulturhistorisch-volkskundliche Studien und Materialien*. Berlin: Akademie-Verlag.

—. 1973b. "Einleitung." In Jacobeit and Mohrmann, eds. 1973a, 7-19.

Jelken, Ernst. 1938. *Die Dichtung des deutschen Arbeiters. Erscheinung und Gestalt*. Jena: Frommann.

Jonas, Gisela, ed. 1988a. *Schiller-Debatte 1905*. Berlin: Akademie-Verlag [= *Textausgaben*, vol. 26].

—. 1988b. "Einleitung." In Jonas, ed. 1988a, ix-xxxii.

Jost, Annette, ed. 1974. "Zwischen Sozialgeschichte und Legitimationswissenschaft: Protokoll einer Tagung über Geschichtsschreibung der Arbeiterbewegung [...]." In *Marxistische Revolutionstheorien* [= *Jahrbuch Arbeiterbewegung*, vol. 2, ed. Claudio Pozzoli]. Frankfurt am Main: S. Fischer, 267-300.

Kaiser, Bruno. 1950. "Über die Entwicklung der politischen Lyrik in Deutschland." In *Das Zwischenspiel* by Erich Weinert. 3rd ed. Berlin: Volk und Welt, 1953, vii-xxvii.

—, ed. 1958. *Die Pariser Kommune im deutschen Gedicht*. Berlin: Dietz.

Kampffmeyer, Paul. 1901. *Die Geschichte und Literatur der deutschen Sozialdemokratie in ihren Hauptzügen*. Nuremberg: Fränkische Verlagsanstalt.

—. 1903. "Der Classenkampf und der Culturfortschritt. Gedanken über die Culturpolitik der größten Partei Deutschlands." *Sozialistische Monatshefte* 9, 667-75.

Kantorowicz, Ludwig. 1922. *Die sozialdemokratische Presse Deutschlands. Eine soziologische Untersuchung*. Tübingen: J. C. B. Mohr.

Kaufmann, Hans, et al. 1974. *Geschichte der deutschen Literatur*. Vol. 9, *Vom Ausgang des 19. Jahrhunderts bis 1917*. Berlin: Volk und Wissen.

Kautsky, Karl. 1890-91. "Der Alkoholismus und seine Bekämpfung" [excerpt]. In Rothe, ed. 1986a, 34-38.

—. 1892. *Das Erfurter Programm in seinem grundsätzlichen Teil*. Stuttgart: Dietz.

—. 1903-04. "Franz Mehring." *Neue Zeit* 22, 97-108.

—. 1904-05. "Die Rebellionen in Schillers Dramen." In Jonas, ed. 1988a, 149-78.

—. 1908-09. "Der Werdegang einer kämpfenden Proletarierin." *Neue Zeit* 27, 313-16.

—. 1909. *Der Weg zur Macht. Politische Betrachtungen über das Hineinwachsen in die Revolution.* Hamburg: Erdmann Dubber.

—. 1911. "Die Aktion der Masse." In *Die Massenstreikdebatte*, ed. Antonia Grunenberg. Frankfurt am Main: Europäische Verlagsanstalt, 1970, 233-63.

—. 1912. "Die neue Taktik." In *Die Massenstreikdebatte*, ed. Antonia Grunenberg. Frankfurt am Main: Europäische Verlagsanstalt, 1970, 295-334.

—. 1913-14. "Heinrich Dietz." *Neue Zeit* 32, 1-9.

—. 1960. *Erinnerungen und Erörterungen.* Ed. Benedikt Kautsky. S-Gravenhage: Mouton.

Kautsky, Minna. 1909. [Autobiographische Skizze]. *In Freien Stunden* 13, no. 2, 23-24.

Keller, Werner. 1972. "Franz Mehring und die Anfänge der marxistischen Literaturkritik in Deutschland." In *Zeiten und Formen in Sprache und Dichtung. Festschrift für Fritz Tschirsch*, ed. Karl-Heinz Schirmer and Bernhard Sowinski. Cologne and Vienna: Böhlau, 307-31.

Kette, Max. 1909. Review of *Jugendgeschichte einer Arbeiterin* [by Adelheid Popp]. *Der Bibliothekar* 1, 40-41.

Klaar, Ernst. 1902. "Max Kegel." *Süddeutscher Postillon* 23, 138.

Kliche, Dieter. 1976. "Zur Literatur- und Kulturauffassung Clara Zetkins." *Weimarer Beiträge* 21, 38-70.

Kliche, Joseph. 1910. "Das Berliner Arbeiterbibliothekswesen." *Vorwärts*, April 15, 291-92 & April 17, 295.

—. 1911. "Arbeiterlektüre." *Sozialistische Monatshefte* 15, 315-19.

—. 1914a. "Vom Feuilleton der Tageszeitungen." *Kunstwart* 27, 127-29.

—. 1914b. "Der Roman in der Parteipresse." *Mitteilungen des Vereins Arbeiterpresse* 15, no. 122, 4-5.

Knilli, Friedrich. 1970a. "'Der Wahre Jakob' — ein linker Supermann?" In *Comic Strips* [exhibition catalogue]. Berlin: Akademie der Künste, 12-20.

—. 1970b. "Das frühe deutsche Arbeitertheater: War es niedere Literatur oder Literatur der Niederen?" In Knilli and Münchow, eds. 1970, 35-53.

— and Ursula Münchow, eds. 1970. *Frühes deutsches Arbeitertheater 1847-1918.* Munich: Carl Hanser.

—. 1973. "Kitsch im Klassenkampf?" In *Arbeiterdichtung*, 76-91.

Koch, Hans. 1959. *Franz Mehrings Beitrag zur marxistischen Literaturtheorie*. Berlin: Dietz.

Koigen, David. 1903. *Die Kulturanschauung des Sozialismus. Ein Beitrag zum Wirklichkeits-Idealismus*. Berlin: Ferd. Dümmler.

Die Kongresse der Sozialistischen Arbeiterpartei Deutschlands unter dem Sozialistengesetz. 1980. Ed. Institut für Marxismus-Leninismus beim ZK der SED. 2 vols. Leipzig: Zentralantiquariat der DDR.

Köppen, Manuel. 1982. *Sozialdemokratische Belletristik vor dem ersten Weltkrieg*. Cologne: Pahl-Rugenstein.

Korn, Karl. 1908. "Proletariat und Klassik." *Neue Zeit* 26, 409-18.

—. 1922. *Die Arbeiterjugendbewegung. Einführung in ihre Geschichte*. Berlin: Arbeiterjugend-Verlag.

Kramer, Dieter. 1973. "Die soziokulturelle Lage und Ideologie der Arbeiterschaft im 19. Jahrhundert." In *Kultureller Wandel im 19. Jahrhundert*, ed. Günter Wiegelmann. Göttingen: Vandenhoeck & Ruprecht, 112-34.

Kreowski, Ernst. 1903. "Soziale Lyrik." *Neue Welt*, 131-2, 148-49.

—. 1907. "Robert Schweichel." *Der Wahre Jacob*, 5406-08.

Krille, Otto. 1904-05. "Die Kunstphrase und die Arbeiterfeste." *Neue Zeit* 23, 459-60.

—. 1905-06. "Kunst und Kapitalismus." *Neue Zeit* 24, 530-34.

—. 1914. *Unter dem Joch. Geschichte einer Jugend*. Ed. Ursula Münchow. Berlin: Akademie-Verlag, 1975 [= *Textausgaben*, vol. 15].

Kuczynski, Jürgen. 1946. *Die Geschichte der Lage der Arbeiter in Deutschland von 1800 bis in die Gegenwart*. Vol. 1, *1800 bis 1932*. Berlin: Die Freie Gewerkschaft.

—. 1981. *Die Geschichte des Alltags des deutschen Volkes 1600 bis 1945*, vol. 4, *1871-1918*. 2d ed. Cologne: Pahl-Rugenstein, 1982.

Kühn, Gudrun. 1974. "Die Sprache im Dienste des Kampfes der Arbeiterklasse." In *Die Sprache des Arbeiters im Klassenkampf*, ed. Dieter Faulseit and Gudrun Kühn. Berlin: Tribüne, 25-75.

Kumpmann, Walter. 1966. *Franz Mehring als Vertreter des historischen Materialismus*. Wiesbaden: Harrassowitz.

Kunert, Marle. 1906. "Ein Dichter der Freiheit." *Neue Welt*, 212, 214.

—. 1907. "Minna Kautsky." *Neue Welt*, 179-80, 182.

Kürbisch, Friedrich G., ed. 1969. *Anklage und Botschaft. Die lyrische Aussage der Arbeiter seit 1900.* Hannover: J. H. W. Dietz Nachf.

"Die Kunst und der Sozialismus." 1895. In Achten, ed. 1980, 60.

Lammel, Inge. 1962. *Das deutsche Arbeiterlied.* Leipzig, Jena and Berlin: Urania.

—, ed. 1971. *Bibliographie der deutschen Arbeiterliederbücher 1833-1945.* Leipzig: VEB Deutscher Verlag für Musik.

Landauer, Gustav. 1891-92. "Die Zukunft und die Kunst." In Rothe, ed. 1986a, 116-21.

Langewiesche, Dieter. 1979. "Arbeiterkultur in Österreich: Aspekte, Tendenzen und Thesen." In Ritter, ed. 1979a, 40-57.

— and Klaus Schönhoven. 1976. "Arbeiterbibliotheken und Arbeiterlektüre im Wilhelminischen Deutschland." *Archiv für Sozialgeschichte* 16, 135-204.

Lassalle, Ferdinand. *Gesammelte Schriften und Reden*, ed. Eduard Bernstein. 12 vols. Berlin: Cassirer, 1919-20.

—. 1863a. *Offenes Antwortschreiben.* In *Gesammelte Schriften*, vol. 3, 41-92.

—. 1863b. *Die Wissenschaft und die Arbeiter.* In *Gesammelte Schriften.* vol. 2, 213-84.

—. 1863c. *Arbeiter-Lesebuch.* In *Gesammelte Schriften*, vol. 3, 179-289.

Laufenberg, Heinrich. 1911. *Geschichte der Arbeiterbewegung in Hamburg, Altona und Umgebung.* Hamburg: Hamburger Buchdruckerei [Auer]. Reprint: Berlin, Bonn and Bad Godesberg: J. H. W. Dietz Nachf. 1977.

Legien, Carl. 1901. *Die deutsche Gewerkschaftsbewegung.* Berlin: Verlag der Sozialistischen Monatshefte.

Der Leipziger Hochverratsprozess vom Jahre 1872. Ed. Karl-Heinz Leidigkeit. Berlin: Rütten und Loening, 1960.

Lenzner, Paul. 1913. "Einiges über den Roman." *Der Bibliothekar* 5, 42-43.

Levenstein, Adolf, ed. 1909a. *Aus der Tiefe: Arbeiterbriefe. Beiträge zur Seelen-Analyse moderner Arbeiter.* Berlin: Morgen.

—, ed. 1909b. *Arbeiter-Philosophen und -Dichter*, Vol. 1. Berlin: Morgen.

—, ed. 1912. *Die Arbeiterfrage. Mit besonderer Berücksichtigung der sozialpsychologischen Seite des modernen Großbetriebes und der psycho-physischen Einwirkungen auf die Arbeiter.* Munich: Ernst Reinhardt. Reprint: New York: Arno Press, 1975.

Lexikon. 1964. *Lexikon sozialistischer deutscher Literatur. Von den Anfängen bis 1945.* Leipzig: Bibliographisches Institut.

Lidtke, Vernon L. 1973. "Die kulturelle Bedeutung der Arbeitervereine." In *Kultureller Wandel im 19. Jahrhundert*, ed. Günter Wiegelmann. Göttingen: Vandenhoeck & Ruprecht, 146-59.

—. 1985. *The Alternative Culture. Socialist Labor in Imperial Germany*. New York and Oxford: Oxford Univ. Press.

Liebknecht, Wilhelm. 1872. "Wissen ist Macht — Macht ist Wissen." In Liebknecht, *Wissen ist Macht — Macht ist Wissen und andere bildungspolitisch-pädagogische Äußerungen*. Ed. Hans Brumme. Berlin: Volk und Wissen, 1968, 51-101.

—. 1890-91. "Brief aus Berlin." *Neue Zeit* 9, 709-11.

—. 1973. *Briefwechsel mit deutschen Sozialdemokraten*. Vol. 1, *1862-1878*, ed. Georg Eckert. Assen: Van Gorcum.

—. 1976. *Erinnerungen eines Soldaten der Revolution*. Ed. Heinrich Gemkow. Berlin: Dietz.

Loeb, Minna. 1932. "Die Ideengehalte der Arbeiterdichtung." Ph.D. diss., Univ. Giessen.

Loreck, Jochen. 1977. *Wie man früher Sozialdemokrat wurde. Das Kommunikationsverhalten in der deutschen Arbeiterbewegung und die Konzeption der sozialistischen Parteipublizistik durch August Bebel*. Bonn/Bad Godesberg: Neue Gesellschaft.

Ludwig, Martin H. 1976. *Arbeiterliteratur in Deutschland*. Stuttgart: Metzler.

Lüdtke, Alf. 1982. "Rekonstruktion von Alltagswirklichkeit — Entpolitisierung der Sozialgeschichte?" In *Klassen und Kultur. Sozialanthropologische Perspektiven in der Geschichtsschreibung*, ed. Robert M. Berdahl, et al. Frankfurt am Main: Syndikat, 321-53.

Lukács, Georg. 1933. "Franz Mehring, 1846-1919." In Lukács, *Beiträge zur Geschichte der Ästhetik*. Berlin: Aufbau-Verlag, 1954, 318-403.

Lützeler, Paul Michael. 1971. "Die marxistische Lessing-Rezeption: Darstellung und Kritik am Beispiel von Mehring und Lukács." *Lessing Yearbook* 3, 173-93.

Luxemburg, Rosa. *Gesammelte Werke*, ed. Institut für Marxismus-Leninismus beim ZK der SED. 5 vols. Berlin: Dietz, 1970-75.

—. 1899a. *Sozialreform oder Revolution?* Leipzig: G. Heinisch. In *Gesammelte Werke*, vol. 1, pt. 1, 367-466.

—. 1899b. "Unser leitendes Zentralorgan." In *Gesammelte Werke*, vol. 1, pt.1, 555-58.

—. 1903. "Stillstand und Fortschritt im Marxismus." In *Gesammelte Werke*, vol. 1, pt. 2, 363-68.

—. 1903-04. "Organisationsfragen der russischen Sozialdemokratie." In *Gesammelte Werke*, vol. 1, pt. 2, 422-44.

—. 1904. "Lassalle und die Revolution." In *Gesammelte Werke*, vol. 1, pt. 2, 417-21.

—. 1904-05. Review of *Schiller. Ein Lebensbild für deutsche Arbeiter* by Franz Mehring. In *Gesammelte Werke*, vol. 1, pt. 2, 533-36.

—. 1905. "Die Debatten in Köln." In *Gesammelte Werke*, vol. 1, pt. 2, 580-86.

—. 1906. *Massenstreik, Partei und Gewerkschaften*. Hamburg: Erdmann Dubber. In *Gesammelte Werke*, vol. 2, 91-170.

—. 1907. "Die Maifeier." In *Gesammelte Werke*, vol. 2, 201-04.

—. 1908. "Tolstoi als sozialer Denker." In *Gesammelte Werke*, vol. 2, 246-53.

—. 1909. "Das Begräbnis der Maifeier." In *Gesammelte Werke*, vol. 2, 269-73.

—. 1912-13. "Tolstois Nachlaß." In *Gesammelte Werke*, vol. 3, 185-90.

—. 1913. "Lassalles Erbschaft." In *Gesammelte Werke*, vol. 3, 220-24.

Mann, Golo. 1958. *Deutsche Geschichte des 19. und 20. Jahrhunderts*. Frankfurt am Main: S. Fischer.

Märten, Lu. 1906. "Kunst, Klasse und Sozialismus." *Neue Welt*, 359.

—. 1911-12. "Zur ästhetisch-literarischen Enquete." In Bürgel, ed. 1987a, 96-101.

Martini, Fritz. 1958. "Arbeiterdichtung." In *Reallexikon der deutschen Literaturgeschichte*, vol. 1. Berlin: Walter De Gruyter, 97-99.

Marx, Karl. 1848. *Manifest der Kommunistischen Partei*. In *MEW*, vol. 4, 459-93.

—. 1857. "Einleitung [zur Kritik der Politischen Ökonomie]." In *MEW*, vol. 13, 615-42.

—. 1864. "Inauguraladresse der Internationalen Arbeiter-Assoziation." In *MEW*, vol. 16, 5-13.

—. 1872. "Nachwort zur zweiten Auflage von *Das Kapital*." In *MEW*, vol. 23, 18-28.

—. 1880a. "Fragebogen für Arbeiter." In *MEW*, vol. 19, 230-7.

—. 1880b. "[Einleitung zum Programm der französischen Arbeiterpartei]" and "Minimalprogramm." In *MEW*, vol. 19, 238, 570-1.

—. 1946. *Kritik des Gothaer Programms*. Berlin: Neuer Weg.

— and Friedrich Engels. 1967-68. *Über Kunst und Literatur*. 2 vols. Ed. Manfred Kliem. Berlin: Dietz.

Mathes, Klaus. 1987. *August Otto-Walster: Schriftsteller und Politiker in der deutschen Arbeiterbewegung*. Frankfurt am Main and Berne: Peter Lang.

Maurenbrecher, Max. 1905-06. "Was ist uns Schiller?" In Jonas, ed. 1988a, 8-13.

—. 1909a. "Schulung der Funktionäre." *Sozialistische Monatshefte* 13, 1405-11.

—. 1909b. "Über die Methode der Bildung." *Sozialistische Monatshefte* 13, 1537-43.

Mehlich, Ernst. 1913-14. "Die Zukunft der Arbeiterbüchereien." *Neue Zeit* 32, 65-69.

Mehring, Franz. *Gesammelte Schriften*, ed. Thomas Höhle, Hans Koch and Josef Schleifstein. 15 vols. Berlin: Dietz, 1960-67.

—. 1887. "Robert Schweichel." In *Gesammelte Schriften*, vol. 11, 453-62.

—. 1891. "Kapital und Presse" [excerpt]. In Rothe, ed. 1986a, 60-65.

—. 1891-93. *Lessing-Legende*. Vol. 9 of *Gesammelte Schriften*.

—. 1892-93. "Der heutige Naturalismus." In *Gesammelte Schriften*, vol. 11, 131-33.

—. 1893a. "Goethes *Egmont*." In *Gesammelte Schriften*, vol. 10, 63-69.

—. 1893b. Review of *Deutsche Arbeiterdichtung*. In *Gesammelte Schriften*, vol. 11, 477-78.

—. 1896. "Kunst und Proletariat." *Gesammelte Schriften*, vol. 11, 134-40.

—. 1897-98. *Geschichte der deutschen Sozialdemokratie*. Vols. 1-2 of *Gesammelte Schriften*.

—. 1898. "Ästhetische Streifzüge." In *Gesammelte Schriften*, vol. 11, 141-226.

—. 1899. "Goethe und die Gegenwart." In *Gesammelte Schriften*, vol. 10, 86-90.

—. 1900. "Leo Tolstoi." In *Gesammelte Schriften*, vol. 12, 131-40.

—. 1901. [Robert Schweichel zum 80. Geburtstag.] In *Gesammelte Schriften*, vol. 11, 463-64.

—. 1902. "Emile Zola." In *Gesammelte Schriften*, vol. 12, 35-39.

—. 1903. Review of *Nachtasyl* by Maxim Gorky. In *Gesammelte Schriften*, vol. 12, 151-55.

—. 1904. Review of *Die Karikatur der europäischen Völker vom Jahre 1848 bis zur Gegenwart* by Eduard Fuchs. In *Gesammelte Schriften*, vol. 12, 181-82.

—. 1904-05. "Schiller und die Gegenwart." In *Gesammelte Schriften*, vol. 10, 282-86.

—. 1905a. *Schiller. Ein Lebensbild für deutsche Arbeiter*. In *Gesammelte Schriften*, vol. 10, 91-241.

—. 1905b. "Schiller und die Arbeiter." In *Gesammelte Schriften*, vol. 10, 278-81.

—. 1906. "Gedenktage." In *Gesammelte Schriften*, vol. 11, 465-66.

—. 1907. Review of *Lebensgeschichte eines modernen Fabrikarbeiters* by William Bromme. In *Gesammelte Schriften*, vol. 11, 494-95.

—. 1908a. Review of *Gesammelte Gedichte* by Clara Müller-Jahnke. In *Gesammelte Schriften*, vol. 11, 486-88.

—. 1908b. Review of *Im Strom der Zeit* by Ernst Preczang. In *Gesammelte Schriften*, vol. 11, 489-90.

—. 1908c. "Karl Marx und das Gleichnis." In *Gesammelte Schriften*, vol. 12, 199-202.

—. 1909a. *"Wilhelm Tell."* In *Gesammelte Schriften*, vol. 10, 259-65.

—. 1909b. Review of *Lebensgang eines deutsch-tschechischen Handarbeiters* by Wenzel Holek. In *Gesammelte Schriften*, vol. 11, 496-500.

—. 1910. "Leo Tolstoi." In *Gesammelte Schriften*, vol. 12, 147-50.

—. 1912a. "Minna Kautsky." In *Gesammelte Schriften*, vol. 11, 451-52.

—. 1913. "Ein Nachzügler." In *Gesammelte Schriften*, vol. 11, 238-43.

—. 1914. "Sozialistische Lyrik." In *Gesammelte Schriften*, vol. 10, 395-421.

MEW. Marx, Karl and Friedrich Engels. *Werke*, ed. Institut für Marxismus-Leninismus beim ZK der SED. 43 vols. Berlin: Dietz, 1961-81.

Michels, Robert. 1910. *Zur Soziologie des Parteiwesens in der modernen Demokratie.* 2nd ed. Leipzig: Alfred Kröner, 1925.

Miller, Susanne. 1964. *Das Problem der Freiheit im Sozialismus. Freiheit, Staat und Revolution in der Programmatik der Sozialdemokratie von Lassalle bis zum Revisionismusstreit.* Frankfurt am Main: Europäische Verlagsanstalt.

Molkenbuhr, Hermann. 1905. "Schillers Einfluß auf die Agitation der Sozialdemokraten." In Jonas, ed. 1988a, 145-47.

Moltrecht, Hans-Jürgen. 1973. "Kultur- und Bildungsarbeit im Leipziger 'Fortbildungsverein für Arbeiter' während des Sozialistengesetzes (1879-1890)." In Jacobeit and Mohrmann, eds. 1973a, 137-58.

Mühlberg, Dietrich. 1983. "Literatur in der Arbeiterklassenkultur. Bemerkungen zu Ansätzen kulturhistorischer Forschung." In Mühlberg and Rosenberg, eds. 1983a, 17-44.

— and Rainer Rosenberg, eds. 1983a. *Literatur und proletarische Kultur. Beiträge zur Kulturgeschichte der deutschen Arbeiterklasse im 19. Jahrhundert.* Berlin: Akademie-Verlag.

— and Rainer Rosenberg. 1983b. "Vorwort." In Mühlberg and Rosenberg, eds. 1983a, 7-16.

Münchow, Ursula. 1963. "Die ersten Anfänge der sozialistischen Dramatik in Deutschland." *Weimarer Beiträge* 9, 729-75.

—. 1964. "Naturalismus und Proletariat." *Weimarer Beiträge* 10, 599-617.

—, ed. 1964-72. *Aus den Anfängen der sozialistischen Dramatik*. 3 vols. Berlin: Akademie-Verlag [= *Textausgaben*, vols. 3, 5, 11].

—. 1970. "Zur Entstehung und Entwicklung des frühen deutschen Arbeitertheaters." In Knilli and Münchow, eds., 1970, 11-33.

—. 1973a. *Frühe deutsche Arbeiterautobiographie*. Berlin: Akademie-Verlag.

—. 1973b. "Das Bild des Arbeiters in der proletarischen Selbstdarstellung." *Weimarer Beiträge* 19, 110-35.

—. 1981. *Arbeiterbewegung und Literatur 1860-1914*. Berlin and Weimar: Aufbau-Verlag.

—. 1982. "Nachwort." In *Des Morgens erste Röte. Sozialistische deutsche Literatur 1860-1918*, ed. Norbert Rothe and Ursula Münchow. Leipzig: Philipp Reclam jun., 405-28.

Na'man, Shlomo. 1970. *Lassalle*. Hannover: Verlag für Literatur und Zeitgeschehen.

— and H.-P. Harstick. 1975. *Die Konstituierung der deutschen Arbeiterbewegung 1862/63*. Assen: Van Gorcum.

Negt, Oskar and Alexander Kluge. 1972. *Öffentlichkeit und Erfahrung. Zur Organisationsanalyse von bürgerlicher und proletarischer Öffentlichkeit*. Frankfurt am Main: Suhrkamp.

Nespital, Margarete. 1932. *Das deutsche Proletariat in seinem Lied*. Rostock: Mecklenburgische Volkszeitung.

Nitschke, Wilhelm. 1913. "Wie und nach welcher Richtung entwickelt sich das Lesebedürfnis der Arbeiterschaft?" *Sozialistische Monatshefte* 17, 364-70.

Noack, Victor. 1909. "Zur Rettung des Proletarierliedes." In *Arbeitshefte* 15, 113.

Olbrich, Harald, ed. 1979a. *Sozialistische deutsche Karikatur 1848-1978*. Berlin: Eulenspiegel Verlag.

—. 1979b. "Vorwort." In Olbrich, ed. 1979a, 7-10.

Osterroth, Franz and Dieter Schuster, eds. 1963. *Chronik der deutschen Sozialdemokratie*. Hannover: J. H. W. Dietz Nachf.

Pannekoek, Anton. 1912. "Massenaktion und Revolution." In *Massenstreikdebatte*, ed. Antonia Grunenberg. Frankfurt am Main: Europäische Verlagsanstalt, 1970, 264-94.

Pehlke, Michael. 1971. "Ein Exempel proletarischer Dramatik. Bemerkungen zu Friedrich Bosses Streikdrama *Im Kampf*." In Horst Albert Glaser, et al., *Literaturwissenschaft und Sozialwissenschaften*. Stuttgart: Metzler, 400-34.

Pforte, Dietger. 1969. "Die Anthologie als Kampfbuch. Vier Lyrikanthologien der frühen deutschen Sozialdemokratie." In *Die deutschsprachige Anthologie*, ed. Joachim Bark and Dietger Pforte, vol. 2. Frankfurt am Main: Vittorio Klostermann, 199-221.

—. 1974. "Die deutsche Sozialdemokratie und die Naturalisten." In *Naturalismus. Bürgerliche Dichtung und soziales Engagement*, ed. Helmut Scheuer. Stuttgart: Kohlhammer, 175-205.

—. 1979. *Von unten auf. Studien zur literarischen Bildungsarbeit der frühen deutschen Sozialdemokratie und zum Verhältnis von Literatur und Arbeiterklasse*. Giessen: Anabas.

Pick, Erika, ed. 1964. *Robert Schweichel: Erzählungen*. Berlin: Akademie-Verlag [= *Textausgaben*, vol. 2].

Piltz, Georg. 1976. *Geschichte der europäischen Karikatur*. Berlin: VEB Deutscher Verlag.

—. "I. 1848-1890." In Olbrich, ed. 1979a, 12-21.

Poensgen-Alberty, Max. 1913. "Vom Rezitieren und Theaterspielen." *Arbeiter-Jugend* 5, 238-39.

Popp, Adelheid. 1909. *Die Jugendgeschichte einer Arbeiterin*. Berlin and Stuttgart: J. H. W. Dietz Nachf., 1922.

PPT. Protokoll über die Verhandlungen des Parteitages der Sozialdemokratischen Partei Deutschlands. 1890-1913. Place varies.

Quatember, Wolfgang. 1988. *Erzählprosa im Umfeld der österreichischen Arbeiterbewegung*. Vienna and Zurich: Europaverlag.

Rabold, Emil. 1913. "Das Feuilleton unserer Parteipresse." *Mitteilungen des Vereins Arbeiterpresse* 14, no. 117, 1-2.

Raddatz, Fritz J. 1979. "Die Mehring-Legende. Über echte wahre Kunst — oder Dekadenz und Fäulnis in der modernen Literatur." In Raddatz, *Revolte und Melancholie. Aufsätze zur Literaturtheorie*. Hamburg: Knaus, 57-100, 294-98.

Rector, Martin. 1980. "Sozialdemokratische Literatur von 1890 bis 1918." In *Geschichte der deutschen Literatur vom 18. Jahrhundert bis zur Gegenwart*, ed. Viktor Žmegač, vol. 2. Königstein/Ts.: Athenäum, 234-55.

Reinelt, Herbert. 1967. "August Otto-Walster 1834-1898. Sein Beitrag zur deutschen sozialistischen Prosaliteratur des 19. Jahrhunderts." Ph.D. diss., Potsdam.

Reisig, Hildegard. 1933. *Die Rolle der Bildung für die Befreiung des Proletariats im politischen Denken der deutschen Arbeiterbewegung von den 40er Jahren bis zum Weltkrieg*. Langensalza: Beyer & Söhne.

Reißmann, Alwin. 1913-14. "Die Arbeiterbibliotheken als Bildungsanstalt." *Neue Zeit* 32, 548-52.

Reutershan, Joan. 1985. *Clara Zetkin und Brot und Rosen: Literaturpolitische Konflikte zwischen Partei und Frauenbewegung in der deutschen Vorkriegssozialdemokratie*. New York, Berne and Frankfurt am Main: Peter Lang.

Review of *Aus der Tiefe* by Adolf Levenstein. 1909. *In Freien Stunden*, 479-80.

Review of *Victoria* by Minna Kautsky. 1889. *Neue Zeit* 7, 235-6.

Ritter, Gerhard A. 1959. *Die Arbeiterbewegung im Wilhelminischen Reich. SPD und Gewerkschaft nach dem Sozialistengesetz*. 2nd ed. Berlin: Colloquium, 1963.

—, ed. 1979a. *Arbeiterkultur*. Königstein/Ts.: Athenäum.

—. 1979b. "Arbeiterkultur im deutschen Kaiserreich: Probleme und Forschungsansätze." In Ritter, ed. 1979a, 15-39.

— and Jürgen Kocka, eds. 1974. *Deutsche Sozialgeschichte: Dokumente und Skizzen*. Vol. 1, *1870-1914*, compiled by Werner Pöls. Munich: C. H. Beck.

Roland. 1914. "Emil Rosenows *Kater Lampe*." *Arbeiter-Jugend* 6, 75-76.

Rosenberg, Rainer. 1983. "Die Literatur der deutschen Arbeiterbewegung als Forschungsgegenstand der Literaturwissenschaft." In Mühlberg and Rosenberg, eds. 1983a, 45-74.

Roßbach, Emil. 1874a. "Die Schulen und die Arbeiter." *Volksstaat* 6 (May 20), 1.

—. 1874b. "Zur Emancipation der Frauen." *Volksstaat* 6 (June 12), 1.

Roßmäßler, Adolf. 1862. "Rede beim Einweihungsfest des Vereins *Vorwärts* am 30. November 1862." In Na'man and Harstick 1975, 346-51.

—. 1863. "An die deutschen Arbeiter!" In Na'man and Harstick 1975, 405-10.

Roth, Guenther. 1963. *The Social Democrats in Imperial Germany. A Study in Working-Class Isolation and National Integration*. Towota, NJ: The Bedminster Press.

Rothe, Norbert, ed. 1986a. *Naturalismus-Debatte 1891-1896*. Berlin: Akademie-Verlag [= *Textausgaben*, vol. 25].

—. 1986b. "Einleitung." In Rothe, ed. 1986a, vii-lxii.

Rüden, Peter von. 1973. *Sozialdemokratisches Arbeitertheater (1848-1914): Ein Beitrag zur Geschichte des politischen Theaters*. Frankfurt am Main: Athenäum.

— and Kurt Kosyk, eds. 1979. *Dokumente und Materialien zur Kulturgeschichte der deutschen Arbeiterbewegung 1848-1918*. Frankfurt am Main, Vienna and Zurich: Büchergilde Gutenberg.

Rühle, Otto. 1907. *Volksbildung, Wissenschaft, Kunst und Sozialdemokratie.* Berlin: Vorwärts.

—. 1930. *Illustrierte Kultur- und Sittengeschichte des Proletariats*, vol. 1. Berlin: Neuer Deutscher Verlag. New ed. Frankfurt am Main: Neue Kritik, 1970.

J. S. and E. F. 1894-95. "Was lesen die organisierten Arbeiter in Deutschland?" *Neue Zeit* 13, 153-55.

Saldern, Adelheid v. 1977. "Wilhelminische Gesellschaft und Arbeiterklasse: Emanzipations- und Integrationsprozesse im kulturellen und sozialen Bereich." *Internationale wissenschaftliche Korrespondenz zur Geschichte der Arbeiterbewegung* 13, 469-505.

Schäfers, Hans-Joachim. 1961. *Zur sozialistischen Arbeiterbildung in Leipzig 1890 bis 1914.* Leipzig: Museum für Geschichte der Leipziger Arbeiterbewegung.

Scharrer, Manfred. 1976. *Arbeiterbewegung im Obrigkeitsstaat. SPD und Gewerkschaft nach dem Sozialistengesetz.* Berlin: Rotbuch.

Schauder, A. 1907. "Das Volkslied und die Gesangvereine." In *Arbeitshefte* 15, 117-18.

Scherer, Herbert. 1974. *Bürgerlich-oppositionelle Literaten und sozialdemokratische Arbeiterbewegung nach 1890. Die 'Friedrichshagener' und ihr Einfluß auf die sozialdemokratische Kulturpolitik.* Stuttgart: Metzler.

Schieder, Wolfgang. 1964. "Zur Geschichte der deutschen Arbeiterbewegung im 19. Jahrhundert." *Neue politische Literatur* 9, 323-38.

Schiller, Dieter. 1977. "Rosa Luxemburg (1971-1919)." In *Positionsbestimmungen. Zur Geschichte marxistischer Theorie von Literatur und Kultur am Ausgang des 19. und zu Beginn des 20. Jahrhunderts*, ed. Dieter Schlenstedt and Klaus Städtke. Frankfurt am Main: Röderberg, 323-68.

Schlaikjer, Erich. 1893-94. "Der Einfluß des Kapitalismus auf die moderne dramatische Kunst." In Rothe, ed. 1986a, 171-83.

—. 1895-96. "Die Befreiung der Kunst." *Neue Zeit* 14, 69-77.

Schmidt, Hugo Ernst. 1896. "Die Kunst und das Volk." *Der sozialistische Akademiker* 2, 159-62.

Schorske, Carl E. 1955. *German Social Democracy 1905-1917.* Cambridge, MA: Harvard Univ. Press.

Schröder, Gustav. 1965. "Das sozialistische deutsche Bühnenstück von den sechziger Jahren des 19. Jahrhunderts bis zum Zusammenbruch der Zweiten Sozialistischen Internationale." Habilitation diss., Potsdam.

—. 1967. "Friedrich Bosse: ein Pionier des deutschen sozialistischen Bühnenstücks." *Wissenschaftliche Zeitschrift der Pädagogischen Hochschule Potsdam* (Gesellsch.-sprachw. Reihe) 11, 105-16.

—, ed. 1972. *Frühes Leipziger Arbeitertheater. Friedrich Bosse*. Berlin: Akademie-Verlag [= *Textausgaben*, vol. 12].

Schröder, Wilhelm. 1910. *Handbuch der sozialdemokratischen Parteitage von 1863 bis 1909*. Munich: G. Birk.

Schult, Johannes. 1914. *Die Hamburger Arbeiterbewegung als Kulturfaktor. Ein Beitrag zur hamburgischen Kulturgeschichte*. Hamburg: Hamburger Druckereigesellschaft Kurt Weltzien.

Schultze, Ernst. 1909. "Selbstmord und Schundliteratur." *In Freien Stunden* 13, no. 1, 359-60.

—. 1910. "Gute und schlechte Kriminalliteratur." *Der Bibliothekar* 2, 156-57.

Schulz, Heinrich. 1900-01. "Sozialdemokratische Jugendliteratur?" *Neue Zeit* 19, 172-77.

—. 1910. "Arbeiterfeste." *Neue Welt*, 137-38.

—. 1931. *Politik und Bildung. Hundert Jahre Arbeiterbildung*. Berlin: Dietz Nachf.

Schulz, Ursula, ed. 1968. *Die deutsche Arbeiterbewegung 1848-1919 in Augenzeugenberichten*. Düsseldorf: Karl Rauch.

Schulze-Delitzsch, Hermann. 1862. "Rede auf der öffentlichen Arbeiterversammlung am 2. November nach dem Bericht der *Nationalzeitung* vom 4.11.1862." In Na'man and Harstick 1975, 210-19.

—. 1863. *Capitel zu einem deutschen Arbeiterkatechismus*. Leipzig: Ernst Keil.

Schütz, Hans J., ed. 1977. *Der wahre Jacob. Ein halbes Jahrhundert in Faksimiles*. Berlin J. H. W. Dietz Nachf.

Schweichel, Robert. 1885. "*Germinal*." *Neue Zeit* 3, 361-70.

—. 1887. "Der naturalistische Roman bei den Russen und Franzosen." *Neue Zeit* 5, 1-14.

—. 1890-91. "Deutschlands jüngste Dichterschule." In Rothe, ed. 1986a, 44-53.

Schweitzer, Jean Baptist v. 1912. *Politische Aufsätze und Reden*, ed. Franz Mehring. Berlin: Buchhandlung Vorwärts.

Schwendter, Rolf. 1973. *Theorie der Subkultur*. 3d ed. Frankfurt am Main: Syndikat, 1981.

Serebrow, N. 1961. "Die literarkritischen Ansichten Rosa Luxemburgs." *Kunst und Literatur* 9, 727-37.

Seybold, Annette. 1986. "Erzählliteratur in der sozialdemokratischen und der konservativen Presse 1892-1914. Eine Untersuchung zur These der Verbürgerlichung der Sozialdemokratie anhand eines Vergleichs der Familienzeitschriften *Die Neue Welt* und *Die Gartenlaube*." Ph.D. diss., Univ. Frankfurt.

Siemering, Hertha. 1911. *Arbeiterbildungswesen in Wien und Berlin. Eine kritische Untersuchung.* Karlsruhe: Braun.

"Skizze zur Geschichte der deutschen Nationalliteratur von den Anfängen der deutschen Arbeiterbewegung bis zur Gegenwart." 1964. *Weimarer Beiträge* 10, 644-812.

Sommer, B. 1912. "Das dramatische Werk Emil Rosenows." *Der Bibliothekar* 4, 469-70.

Sperber, Heinz [Herman Heijermans]. 1910a. "Kunst und Industrie." In Bürgel, ed. 1987a, 3-10.

—. 1910b. "Tendenziöse Kunst." In Bürgel, ed. 1987a, 10-14.

—. 1910c. "Missa Solemnis ..." In Bürgel, ed. 1987a, 21-24.

—. 1911a. "Vorpostengefechte." In Bürgel, ed. 1987a, 49-53.

—. 1911b. "Die Theatersaison." In Bürgel, ed. 1987a, 57-58.

—. 1911c. "Klasseninstinkt und Kunstverständnis." In Bürgel, ed. 1987a, 64-67.

F. St. 1902. "Maipredigt." In Achten, ed. 1980, 113.

Stampfer, Friedrich. 1903. "Das Theater und die Revolution." *Neue Welt*, 115-16, 126.

—. 1904-05. "Zwei Dramen einer deutschen Arbeiterin." *Neue Zeit* 23, 389-91.

—. 1905. "Werden und Vergehen." In Jonas, ed. 1988a, 109-17.

—. 1911a. "Kunst und Klassenkampf." In Bürgel, ed. 1987a, 53-57.

—. 1911b. "Klasseninstinkt und Kunstverständnis." In Bürgel, ed. 1987a, 61-64.

Steiger, Edgar. 1896a. "Das arbeitende Volk und die Kunst." In Rothe, ed. 1986a, 185-91.

—. 1896b. "Das *Hamburger Echo* und die Kunst." In Rothe, ed. 1986a, 202-06.

—. 1896c. "Kunst und Sittlichkeit." In Rothe, ed. 1986a, 206-09.

Steinberg, Hans-Josef. 1967. *Sozialismus und deutsche Sozialdemokratie. Zur Ideologie der Partei vor dem 1. Weltkrieg.* Hannover: Verlag für Literatur und Zeitgeschehen.

Stephan, Cora. 1981. "Bemerkungen zur Rezeption Ferdinand Lassalles." In *Ferdinand Lassalle — Allgemeiner Deutscher Arbeiterverein. Bibliographie ihrer Schriften und der Literatur über sie 1840 bis 1975*, ed. Bert Andreas. Bonn: Neue Gesellschaft, 9-25.

Stieg, Gerald. 1973. "Thesen zur Arbeiterlyrik von 1863 bis 1933." In *Arbeiterdichtung*, 26-36.

— and Bernd Witte. 1973. *Abriß einer Geschichte der deutschen Arbeiterliteratur.* Stuttgart: Ernst Klett.

Stirner, Hartmut. 1979. *Die Agitation und Rhetorik Ferdinand Lassalles*. Marburg: Verlag Arbeiterbewegung und Gesellschaftswissenschaft.

Strasser, Charlot. 1930. *Arbeiterdichtung*. Zurich: Genossenschaftsdruckerei.

Ströbel, Heinrich. 1910. "Humor." In Bürgel, ed. 1987a, 29-34.

—. 1910-11. "Eine ästhetische Werttheorie." In Bürgel, ed. 1987a, 40-49.

—. 1911-12. "Kunst und Proletariat." In Bürgel, ed. 1987a, 89-96.

Thalheimer, August. 1929. "Einleitung." In Franz Mehring, *Zur Literaturgeschichte von Calderon bis Heine*, ed. Eduard Fuchs. Berlin: Soziologische Verlagsanstalt, 15-32.

Tenfelde, Klaus. 1979a. "Bergarbeiterkultur in Deutschland. Ein Überblick." In *Geschichte und Gesellschaft* 5, 12-53.

—. 1979b. "Das Fest der Bergleute: Studien zur Geselligkeit der Arbeiterschaft während der Industrialisierung am Beispiel des deutschen Bergbaus." In Ritter, ed. 1979a, 209-45.

—. 1982. "Anmerkungen zur Arbeiterkultur." In *Erinnerungsarbeit. Geschichte und demokratische Identität in Deutschland*, ed. Wolfgang Ruppert. Opladen: Leske Verlag + Budrich, 107-34.

Textausgaben zur frühen sozialistischen Literatur in Deutschland, ed. Bruno Kaiser, Manfred Häckel and Ursula Münchow. Berlin: Akademie-Verlag [= *Textausgaben*].

"Das Theater als Bildungsmittel." 1911. *Arbeiter-Jugend* 3, 404-06.

Trempenau, Dietmar. 1979. *Frühe sozialdemokratische und sozialistische Arbeiterdramatik (1890 bis 1914)*. Stuttgart: Metzler.

Trommler, Frank. 1976a. *Sozialistische Literatur in Deutschland*. Stuttgart: Alfred Kröner.

—. 1976b. "Die Kulturpolitik der DDR und die kulturelle Tradition des deutschen Sozialismus." In *Literatur und Literaturtheorie in der DDR*, ed. Peter Uwe Hohendahl and Patricia Herminghouse. Frankfurt am Main: Suhrkamp, 13-72.

Trunz, Cecilia A. 1934. *Die Autobiographien von deutschen Industriearbeitern*. Freiburg: Herder.

"Über die Schaubühne und ihre Zukunft." 1875. *Volksstaat* 7 (April 30), 1-2; (May 5), 1; (May 7), 1-2; (May 9), 1.

Ullrich, Volker. 1972. "Emanzipation durch Integration? Zur Kritik der bürgerlichen Geschichtsschreibung über die Arbeiterbewegung bis 1914." In *Das Argument* 75, 104-47.

Varein, Heinz Josef. 1956. *Freie Gewerkschaften, Sozialdemokratie und Staat. Die Politik der Generalkommission unter der Führung Carl Legiens (1890-1920)*. Düsseldorf: Droste.

Vaßen, Florian. 1980. "Sozialistische Literatur von 1849 bis 1890." In *Geschichte der deutschen Literatur vom 18. Jahrhundert bis zur Gegenwart*, ed. Viktor Žmegač, vol. 2. Königstein/Ts.: Athenäum, 109-39.

Vogtmeier, Michael. 1984. *Die proletarische Autobiographie 1903-1914. Studien zur Gattungs- und Funktionsgeschichte der Autobiographie*. Frankfurt am Main, Berne and New York: Peter Lang.

Völkerling, Klaus. 1962. "Der Crimmitschauer Textilarbeiterstreik von 1903/04 in der frühen sozialistischen Literatur und im revolutionären Arbeiterlied." *Weimarer Beiträge* 8, 614-40.

—. 1969. "Die politisch-satirischen Zeitschriften *Süddeutscher Postillon* (München) und *Der Wahre Jakob* (Stuttgart)." Ph.D. diss., Potsdam.

Vollmar, Georg v. 1891. *Über die nächsten Aufgaben der Sozialdemokratie*. 2nd ed. Munich: M. Ernst.

Wagner, Richard. 1910. "Proletarische Poesie." *Arbeiter-Jugend* 2, 295-96.

Wendel, Hermann. 1911-12. Review of *Gesammelte Dramen* by Emil Rosenow. *Neue Zeit* 30, 644-46.

Wendemuth, Karl. 1913-14. "Nachdenkliches zum Fall Rosenow." *Neue Zeit* 32, 636-38.

Wendorf, Werner. 1978. *Schule und Bildung in der Politik von Wilhelm Liebknecht*. Berlin: Colloquium.

Wiese, Benno von. 1931. *Politische Dichtung Deutschlands*. Berlin: Junker und Dünnhaupt.

Witte, Bernd. 1973. "Arbeiterautobiographien." In *Arbeiterdichtung* 1973, 37-46.

—. 1977a. "Literatur der Opposition. Über Geschichte, Funktion und Wirkmittel der frühen Arbeiterliteratur." In Arnold, ed. 1977, vol. 1, 7-45.

—, ed. 1977b. *Deutsche Arbeiterliteratur von den Anfängen bis 1914*. Stuttgart: Philip Reclam jun.

Wittner, Otto. 1913. "Der Roman des Proletariats." *Gleichheit* 23, 89-90.

Wunderer, Hartmann. 1980. *Arbeitervereine und Arbeiterparteien. Kultur- und Massenorganisationen in der Arbeiterbewegung (1890-1933)*. Frankfurt am Main and New York: Campus.

Wurm, Emmanuel. 1907. "Tendenzlieder." In *Arbeitshefte* 15, 111-13.

Zadek, Ignaz. 1884. "Die neueste deutsche Belletristik." *Neue Zeit* 2, 241-52.

Zadek, Julie. 1884. Review of *Die Alten und die Neuen* by Minna Kautsky. In C. Friedrich, ed. 1964, 152-59.

Zepler, Wally. 1910. "Die psychischen Grundlagen der Arbeiterbildung." *Sozialistische Monatshefte* 14, 1551-59.

Zerges, Kristina. 1980. *Was haben die Arbeiter gelesen?* Siegen: Gesamthochschule.

—. 1982. *Sozialdemokratische Presse und Literatur. Empirische Untersuchung zur Literaturvermittlung in der sozialdemokratischen Presse 1876 bis 1933.* Stuttgart: Metzler.

Zetkin, Clara. 1899. "Eine Dichterin der Freiheit." *Gleichheit* 9, 44-46, 52-54, 60-63.

—. 1904a. Letter to Franz Mehring (September 14). In Mehring, *Gesammelte Schriften*, vol. 11, 596.

—. 1904b. "Vorwort." In Otto Krille, *Aus engen Gassen*. Berlin: Johann Sassenbach, 3-5.

—. 1906a. "Henrik Ibsen." In Clara Zetkin, *Über Literatur und Kunst*, ed. Emilia Zetkin-Milowidowa. Berlin: Henschel, 1955, 33-43.

—. 1906b. "An die Eltern!" In *Für unsere Kinder. Weihnachtsbuch der Gleichheit*, ed. Clara Zetkin (Zundel). Stuttgart: Paul Singer, [1-2].

—. 1909-10. "Friedrich Schiller." In Jonas, ed. 1988a, 245-61.

—. 1910. "Ein Dichter der Revolution." *Gleichheit* 20, 73-74.

—. 1911. "Kunst und Proletariat." In Clara Zetkin, *Ausgewählte Reden und Schriften*, ed. Institut für Marxismus-Leninismus beim ZK der SED. Berlin: Dietz, 1957, 490-505.

—. 1912. "Ein Arbeiterdrama" [review of *Bergarbeiter* by Lu Märten]. *Gleichheit* 16, 61-63.

Index

Abendroth, Wolfgang 32
Achten, Udo 59, 91
Advocatus [Paul Vogt] 83
Alexander, Gertrud 69
Almsroth, Ernst [Heinrich Schulz] 81
Andersen Nexø, Martin 85, 109, 110
Audorf, Jakob 85, 97, 100
Auer, Ignaz 35, 86
Avenarius, Ferdinand 81

Baake, Kurt 89
Bab, Julius 93
Bachmann, Ingeborg 7, 20
Bader, Paul 105
Balser, Frolinde 24
Balzac, Honoré de 111
Bär, Adam 81, 84
Bausinger, Hermann 53
Bebel, Agust 1, 2, 26, 27, 28, 29, 33, 34, 36, 40, 54, 56, 72, 76, 85, 86, 118, 120
Bellamy, Edward 34
Belli, Joseph 85
Benjamin, Walter 46, 64, 77
Benn, Gottfried 7, 20
Bérard, R. 76
Bernstein, Eduard 1, 3, 34, 35, 37, 38, 40, 45, 47, 71, 74, 79, 80, 99
Birker, Karl 56
Bismarck, Otto v. 28, 29, 30
K. Bl. 80, 81
Blos, Wilhelm 40, 59, 109
Böhme, Helmut 24
Bohnen, Klaus 64, 70
Bollenbeck, Georg 101, 117, 119, 120
Born, Stephan 24
Bosse, Friedrich 55, 56, 103, 104, 106, 107
Böttcher, Kurt 94, 100, 112, 113
Braun, Lily 73
Brauneck, Manfred 77, 80
Brecht, Bertolt 107
Bröger, Karl 93
Bromme, Moritz William 116, 118, 119, 120
Brückner, Peter 49, 82
Brüggemeier, Franz J. 51
Buck, Theo 62
Buckle, Henry Thomas 33
Bürgel, Tanja 78, 80, 113, 114
Burggraf, Uta 82

Carpin 109, 111
Cohen, Hermann 37
Conze, Werner 34, 41

Dammer, Otto 25
Darwin, Charles 2, 33, 59
David, Eduard 48, 73
Demetz, Peter 63
Diederich, Franz 74, 85, 97, 98, 105
Dietz, Johann Heinrich 85, 97
Dikreiter, Heinrich Georg 117, 120
Döring, E. 82
Dowe, Dieter 57, 98
Dumas, Alexandre (père) 83
Duncker, Hermann 99
Duncker, Käte 81
Düvell, Fritz 98

Ecks, Karl 93
Eichhorn, Emil 89
Eisner, Kurt 37, 58, 73, 74, 76, 77, 83
Emig, Brigitte 41, 49, 59
Emmerich, Wolfgang 119, 120
Engelbert, Ernst 69
Engelke, Gerrit 93
Engels, Friedrich 1, 2, 29, 31, 32, 33, 35, 43, 50, 51, 68, 106, 107, 111, 112, 113, 114, 120
Engelsing, Rolf 88
Escarpit, Robert 7
Eschstruth, Nataly 84

E. F. 83
Feddersen, Harald 87, 88
Feidel-Mertz, Hildegard 49
Fendrich, Anton 81
Fischer, Edmund 33
Fischer, Franz Louis 116
Fischer, Karl 116, 117, 118, 119, 120
Fischer, Richard 86
Fish, Stanley 6
Frank, Ludwig 80
Franke, Arno 87, 108
Franz, Rudolf 79, 98
Freiligrath, Ferdinand 4, 80, 96
Fricke, Dieter 86, 88
Friedrich, Cäcilia 88, 112
Friedrich, Wolfgang 45, 99, 100, 113
Fritzsche, Wilhelm 25

Frohme, Karl Egon 76, 85, 97
Fuchs, Eduard 89, 90, 91, 97, 108
Füllberth, Georg 32, 35, 41, 69, 70, 74, 77, 80, 84, 85

A. G. 98
Gadamer, Hans-Georg 6, 7
Gebauer, Horst 84
Ger, A. [Karl Alwin Gerisch] 85, 90, 110
Geib, August 58
Gille, Klaus F. 70
Girnus, Werner 70
Goethe, Johann Wolfgang 5, 7, 15, 19, 63, 68, 83
Göhre, Paul 34, 50, 116, 118, 119
Gorky, Maxim 71, 110
Greulich, Hermann 93
Groh, Dieter 33
Groschopp, Horst 50, 55, 58, 94
Grötzsch, Robert 79
Gumpert, Fritz 48

J. H. 72
R. H. 82
Häckel, Manfred 91
Haenisch, Konrad 87
Hagen, Wolfgang 41, 49, 74
Hanauer 82
Harkness, Margaret 112
Hart, Julius 75
Hasenclever, Wilhelm 85, 97
Hauptmann, Gerhart 9, 63, 75, 104
Hegeler, Wilhelm 117
Heid, Elisabeth 101
Heid, Ludger 101
Heine, Heinrich 4, 96
Henckell, Karl 85, 97
Hepner, Adolf 28
Hermand, Jost 67, 117, 118, 119
Hermes, Gertrud 49, 50, 93
Herwegh, Georg 4, 80, 96
Hobsbawm, E. J. 48
Höchberg, Karl 37
Hochdorf, Max 109
Hoernle, Edwin 81
Hoffmann, Dirk 85, 87, 88, 89
Hoggart, Richard 94
Hohendahl, Peter Uwe 101
Holek, Heinrich 83
Holek, Wenzel 116, 117, 118, 119, 120
Hollweck, Ludwig 91
Horn, Robert 73
Huyssen, Andreas 77

Ibsen, Henrik 71, 75, 104

Jacobeit, Wolfgang 51, 94
Jacoby, Johann 37
Jacoby, Leopold 93, 97
Jauss, Hans Robert 6, 7
Jelken, Ernst 93
Jonas, Gisela 73, 74

Kaiser, Bruno 28, 77, 97
Kämpchen, Heinrich 93, 98
Kampffmeyer, Paul 45, 51
Kant, Immanuel 67
Kantorowicz, Ludwig 86
Kapell, August 102, 103
Kaufmann, Hans 94, 100, 101, 118
Kautsky, Karl 1, 31, 32, 33, 34, 35, 37, 38, 40, 65, 72, 74, 75, 108, 117
Kautsky, Minna 68, 85, 88, 90, 110, 111, 112, 113, 114, 115
Kegel, Max 85, 88, 91, 97, 98, 100, 102
Keller, Werner 70
Kette, Max 117
Klaar, Ernst 91, 98
Kliche, Dieter 71
Kliche, Joseph 83, 84, 87, 89
Kluge, Alexander 53
Knilli, Friedrich 91, 103, 104, 105, 106
Koch, Hans 69, 70
Kocka, Jürgen 57
Koigen, David 47
Köppen, Manuel 115, 120
Korn, Karl 47, 59, 73
Kramer, Dieter 54
Kreowski, Ernst 97, 110
Krille, Otto 71, 72, 117, 119
Kuczynski, Jürgen 25, 41, 50, 51, 53
Kumpmann, Walter 65, 69, 70
Kunert, Marie 110, 111
Kürbisch, Friedrich G. 93

Lammel, Inge 101
Landauer, Gustav 75
Lange, F. A. 37
Lange, Heinrich 57
Langewiesche, Dieter 52, 56, 83, 84
Lassalle, Ferdinand 1, 2, 3, 4, 25-27, 28, 29, 30, 31, 34, 43, 44, 45, 58, 59, 102, 111
Lavant, Rudolf [Richard Cramer] 85, 91, 97
Legien, Karl 36
Lenin, Vladimir Illyich 11, 39, 119
Lenzner, Paul 109, 110, 111

Lepp, Adolf 85, 100
Lersch, Heinrich 93
Lessen, Ludwig 98, 117
Lessing, Gotthold Ephraim 15, 19, 63, 64, 68, 70
Levenstein, Adolf 51, 116, 117
Lidtke, Vernon L. 46, 47, 55, 56, 57, 58, 59, 60, 94, 101, 102
Liebknecht, Karl 80
Liebknecht, Wilhelm 1, 2, 17, 27, 28, 33, 36, 43, 45-46, 71, 75, 102, 110
Loeb, Minna 93
Loreck, Jochen 17, 86
Lübeck, Carl 88
Lüdtke, Alf 52
Ludwig, Martin H. 101, 103, 114
Lukács, Georg 61, 66, 69, 70, 114, 120
Lützeler, Paul Michael 70
Luxemburg, Rosa 1, 2, 3, 16, 26, 37, 38, 39, 45, 71, 72, 73, 74, 78

Mann, Golo 24
Marlitt, Eugenie 84
Märten, Lu 71, 72, 73, 79, 85, 104, 105, 106, 117
Martini, Fritz 93
Marx, Karl 1, 2, 3, 4, 5, 24, 26, 27, 29, 30, 31, 32, 33, 34, 36, 38, 44, 50, 51, 59, 61, 62, 68, 77, 83, 102, 107, 110
Mathes, Klaus 111
Maurenbrecher, Max 47, 74
May, Karl 84
Mehlich, Ernst 84
Mehring, Franz 1, 12, 13, 14, 15, 16, 21, 26, 34, 40, 44, 45, 46, 47, 54, 61-70, 71, 72, 73, 74, 75, 77, 78, 79, 82, 83, 95, 97, 98, 103, 104, 105, 110, 111, 116, 117, 118, 119
Michels, Robert 36
Miller, Susanne 30, 32, 41
Mohrmann, Ute 51, 94
Moltrecht, Hans-Jürgen 49
Molkenbuhr, Hermann 73, 74
Mühlberg, Dietrich 94, 114
Müller-Jahnke, Clara 68, 71, 91, 98
Münchow, Ursula 74, 77, 100, 103, 104, 105, 106, 107, 113, 118, 119, 120

Na'man, Shlomo 26
Napoleon III 27
Negt, Oskar 53
Nespital, Robert 104, 105
Naumann, Friedrich 116

Naumann, Manfred 94
Niethammer, Lutz 51
Nitschke, Wilhelm 83, 84
Noack, Victor 99

Otto-Walster, August 85, 88, 96, 102, 109, 110, 111, 113

Pehlke, Michael 107
Petzold, Alfons 98, 117, 119
Pick, Erika 113
Piltz, Georg 91
Pforte, Dietger 77, 97
Poensgen-Alberty, Max 105
Popp, Adelheid 54, 85, 116, 117, 118, 120
Preczang, Ernst 85, 90, 96, 98, 104, 106, 107, 110, 119

Quatember, Wolfgang 114, 120

Rabold, Emil 87
Raddatz, Fritz J. 70
Rector, Martin 104, 114
Rehbein, Franz 116, 118, 120
Reinelt, Herbert 113
Reisig, Hildegard 49
Reißmann, Alwin 83
Reutershan, Joan 71
Rhenanus 88
Ricke, Gabriele 49, 82
Riha, Karl 101
Ritter, Gerhard A. 36, 49, 51, 57, 119
Roland 105
Rosenberg, Rainer 94, 95, 114
Rosenow, Emil 104, 105, 106
Roßbach, Emil 45
Roßmäßler, Adolf 25, 56
Roth, Guenther 49, 55
Rothe, Norbert 76, 77
Rüden, Peter v. 104, 107
Rühle, Otto 24, 47, 52, 56, 71

J. S. 83
Sachs, Hans 105
Scävola, G. M. 98
Schäfers, Hans-Joachim 48, 55
Scharrer, Manfred 31, 33, 39, 41, 119
Schauder, A. 99
Scherer, Herbert 75, 77
Scheu, Andreas 85, 93, 97
Schieder, Wolfgang 34
Schikowski, John 73
Schiller, Dieter 71

Schiller, Friedrich 5, 7, 15, 16, 19, 49, 63, 64, 67, 73, 74
Schlaikjer, Erich 67, 69, 75, 76
Schmidt, Hugo Ernst 76
Schönhoven, Klaus 83, 84
Schönlank, Bruno 76, 91
Schorske, Carl E. 30, 32
Schröder, Gustav 56, 105, 106, 107
Schult, Johannes 52, 99
Schultze, Ernst 81
Schulz, Heinrich 43, 46, 47, 57, 58, 81
Schulz, Ursula 28
Schulze-Delitzsch, Hermann 25
Schütz, Hans J. 91
Schweichel, Robert 68, 75, 85, 88, 110, 113, 114
Schweitzer, Jean Baptist v. 95, 102, 111
Schwendter, Rolf 52
Seidel, Robert 91, 98
Serebrow, N. 71
Seybold, Annette 89, 90
Siemering, Hertha 48, 84
Sommer, B. 105
Sperber, Heinz [Herman Heijermans] 78, 79, 80
Stalin, Joseph 69
Stampfer, Friedrich 37, 73, 74, 79
Starosson, Franz 104, 105
Steiger, Edgar 76, 87
Steinberg, Hans-Josef 31, 33, 34, 37, 41, 84, 85
Stern, Jakob 85
Stieg, Gerald 101, 116
Stirner, Hartmut 44
Strasser, Charlot 93, 118
Ströbel, Heinrich 79
Sudermann, Hermann 104
Sue, Eugène 111

Taine, Hippolyte 64
Tenfelde, Klaus 48, 52, 53, 54, 57, 58
Thalheimer, August 69
Thompson, Edward P. 94
Tolstoy, Leo 71, 75, 104
Trempenau, Dietmar 107
Trommler, Frank 49, 65, 69, 71, 77, 81, 82, 95, 101, 107, 108, 114, 117, 118, 120
Trunz, Cecilia A. 118

Ulbricht, Walter 119
Ullrich, Volker 41

Vahlteich, Julius 25

Varein, Heinz Josef 36
Vaßen, Florian 101, 114, 116
Vinschen, Klaus-Dieter 101
Vogtmeier, Michael 116, 117, 120, 121
Vollmar, Georg v. 34, 35, 37
Völkerling, Klaus 90, 91, 97

Wagner, Richard 97
Weber, Max 117, 118
Weerth, Georg 4, 96
Wendel, Hermann 105
Wendemuth, Karl 105
Wiese, Benno v. 93
Williams, Raymond 94
Witte, Bernd 93, 101, 107, 114, 116, 119
Wittich, Manfred 103
Wittner, Otto 109, 110, 111
Wolgast, Heinrich 81
Wunderer, Hartmann 50
Wurm, Emmanuel 99

Zadek, Ignaz 75
Zadek, Julie 111
Zepler, Wally 48
Zerges, Kristina 89, 90

Zetkin, Clara 1, 34, 43, 46, 47, 54, 59, 71, 72, 74, 80, 81, 97, 98
Zola, Emile 75, 85, 109, 110, 111
predicament

OHIO UNIVERSITY LIBRARY

Please return this book as soon as you have finished with it. In order to avoid a fine it must be returned by the latest date stamped below. All books are subject to recall after two weeks or immediately if needed for reserve.

FEB 0 2 1994